HUMOR AND
INFORMATION LITERACY

HUMOR AND INFORMATION LITERACY

*Practical Techniques for
Library Instruction*

Joshua Vossler and Scott Sheidlower

LIBRARIES UNLIMITED

AN IMPRINT OF ABC-CLIO, LLC
Santa Barbara, California • Denver, Colorado • Oxford, England

KH

Library of Congress Cataloging-in-Publication Data

Vossler, Joshua J.
    Humor and information literacy : practical techniques for library instruction / Joshua Vossler and Scott Sheidlower.
        p. cm.
    Includes bibliographical references and index.
    ISBN 978–1–59884–532–7 (pbk. : acid-free paper) — ISBN 978–1–59884–533–4 (ebook)
1. Information literacy—Study and teaching (Higher) 2. Library orientation for college students.
3. Wit and humor in education. I. Sheidlower, Scott. II. Title.
ZA3075.V64   2011
028.7071′1—dc23   2011025415

ISBN: 978–1–59884–532–7
EISBN: 978–1–59884–533–4

15 14 13 12 11   1 2 3 4 5

This book is also available on the World Wide Web as an eBook.
Visit www.abc-clio.com for details.

Libraries Unlimited
An Imprint of ABC-CLIO, LLC

ABC-CLIO, LLC
130 Cremona Drive, P.O. Box 1911
Santa Barbara, California 93116-1911

This book is printed on acid-free paper ∞

Manufactured in the United States of America

3/6/12

Contents

Acknowledgments

Scott Sheidlower would like to thank his colleagues at York College in Jamaica, Queens, and throughout the City University of New York for their support during the writing of this book. He would especially like to thank Ms. Grace Avila, Mr. Daniel Cleary, Professor John Drobnicki, Mr. Travis Hilton, Professor Njoki Kinyatti, Dean Curtis Kendrick, the chief librarian of the City University of New York, Mr. Kenneth Krepp, Professor Robert Machalow, Ms. Christina Miller, Professor Di Su, Ms. Sandra Urban, and Professor Hope Young. He would also like to thank his friends and family who helped him write through their support: Mr. Charles Fineman, now retired but formerly of Harvard University; Mrs. Ruth Sheidlower, my mom; Mr. David Sheidlower, my brother; Mr. Isaac Sheidlower, my nephew; and Mr. Nathaniel Sheidlower, my other nephew. Finally, I want to thank the clergy and congregation of the Stephen Wise Free Synagogue, all of whom were very supportive. Anyone I forgot to include, please forgive me and know that when you read this book you helped to bring it to fruition.

Joshua Vossler would like to thank his colleagues at Kimbel Library and Coastal Carolina University for picking up his slack and giving him time to write. I would also like to thank my former colleagues at the University of Texas at Arlington for tolerating my sense of humor for nearly three years; Chad Chisholm for never doubting that the study of humor was a serious matter; John Watts for never letting me forget to laugh, even in the dark times—like night; Barbara Burd for hiring me even after I told her what I was writing a book about; Ric Simmons and the Simmons clan for their boundless warmth; Sherman Normandin, Erik Little, Randy Bratvold, Jack Maney, and Carl Olimb, for your support; SEH, for inspiring me to write about pirates; and my parents, all three, for always being there.

Finally, both authors would jointly like to thank and acknowledge those contributors who generously agreed to share their techniques in using humor to teach information literacy. These contributors, who are mainly librarians, along with their titles and their institutions and locations, are laid out in alphabetical order, by the contributor's last name, in the following list:

John E. Adkins, the director of the Schoenbaum Library at the University of Charleston in Charleston, West Virginia; Professor Michelle Blackman, instruction librarian at Grossmont College in El Cajon, California; Sarah Blakeslee, interim university librarian at the Meriam Library at California State University located in Chico, California; Norman Boyd, assistant librarian in the Customer Services Division of Anglia Ruskin University, located on campuses in both Cambridge and Chelmsford in the United Kingdom, who formerly worked at Barking College near London; Tamara Brathwaite, librarian II at the Institute of International Relations, University of the West Indies, St. Augustine Campus, St. Augustine, Trinidad & Tobago, the West Indies; Antony Brewerton, the head of academic services in the library at the University of Warwick in Coventry, United Kingdom; Monique Delatte, adjunct librarian at the library at Rio Hondo College in Whittier, California and librarian—Acquisitions at the library at Fullerton College in Fullerton, California; Anne Driscoll, the lead reference librarian in the Frederick Douglass Library at the University of Maryland Eastern Shore in Princess Anne, Maryland; Dr. David Ettinger, international affairs and political science librarian in the Gelman Library at George Washington University in Washington, D.C.; Jason Eyre, assistant librarian at De Montfort University in Leicester, United Kingdom; Linda J. Goff, the head of instructional services at California State University in Sacramento, California; Margaret G. Grotti, both assistant librarian and coordinator of library instruction at the Morris Library at the University of Delaware in Newark, Delaware; Kathleen Irvine, subject librarian at the Highland Health Sciences Library, which is part of the University of Stirling's Centre for Health Science in Inverness, United Kingdom; Professor Beth Lander, director of library services at the Basileiad Library located at Manor College in Jenkintown, Pennsylvania; Ian McCracken, the Learning Resource Centre manager at Govan High School in Glasgow, United Kingdom; Joshua McKain, the college librarian for the Fisher College library at Fisher College in Boston, Massachusetts; Els Mertens, librarian at the Centrale Mediatheek of the Katholieke Hogeschool Kempen located in Geel, Belgium; Sara D. Miller, assistant library instruction coordinator at the libraries at Michigan State University in East Lansing, Michigan; Janet Morton, the faculty team librarian at the University of Leeds in the United Kingdom; Heather Nicholson, MLIS candidate, who is a library intern at the University of Lethbridge Library in Lethbridge, Alberta, Canada; Bonnie Petry, reference librarian for the College of Natural Sciences in the John M. Pfau Library at California State University at San Bernardino, California; Stephanie Rosenblatt of the Pollak Library located on the campus of California State University at Fullerton in Fullerton, California; Kate Rubick, reference and instruction librarian at the Watzek Library at Lewis & Clark College, located in Portland, Oregon; Jenna Ryan, assistant librarian for reference and instruction at Louisiana State University in Baton Rouge, Louisiana; Tracey Simon, the director of the Floral Park Public Library in Floral Park, New York; Amy Springer, government and business information librarian at the Alcuin Library at the College of St. Benedict and St. John's University in Collegeville, Minnesota; Corrine Syster, reference and instruction librarian in the McCormick Library located at Harrisburg Area Community College in Harrisburg, Pennsylvania; Professor Shea A. Taylor, the chief of reference of the Cohen Library at the City College of New York, which is part of the City University of New York and is located in Manhattan, New York City; Professor Jan Turner, reference librarian at Regis University in Denver, Colorado; Professor Dale Vidmar, the library instruction coordinator and education, communication, health, and physical education librarian at the Lenn and Dixie Hannon Library of

Southern Oregon University in Ashland, Oregon; Billie E. Walker, reference librarian at the Thun Library located on the Berks Campus of Penn State University in Reading, Pennsylvania; Mr. John Watts, the outreach and reference librarian in the Kimbel Library located at Carolina Coastal University in Conway, South Carolina; Dr. Kwasi Sarkodie-Mensah, manager of the instructional services at Boston College.

Introduction

WHY WRITE A BOOK ABOUT USING HUMOR TO TEACH INFORMATION LITERACY?

Above anything else, this book is about being a good teacher. We leave to others the task of analyzing how best to compose a lesson and present it to a class. Instead, we speak to the moment-to-moment social relationship we create while we stand in front of our students: building rapport with them during the first moments at the beginning of the hour, and then engaging their attention strongly enough that some of our passion for learning passes on to them. Humor, we believe, is key. It is through sharing our sense of humor with students that we begin to reveal ourselves to them and rapport develops. This requires taking a risk: a sense of humor is deeply personal, and sharing it makes us vulnerable. A willingness to be vulnerable, however, is one of the first steps toward building rapport. For mutual trust to be built, someone must make that first genuine gesture, and that someone should be the teacher. It also can help convey our enthusiasm and our personal commitment to our subject matter. The authors believe that the right touch of humor in the classroom can make an otherwise humdrum lesson interesting and memorable at the very least, and at its best also impart energy and excitement. Humor accomplishes all of these things instantaneously. That makes it a powerful tool that any teacher should consider, but it is especially relevant for teachers who work with subjects that students rarely find compelling.

Library instruction is such a subject. It can be tedious for instructor and student alike. However, if humor was an uncomplicated solution that instantly made tedious subjects interesting, there would be no need for a book on humor. There would just be a short memo: Be funny. The situation, unfortunately, is not simple; it is indeed rather complicated. To begin with, just coaxing an audience to laugh can be a challenge. Add on the demands of using humor in a college classroom to support educational goals, and that challenge becomes magnified.

Humor has the capacity to divide as well as unite. Failed humor carries undesirable consequences, just as successful humor imparts rewards. It is a high-stakes endeavor, and because of that risk we think it bears noting that this book approaches the subject of humor in the classroom with a definite bias in favor of humor. Humor carries risk, but we believe it is a risk worth taking. Loving humor, however, does not preclude asking how, where, and why humor is best implemented in a learning environment. We are always teachers first and comedians second. Laughter is a fine thing, but if our students are not learning, we are wasting their time as well as our own. Fortunately, students cannot learn what they ignore, and one of humor's strengths lies in making boring subjects (as much as we disagree, that includes information literacy) more tolerable. As educators, we want to transmit at least some of the passion we feel for our subjects into the hearts of our students. Humor gives us the ideal medium for this transmission. As Victor Borge said, "Laughter is the shortest distance between two people" (Buxman 2000). It is our hope that this book will help you find the shortest distance between yourself and all the students you will encounter in your teaching career.

Shortening that distance may require a shift in mindset about what teaching actually is. An underlying assumption of this book is that teaching, especially in the context of one-shot information literacy instruction, is a performance. Librarians tend to think of themselves as mentors or guides but not as performers. Outside of the classroom, especially when consulting with students individually, this is indeed the role we play. In the classroom, however, it is not adaptive to conceive of ourselves as such. Unlike the teachers of semester-long classes, instruction librarians are given only an hour or so with any given group of students. Being a mentor takes time and one-on-one interaction. The behaviors that lead to a successful mentoring relationship do not have the time to work in an hour-long instruction session. It is only by acknowledging our role as performers that we are able to take conscious control of how our students perceive us and react to the personas that we reveal to them as we teach.

WHAT DO WE MEAN BY "HUMOR"?

For the purposes of this book, we are defining humor rather broadly. Humor, in our eyes, is about more than just jokes or funny anecdotes that make an audience laugh, although those are indeed important aspects worth consideration. Humor, at its heart, encompasses any technique that demonstrates a warm, friendly personality or that reveals yourself to your students in a way that makes them feel closer to you. Attitude is just as important as technique. Using humor in the classroom means you are finding ways to enjoy yourself and to pass that enjoyment on to your students, even if that enjoyment never results in a single chuckle. Humor can be noisy and obvious, such as a series of jokes told at the beginning of class to get everyone laughing and feeling relaxed. It can also be subtle, such as smiling to students as they file into class or, as Sheidlower does, suggesting that your students call you by your first name. Sheidlower has found his last name to be a barrier to some students and that going by his first name can be a pleasant, humanizing touch. We are not, of course, implying that everyone should dispense with formal address and go on a first-name basis with their students. In Sheidlower's case, this relaxation of formality is just another way to let his personality shine through, and it works for him.

Conversely, Vossler introduces himself as "Mr. Vossler," but also executes the occasional one-handed cartwheel during class to illustrate how he is "head over heels" for research. There is no one right way to use humor, and what works for one teacher might be disruptive and useless for another teacher. Whether you want to make your students burst into howls of laughter or just want them to leave an instruction session feeling good about themselves and the library, rest assured your interests will be represented here.

LIBRARY INSTRUCTION SESSIONS PRESENT A DIFFERENT EDUCATIONAL ENVIRONMENT FROM SEMESTER-LONG CLASSES

Presently, research on humor in information literacy instruction focuses primarily on humor's value as a teaching tool, often to the exclusion of specific techniques for implementing humor in the classroom. Nonetheless, there are some fine volumes on using humor in the college classroom, most notably Ronald Berk's *Professors are from Mars, students are from Snickers* (2003) and *Humor as an instructional defibrillator* (2002), but these works focus on humor in the typical college classroom, especially semester-long classes on a single academic subject. It is our contention that library instruction sessions, where information literacy is most often taught, are not typical college classrooms. They unquestionably share superficial traits, but key differences between the two alter the social landscape.

Instruction librarians are usually guest speakers, so they enter the classroom with none of the trust or rapport enjoyed by teachers who meet with a class over the duration of an entire semester (MacAdam, 1985). For us, every day of class is the first day of class and the last day of class combined. Whereas a "regular" teacher can walk into class and begin the lesson right away, the instruction librarian has a number of other tasks to attend to. As a stranger in front of an audience that has a shared history of being in a class together for weeks or months, breaking the ice is a crucial first step. From there, effort must be made to quickly build a rapport with the class as well as to demonstrate competence. If the students do not like us, they probably will not want to listen seriously to anything we have to say. Librarians, who are seen by our students as having an old-fashioned set of skills, must establish themselves as having formidable research skills that are worth aspiring to, especially in the age of Google. Finally, we also need to make ourselves approachable so that students will not hesitate to reach out to us in the future. All of these goals are in addition to the instruction session's educational goals, which are often extensive.

Library instruction sessions normally have a larger number of concrete educational goals than an equivalently long class session in a semester-long class. This is caused, at least in part, by supply and demand. Few universities have the large number of librarians it would take to offer more than a single instruction session per class per semester. Except in schools that have an information studies major or minor, such as Baruch College of the City University of New York, a single session with a librarian is all most classes can get. Information literacy being as broad-reaching as it is, that single session is woefully insufficient. The limited class time combined with the breadth of information literacy inspires many of us to cram every last bit of information into that session, resulting in the information equivalent of drinking from a fire hose. There is just so much for our students to learn, and so little time. Because of the greater expectations for learning, there is an even greater need to quickly establish a productive learning environment (MacAdam 1985). For greater-than-usual educational goals to be achieved, both the instructor and the students have to be willing participants. Motivating students to take a willing and active role in a library instruction session, however, is another challenge.

Grades motivate many students, and instruction librarians have little influence over student's grades. On the occasions they do, the grades involved are relatively unimportant.

Even our indirect influence over grades, such as the advantages imparted by locating and using high-quality research, is often mitigated by lack of significant professorial buy-in: the punishment for using poor sources is not usually severe enough to engender much desire to learn more effective research methods. Consequently, there is little of either intrinsic or extrinsic motivation for students to take library instruction as seriously as they take the information presented in their semester-long classes. Without a long-term stick or carrot to directly influence student interest in information literacy, instruction librarians are left to rely on whatever rhetoric we can bring to bear. These drawbacks are significant, but they are at least partially mitigated by one of the advantages unique to library instruction. Because we teach the same handful of lessons plans again and again, we can afford to put more effort into polishing them.

This repetition of instruction allows instruction librarians to hone our lesson plans much more quickly than the teachers of a semester-long class. As part of a busy instruction program, a librarian might conduct the same session 30 or more times in the course of one month. Teaching a single lesson 30 times might take the teacher of a semester-long course years or possibly even decades to achieve. Semester-long courses contain a great deal more material than any instruction session, so teachers of those courses are pressed to become familiar with a much broader body of knowledge. This disparity yields two advantages. One, the rapid accretion of experience allows the instruction librarian to approach the development of each lesson plan from an informed position, and can hence implement rapid cycles of trial and error. Two, with fewer lesson plans comes more freedom to put time and effort into developing each one. Each lesson can be looked at from a more granular perspective; it can be broken down minute by minute.

More resources can be expended developing supporting instructional materials as well. Extra time can be put in to finding just the right examples, coming up with apt analogies, or designing excellent group activities. There is also more motivation to devote time and effort in this direction: once developed, an excellent lesson plan can be used for years and shared among colleagues. A well-designed lesson plan is also of material advantage to a library instruction program, whose reputation on campus will be tied to the efficacy of its instruction. For the teacher of a semester-long course, having fine lesson plans is naturally also to be desired. However, the breadth of instruction deters the teacher from investing too much time and energy into any single lesson plan, when there are dozens more still to be developed.

THE DIFFERENCES IN THE EDUCATIONAL ENVIRONMENT INFLUENCE HOW HUMOR SHOULD BE IMPLEMENTED

Over the course of a semester, students in a class will get to know each other as well as the professor. These relationships create comfort and provide a context in which humor can readily occur. This context can also act as a safety net: by knowing your audience, you are less likely to make jokes they will interpret as being in poor taste, and conversely you can get a feeling for the jokes they are most likely to welcome. In library instruction, you do not have these relationships to either guide you or to supply you with humorous material. Humor, then, must be drawn from what remains: the instructor, current events, and the immediate environment of the classroom or university. The teacher of a semester-long class can use humor as someone might use it with a group of casual acquaintances. The instruction librarian, however, shares more in common with stand-up comics, who draw from the aforementioned three topics. As a consequence, the instruction librarian's humor needs to be more internally focused. For example, self-deprecating humor; humor that draws from the librarian's personality quirks, real or imagined; or humor that draws from physical traits will be much easier to pull off than humor that references shared experiences or relationships. The librarian can surely hypothesize that most students do not love spending large quantities of time conducting research, but making a joke using that presupposition is more likely to flop than a joke about how you, the instructor, will probably die alone because you enjoy research so very dearly. This difference can be advantageous for instruction librarians interested in learning more about humor, given that there are some excellent books on the subject of stand-up comedy that can supplement the sparse literature on using humor in the classroom (Ajaye, 2002; Allen, 1987; Carter, 1989, 2001).

Also in a similar manner to a stand-up comic, the instruction librarian only spends a limited amount of time with any given audience. This limited time frame gives the librarian both the freedom and the need to implement a stage personality, or a persona. Teachers of a semester-long course will spend enough time around each of their audiences that they will not have the need or the energy to maintain a persona. Personas can be exhausting to maintain, even if they are just a heightened version of who you really are. Keeping one in place over the course of dozens of classes with the same audience would be soul-crushing and potentially damaging to your credibility. If the audience glimpses your persona slipping, they might interpret that information as evidence of disingenuousness. Fortunately, in the semester-long class, maintaining a persona is not really necessary, because students have the time they need to get to know the teacher naturally. When time with an audience is limited, they cannot naturally get to know the presenter. Adopting an artificial persona speeds the process of acquaintance by exaggerating specific personality traits so that the audience has an easier time figuring out what kind of person they are facing. Instead of spending precious time and mental energy evaluating the presenter, they are free to focus on the material being presented. A clearly communicated persona also makes humor much easier to deliver because it provides a context to work from. For example, if your persona is nervous and high energy, a reference to not being able to wait very long can be immediately funny, especially if it is in regard to something that happens quickly, such as a three-second loading time on a web page.

As already observed, library instruction sessions are normally rather tightly packed with educational content. Fitting humor into a session of around 50 or 80 minutes that are already bursting with content can be difficult. It is easiest if the humor can be intertwined with the subject matter so no educational content needs to be sacrificed at the expense of humor. While this approach is certainly possible in semester-long classes, the impetus for doing so is not as powerful. While certainly not the case everywhere, it is our observation that semester-long classes are usually less packed with learning objectives on a day-to-day basis than is the typical library instruction session. A lesson plan that does not demand every minute of a class leaves room for humor unrelated to the subject matter. Unrelated humor is easier to produce and implement and has the added advantage of being modular. A good joke of any kind on any subject, once written, can be reused in other classes, even while teaching other topics. It is certainly possible to use unrelated humor during library instruction, but humor that is directly integrated into the subject matter tends to make a much more efficient use of the limited amount of time allotted for the session.

Teaching from the same handful of lesson plans provides the same advantages for humor as it does for pedagogy. The quantities of humorous material needed are much smaller than what is needed to fill a semester-long class. Humor, especially good humor, is difficult to produce either quickly or in large quantities. The need for small quantities means more freedom to pick and choose from only your best material. This also translates into more time for practicing your delivery. The reader may feel that the repetition of the same bits of humor might seem to put the humor at risk of becoming stale, but you can trust the energy of each new audience to help keep each delivery fresh so you will only get better after every performance of it (Ajaye, 2002). Just as it is with all comics, including stand-up comics, practice is always a good thing. The familiarity built by that repetition also opens doors to successful ad-libbing. Because your material is so well-rehearsed, your conscious mind is free to pay more attention to the audience and to experiment with new ideas and new styles of delivery. By repeating the old jokes again and again, you increase the odds of coming up with something new and improved.

Because professors often accompany their classes to library instruction sessions, and indeed that is a prerequisite of library instruction at some institutions, instruction librarians face two different audiences with different motivations and tastes. What is funny and appropriate for one audience might not be the same for the other. Making the matter more complicated, both audiences are equally important. We want the students to have a good time, to learn, and to leave the session thinking well of the library and of librarians. But we also want the professor to continue bringing classes to the library in future semesters and to speak well of our services to their friends and their colleagues. This constraint requires careful consideration. Contemporary pop culture references might work well with students, but a professor might not understand them or, worse, find them irrelevant, unprofessional, and possibly even insulting. Conversely, references to pop culture from a decade or two ago might have the professor rolling on the floor, but leave the class scratching their heads and dismissing you both as out-of-touch old codgers. An even more prevalent problem is how humor tends to evolve, especially when it evolves by pushing boundaries. Students today are accustomed to humor that is much more controversial and potentially offensive than humor from a decade ago, just as humor from a decade ago was more controversial and offensive than humor a decade before that, and so on. Humor that appeals to people under the age of 20 is almost certainly going to make people over the age of 40 uncomfortable, especially in an educational setting. The challenge, then, lies in how to skirt that boundary. The librarian needs to try to use humor that appeals to the students but, on the other hand, does not alienate the professor.

Finally, only meeting once with any given class makes each instruction session essentially an extended first impression. There are no (or at least very few) guaranteed future interactions, so that impression, once made, will stick. From any perspective, but especially from the perspective of a comic, this raises the stakes for failed humor. There will be no future opportunity to live anything down. The humor has to work the first time through, or that group of students will leave the session disinclined to reach out for in-person assistance at the library in the future. In a semester-long course, failed humor can sour a class period, but any damage done can be either repaired or at least addressed in future meetings. The relationship between the professor and the students also lends more flexibility to what the class is willing to tolerate and speeds forgiveness of perceived slights. However, this ongoing relationship also places pressure on the professor to maintain at least a modicum of dignity to maintain the respect of the class. Instruction librarians, for better or for worse, are under no such obligation. We are freer to make buffoons of ourselves, so long as we do it in such a way that students leave the session feeling like they can come to us (and by extension, other librarians) for assistance.

STRUCTURE OF THIS BOOK

In writing this book, we wanted to ask questions about using humor that pertain explicitly to instruction librarians and the challenges they face. We wanted to get answers that require no adaptation or adjustment to make sense for teaching information literacy, especially in the environment of the one-shot session. This book is written specifically for academic librarians, but applies to professors, lecturers, and anyone else who engages in information literacy instruction. While the emphasis is usually on applying humor in the one-shot library instruction session, this book can be of use to anyone with an interest in being funny in an educational environment. If you ever plan to be a guest speaker and wish to use humor to facilitate your speech, this book is for you. The purpose of this book is to examine existing research on humor across a variety of disciplines as well as to provide practical, effective techniques for integrating humor into information literacy instruction. Whether you are a beginner to humor or an experienced cut-up, this book will help you understand how humor works and how to better employ it in your own classes.

We conceived of this book in two parts. The first part consists of literature reviews. Previous research on humor and information literacy is relatively limited: less than two dozen articles have ever been published on this subject. Much of the research cited in those articles comes from other fields. Consequently, it seemed sensible to directly consult those other fields for further information. Psychology, education, communication, and professional comedy all bring valuable perspectives to the use of humor in the classroom. Together, they help us cobble together a useful understanding of this rather slippery topic. Part of what makes humor a slippery topic is its interdisciplinary and paradoxical nature: it is something so fundamental to being human that it resists being pigeonholed and analyzed. Humor acts as social glue but can also be divisive. It is timeless, but each generation has its own distinctive tastes and preferences.

We begin with a review of humor in library science. It establishes the context for the other three literature reviews and clarifies library science's debt to the disciplines of education and of psychology and communication, whose literature reviews come next. The final review explores what professional comedians have written about being funny. We recommend reading these chapters in order, but you can feel free to skip around. Each chapter is written to stand on its own. While the literature reviews that make up these three chapters are extensive, none are exhaustive. This is due to the "file drawer problem," a problem that arises in all meta-analysis such as was done in these chapters. In short, this problem exists because "not all studies of a given topic are published [and] that only statistically significant results are presented in those that are published" (Romal, 2008, p. 88). It should also be noted that the study of humor is still very much a growing one, and there is much work yet to be done on humor and its role in human relationships.

The second part of this book consists of techniques for using humor in the library instruction classroom. Each technique has been tested in real-world conditions and found to work, and we encourage you to try them out for yourself. One caveat: Be sure each technique you use suits your in-class persona, your learning objectives, and your audience. We provide suggestions and raw material for you to work with. You need to provide good judgment and the patience to develop lesson plans that integrate humor in a way that supports the creation of a constructive, safe, and comfortable learning environment. These techniques were contributed by experienced instruction librarians, who were reached through listservs, emails, and word of mouth. The ideas remain unchanged; we tried to keep the original language intact and only altered the wording when absolutely necessary to prevent confusion. Please feel free to reach out to either of the authors of this book, Joshua Vossler and Scott Sheidlower, as well as any of our contributors, if you have questions, require clarification, or desire elaboration in regard to the ideas presented here.

THE HIDDEN OBJECTIVE

Instruction librarians teach in a variety of environments. Sometimes we teach in a library instruction room. Sometimes we teach as guests in college classrooms. Other times we teach online or one on one. Besides being influenced by the particular setting we find ourselves in at the moment, how we approach teaching depends on how formal or informal we wish to be. Some of us prefer a "sage on stage" model that emphasizes our role as authority figure while others sidestep the hierarchy by trying to be the students' friend. Regardless of setting and personal inclinations, we all arrive at the classroom door with a lesson plan in mind. This plan may be highly formal with the structure already laid out—complete with student learning outcomes and assessment measures—or it may be quite informal, even to the point that the librarian ad libs based on previous similar lessons. However tightly or loosely structured, the plan invariably will have a set of learning objectives connected to it. These objectives dictate the content of the instruction session, specifying what the students presumably will have learned by the end of the lesson. Missing from most lesson plans is any mention of how the students will behave during the lesson. Even if it is not written down, every lesson plan in the world has at least one hidden objective that must be in place before any of the learning objectives can be met (Berk, 2008). For this lesson plan, the hidden objective is this: students will pay attention, develop some measure of rapport with the instructor, and maybe even enjoy the experience.

If students do not pay attention, they will not remember what is taught, and both faculty and student time is wasted. Even if students pay attention, if they do not enjoy the experience or if they actively dislike it, they will probably not leave the lesson thinking well of either the subject or the instructor. An opportunity to forge a connection is squandered. The hidden objective needs to be taken into account because almost half of first-year students report feeling boredom in their classes (Berk 2008). Students are responsible for their own educations, but teachers are responsible for facilitating those educations. It is our contention that integrating humor into information literacy instruction can successfully address the hidden objectives and help facilitate our students' educations.

BARRIERS TO OVERCOME

Mobile communications devices are the first major barrier. According to an interview with S. Craig Watkins, professor of radio, television, and film at the University of Texas at Austin, the current crop of college students extensively uses the Internet to organize their social lives. Between mobile Internet devices and wired classrooms, students constantly face the temptation to monitor the latest developments in their social networks (Beja, 2009). That temptation can be overwhelming, and few college classes can offer subject matter juicy enough to compete. Based upon Watkins' observation and the relatively bland nature of information literacy as a subject, it is reasonably certain that your students will not struggle overmuch with the decision of whether to focus on library instruction or on their social networks. As librarians and teachers, we not only have to compete with mobile communications devices constantly distracting our students, but we also must deal with preexisting student stereotypes of librarians as well as, in many cases, a generation gap.

The popular stereotype of a librarian is not flattering. It interferes with our efforts to connect with our students and even to appear relevant to them. M. L. Radford and Radford (2003) characterize the librarian stereotype:

An obsession with order, sexual repression, matronly appearance, dowdy dress, fussiness, dour facial expressions, and monosyllabic speech. In media representations of professional librarians there are three predominant activities in which librarians engage: Shelving, stamping, and shushing. Occasionally they are also seen to be pushing carts of books around, pointing library users to the stacks in a desultory fashion, or rebuking users for failure to follow library procedures. (M. L. Radford & G. P. Radford, 1999)

While it is fairly certain that librarians are rather more aware of librarian stereotypes than the general population, those stereotypes do indeed have an effect on how we are perceived (Peresie & Alexander, 2005). Even though most students are probably not overtly contemplating librarian stereotypes upon entering the library, these unflattering images more than likely influence their expectations. That effect makes an already difficult task, that of gaining the attention of and building rapport with a group of unfamiliar students, even more difficult. As if this was not bad enough, libraries themselves are also the subject of negative stereotypes, with popular culture portraying libraries as places that range from confusing to terrifying (G. P. Radford & Radford, 2001). In light of these unfortunate misconceptions, it is not surprising that students dread library instruction (Petry, 1998). It was not by accident that the most frightening scene in the film *Ghostbusters* takes place in a library.

There is a generation gap that further distances librarians from students. Stanley Wilder (1996), assistant dean for technical and financial services in the Louisiana State University Libraries, writing about retirement projections for librarians for the Association of Research Libraries (ARL), noted that between 2005 and 2010, 24 percent of the ARL population was expected to retire. From 2010 to 2020, 27 percent is expected to retire. Based upon this information and assuming that they will retire at age 65, one can conclude that most librarians currently working are over the age of 50, born around the middle of the twentieth century. Most students currently entering college are between the ages of 18 and 20, which means they were born in the early 1990s. The average librarian is older than many of our students' parents. We will avoid discussions of generational traits as they often devolve into their own unfortunate stereotypes, but surely it is safe to say that a 30- to 40-year age gap will be characterized by dramatically different worldviews and stage-of-life issues. In a number of readily apparent ways, librarians are very different from undergraduate students. These differences must be minimized in order to successfully build rapport with these students.

SOLUTIONS

Any instruction librarian who hopes to be successful in the classroom must overcome, or at least mitigate, the problems presented by mobile communications, negative stereotypes, and, when applicable, age differences. While surely there are a variety of solutions to these problems, humor is convenient because it is capable of addressing all of these problems simultaneously. Most of the problems facing information literacy instruction are social in nature, so a social solution seems to be in order. According to Ziv, an Israeli clinical psychologist from Tel Aviv University who specializes in the study of humor, it "help[s] an individual climb the ladder of social hierarchy—to be *accepted*, to win affection, and to gain status" (1984, p. 30, emphasis added). In essence, funny people are easy to like, even if they are different from us. This is especially desirable in library instruction, in which one of the primary goals is to forge connections with students that will endure over time and result in voluntary return visits and positive word-of-mouth advertising for the library and librarians.

Mobile communications devices are not really the problem; they are just a symptom. The problem is that students find class material less stimulating than their social lives, as most students probably always have. The difference today is that mobile communications technology has opened up the option to discreetly interact online from anywhere a wireless signal can penetrate. The moment students cease to be interested by the class, the temptation to interact online can be too great to resist. Humor offers a solution because it engages the mind and provides the stimulation that our students' overstimulated brains crave. Once a class has determined that the teacher is offering up humorous content worth listening to, their attention will focus and the mobile devices will go dark.

Funny people are also a lot easier to pay attention to than boring people. Tierney (2010) reported on a study in *Science* magazine on the subject of daydreaming. The study found that most people tend to daydream about things they are not involved in during their days. According to this study, based upon 250,000 responses, people daydreamed the least while having sex, followed by "exercising, conversation, listening to music, taking a walk, eating, praying and meditating, cooking, shopping, taking care of one's children and reading." The *Science* study further revealed that people daydreamed the most during "personal grooming, [while] commuting and [while] working" (Tierney, 2010). The study further revealed that people's minds wandered nearly 50 percent of the time. Furthermore, "the rate of mind-wandering is lower for more enjoyable activities" (Tierney, 2010). This being the case, it is easy to draw the conclusion that the more worklike an activity is, the more one's mind will wander and the less one will either pay attention to it or absorb what is happening. Therefore, humor is an essential in an information literacy class. The less interesting and entertaining we are, the less attention students will pay to us. The more we make information literacy enjoyable and stimulating, the more students will pay attention. When students find an experience like library instruction stimulating that they expected to be profoundly boring, they get surprised, and that surprise helps dispel stereotypes. Students do not expect to have any fun during library instruction. They expect it to be dull, and they expect the librarian to be equally dull, if they trouble themselves to have any expectations of us at all.

The negative librarian stereotype probably gets far more attention than it deserves. However, there are widespread and unflattering notions about librarians that are perpetuated in popular culture, and whether or not students consciously consider them they almost certainly have some kind of effect on how our students perceive us. These notions are less of a problem in situations that we interact with students one-on-one with no time limit. The student probably signed up for a research consultation by choice and already values the help we can provide. Even if the student is not there by choice, the personal interaction gives us every opportunity to impress the student with our abilities and helpful demeanors. With a pile of learning objectives to work through and a running clock, however, negative stereotypes are harder to dispel. This is where humor comes in. Students will not expect a librarian to be funny or personable. By deviating from their expectations and making a more positive impression than they anticipated we can overcome those stereotypes if they are present. Conveniently, even if nobody in the room has ever thought ill of librarians, this approach will have essentially the same effect: the audience will enjoy spending time with us.

The last major barrier is the generation gap between librarians and students. To our students, many of the approaches to gathering and evaluating information we advocate appear unnecessarily cumbersome or antiquated. If that message was coming from a trusted peer, it would still be a tough sell, but coming from someone who remembers when typewriters were ascendant it is even worse. After all, we are telling them to avoid free search engines and crowd-sourced encyclopedias, both of which have worked swimmingly for their information needs for more than half of their lives. Most of the people they encounter who do not rely on these services are either ignorant of them or not technologically savvy enough to actually use them. From that perspective, it must be tempting for them to simply dismiss us as irrelevant relics who are hopelessly behind the times and want to hold them back with us. They see our withered claws clutching at them as we vanish into the quicksand of the past, and they want no part of it.

Fortunately, humor can circumvent that age difference, but only if it is calibrated to appeal to the students and not our own tastes. The underlying problem here has to do with relevance. Our visibly more advanced age is the first piece of evidence our students gather about us. Combined with the seemingly backward information-seeking behaviors we are advocating, they have all the evidence they need to dismiss us as not in possession of knowledge relevant to their lives. They think people significantly older than they are must be out of touch with the modern world. If we can entertain them, however, we can force them to reevaluate their judgments of us or prevent them from making those judgments in the first place. The ability to deliver material that is entertaining or humorous to them demonstrates that we are intellectually sharp and alert. By making that kind of impression, our message stands a better chance of being received.

WHY THE RESISTANCE?

Our personal experiences suggest, and research has confirmed, that the problems presented by mobile communications, negative stereotypes, and age differences can all be mitigated through the use of humor in the classroom. Yet there exists a lot of hesitation about using humor, and formal implementations of humor are unheard of at the programmatic level. We have this powerful tool at our disposal, but in this instance we believe that it is our own reluctance that holds us back. It is our assumption that this inhibition results from the notion that intentionally using humor in the classroom is somehow inappropriate, that it is, essentially beneath our dignity. After all, being an educator, and at the college level especially, is an august position in today's world, and humor in the classroom is a recent development. Korobkin (1988) observed that humor in the classroom as a teaching technique is less than a century old, and prior to that humor was considered to be antithetical to teaching. In that tradition, humor was a distraction, something that could only detract from the serious nature of scholarship. There was no need to inject entertainment value into lesson plans; traditional subject matter and lessons were supposed to keep students interested (Wandersee, 1982). This attitude goes back to the medieval origins of the institution of higher education, origins that are acknowledged at universities and colleges at least once a year at commencement, when faculty and students don medieval garb. This venerable convention reflects the ancient roots of our educational system. Although we are in the twenty-first century, remnants of the attitudes from those past ages are at least partially to blame for our reluctance to embrace humor, despite the advantages it offers.

While a historically levity-hostile university tradition contributes to many teachers' reluctance to use humor in their classes, the more immediate reason is concern over how colleagues and students will perceive them. Fear of being dismissed as a clown is powerful motivation for maintaining a serious tone. In an institution where humor has been rejected for centuries, this is an especially reasonable concern. However, nearly half of college-level instructors routinely use humor in their classes, so it is only by never using humor of any kind that will make you unusual (Osborne, 1992). Even if you were to be found guilty of being silly (perish the thought), we submit that it is a good thing to be thought of as a clown and have your students enjoy your classes and maybe even have a little bit of your passion for learning rub off on them—that is, if the alternative is to be a dour, humorless, and thoroughly respectable teacher whose students dread coming to class, or worse, attend class without engaging in the material. Of course there are more options out there than these two, but we offer this dichotomy to illustrate the point that it is our students who should be the focus of our efforts. Their needs should outweigh our vanity.

A number of librarians we have spoken with have expressed one other concern over using humor in the classroom: they do not want to draw attention to themselves. Students should focus on the subject matter at hand, their reasoning goes, and not on the instructor. Some of these librarians also intimated that they did not consider themselves to be especially interesting or remarkable people and that they like to avoid the spotlight. In reply to everyone who does not want to be singled out of the crowd, we have this to say to you: Too late. Anyone who stands up in front of a class is already in the spotlight, whether you want to think of it in that way or not. The students in your classes take inventory of you and pay attention to you, at least until they get distracted by the latest developments in their social lives. In this context, there is only one difference between the teachers who use humor and the ones who avoid it. The ones who use humor have chosen to take control of how they are perceived by their students. The ones who avoid humor have relinquished their control. Our students will put together first impressions of us no matter what we do, so it is best to do something that will help shape that impression into something positive.

Even if opening yourself up by revealing your sense of humor to strangers is a terrifying prospect, the potential rewards should give you pause. Sheidlower remembers only one individual lesson from eighth grade, which he completed more than 40 years ago. During a biology lesson, his teacher taught the difference between heredity and environment by telling a joke: A newlywed couple moves into a new neighborhood. Nine months later they have a baby. If that baby looks like the husband, that's heredity. If it looks like the mailman, that's environment. Sheidlower heard that joke over 40 years ago and still remembers it and the lesson it was designed to illustrate. Humor can, in some instances, help students form indelible memories. That kind of reward is worth some risk.

Part I

1

Information Literacy Instruction and Humor

INTRODUCTION

The purpose of this literature review is to examine research on humor as it pertains to library instruction. Because some of the relevant research predates the widespread adoption of the phrase *information literacy*, the phrase *library instruction* will be used to refer to information literacy as well as the older concept of bibliographic instruction. This is not to suggest the two concepts are interchangeable, as information literacy focuses on underlying concepts of information use and bibliographic instruction traditionally deals with the library as a physical location, as well as its services. This mingling of terminology is because humor, as it is dealt with in the literature, applies equally well to both information literacy and bibliographic instruction. There are 15 articles dealing with the subject of humor in library instruction published between 1985 and 2008, with the majority published between 1998 and 2008. Broadly speaking, most of the research focuses on the value or efficacy of humor in the classroom, with a minority of articles supplying advice on methods for using humor. Looking at the research as a whole, it is possible to synthesize the ideas expressed in the 15 articles into a cohesive statement about how the field of library science approaches the subject of humor in the library instruction classroom.

Literature on the subject of humor in libraries and library instruction reveals collective dissatisfaction with how instruction librarians relate to students. It suggests that librarians are responsible for this unsatisfactory relationship and that integrating humor into library instruction is likely to improve the relationship between library instructors and their students. Humor can be a double-edged sword, however, offering both peril and reward. Used properly, humor provides a number of benefits to both instructor and student. Misused, humor can be detrimental to the student-teacher relationship. While educational benefits are frequently referenced, the primary value of integrating humor into library instruction is social, as are the primary risks. There is much to lose from humor backfiring in the individual library instruction session, but at a broader level implementation of humor contributes to a more pleasant and stimulating work environment for the instruction librarian, who otherwise faces a repetitive and possibly tedious curriculum. It also helps to create a more pleasant learning environment that promotes rapport between teacher and student. These advantages outweigh the risks, but humor is a skill and must be learned and improved through trial and error. Humorous techniques can fail to work well the first few times and often require experimentation to succeed. During this period of experimentation in front of a live audience, failures can seem disproportionately devastating, so steely resolve on the part of the librarian is beneficial. For this reason, despite its potential benefits, humor in the classroom should only be undertaken by librarians who are comfortable with the challenges humor presents and are committed to investing the time and energy needed to produce quality results.

While the literature indeed takes varying positions on humor in the classroom, there are sufficient commonalities present to cobble together coherent useful descriptions of the state of humor in library instruction as pictured across the past 25 years. This review begins with an examination of how instruction librarians see themselves and how they see their students before moving on to discuss the myriad claims about the advantages conferred by effective use of humor in the classroom. The review closes with discussions on humor as a learned skill versus an inborn talent, the differences between spontaneous and planned humor, and what kinds of humor to use or avoid in the classroom.

PICTURE OF THE INSTRUCTION LIBRARIAN

In general, literature on humor in library instruction paints a grim picture of the present state of instruction librarians: They are strange, unapproachable people who inhabit the library, which is itself an unwelcoming, unpleasant place to spend time (Arnsan, 2000). If librarians are funny, it is most likely unintentional, and they take themselves too seriously in general (Fulton, 1985). They describe their classes as boring and themselves as not being funny, even though laughing among friends is one of the most normal human behaviors there is (Walker, 2005). Librarians who avoid using humor have no shortage of good reasons to not introduce it in their classrooms. Some librarians express anxiety over the possibility that levity in the classroom will lead to a "complete loss of control" (Walker, 2005, p. 120). Others are concerned that they and their message will be dismissed as frivolous entertainment without any meaningful substance (MacAdam, 1985). There is also the assumption that humor is not a skill that can be learned: one is either funny and able to adroitly use humor or one is not (Sarkodie-Mensah 1998).

It is no surprise, then, that "library instruction can be boring to teach and boring to listen to" (Trefts & Blakeslee, 2000, p. 369). Even when a library instructor might be inclined to experiment with humor, there are some fairly compelling reasons to resist the urge. Similar observations are made about library instruction classes, although the blame, when it is placed, falls on the instruction librarian and not the material. As Warnken and Young (1991) noted, making an instruction session more entertaining (or at least less dull) "require[s] that librarians have a sense of humor, something too often lacking in library instruction" (p. 94). There is no evidence that observations like that one are being made because library instruction classes in general are pretty stimulating but just aren't quite stimulating enough. Rather, it is evident that the library instruction classes these authors have in mind are mind-numbingly dull indeed.

Instruction librarians and their classes as they are glimpsed through the literature seem drab and grim, but there is hope. Librarians mentioned in these articles expressed concerns about using humor themselves, but they also "agreed that using humor was a successful strategy" (Walker, 2005, p. 119). Furthermore, every article surveyed expressed the importance for library instruction classes to be fun, to include humor. Not a single article decried the use of humor or tried to argue that library instruction was already sufficiently stimulating. At the very least, these sentiments reveal an awareness of the value of improvement and a desire to make library instruction better than it is. While many library instruction sessions might continue to be tedious and dull for the time being, the motivation is there for improvement to occur. That improvement might be reached as easily as by making humor a consistent feature in library instruction (Warnken & Young, 1991). Bolstering this positive undercurrent is the belief that the subject matter is not to blame for library instruction being boring: if anything is responsible for tedium in the classroom, it is the instructor's behavior. While this focus on the librarian as the cause of the problem can seem hostile or negative, it is actually heartening. The subject matter for library instruction is much less capable of change than the person presenting it. Research methods and infrastructure gradually change, but they are essentially static in comparison with the effectively limitless ways that those methods can be introduced to students.

PICTURE OF THE STUDENTS AND THEIR ATTITUDES

Although students attending library instruction sessions can vary from first-year students to upperclassmen or graduate students, one commonality they share is that library instruction bores them (Trefts & Blakeslee, 2000; Petry, 1998; Sarkodie-Mensah, 1998). Instead of being a reason for the library instructor to despair (and perhaps seek work gutting fish in Alaska), our students' uniform boredom serves as a fine reason to employ humor: "An early manifestation of humor not only dispels the belief that, 'neither libraries nor librarians are especially interesting,' but also ensures students that the session *is* bound to be useful and fun" (Sarkodie-Mensah, 1998, p. 27). There is a consensus that students enter the library instruction classroom without much hope for anything stimulating to happen during the next hour of their lives. They are at best bored and at worst irritated about being forced to sit through something they feel they already know and hostile toward the person at the front of the classroom who seems responsible for this waste of time.

All is not lost, however. The audience might be bored and possibly hostile, but knowing that in advance has value, and that knowledge can be capitalized on. In terms of their expectations for the next hour or so, the bar is set low enough to trip over. In stark contrast, imagine for a moment trying to perform in front of the same group of people at a comedy club. Because they expect to have a good time (and paid good money) they will not be surprised when they enjoy themselves. Now consider the stereotypical library instruction class: bored, possibly convinced they will learn nothing of value. For someone in such a state of mind, humor's "surprise power is tremendous" (Fulton, 1985, p. 5). Because expectations for enjoyment are low, there is great potential for disrupting those expectations and thereby gaining these students' attention and, possibly even better, their goodwill. Arguably, the instruction librarian's effort to integrate humor into the classroom is made easier by the students' negative preconceived notions.

REASONS FOR USING HUMOR

If library instruction is indeed often tedious, and if librarians are indeed to blame for that, then at least there is hope. The literature contains a constellation of claims about the numerous palliative effects successful implementation of humor can deliver. In fact, there are so many different positive effects ascribed to the use of humor that nearly all of these articles feature a section containing a laundry list of desirable results. This practice suggests a common feeling that the use of humor warrants defending, but based on the wide-ranging salubrious side effects of humor that tend to get cited whatever it is that these scholars are defending themselves against seems to be rather unfocused. These reasons supporting the use of humor often feel tacked on, as if the researchers decided they approved of humor (who wouldn't?), and then went hunting for reasons why humor is good (the age-old practice of searching for evidence to support a conclusion that has already been reached).

The reasons cited for using humor in the library instruction classroom can be collapsed into eight basic categories: expressing personality, establishing trust, improving delivery and apparent competence, reducing student anxiety, gaining and maintaining student attention, fighting instructor burnout, promoting understanding and information retention, and undermining negative library or librarian stereotypes. It would be convenient if these categories fit neatly into a hierarchy, with some categories bearing greater significance or merit than others. That does not appear to be the case here. Some categories, such as establishing trust, do indeed receive more attention than others, such as fighting negative stereotypes. Apart from greater attention across the literature, there are no other indications that some reasons are more important than others.

Expressing Personality

Although the library instructors take most of the blame for failing to relate to students and delivering uninspiring instruction sessions, it is not necessarily because they are boring people. Rather, the problem lies with relating to the students more successfully. Audiences gather an impression of who an instructor is, decide if they like the instructor, and from there determine if they are worth listening to, whether or not the instructor consciously makes an attempt to influence that decision. In the absence of personality-conveying devices such as humor, the only information about the instructor's personality available to students will be what they can glean from a cursory visual inspection and introductory statements made by the instructor. It is dangerous to leave it up to students to cobble together a picture of who the instruction librarian is, especially when there is a device like humor available, which is a fundamental social skill adapted to facilitate communication (Walker, 2005). Using humor can shape how an audience perceives who instructors are as people, which can influence how their message is received. Given the recurring statements in the literature relating to the process of building ethos and teacher personality that exhort the librarian to use humor in order to better transmit personality, it can be inferred that librarians' personalities work to their advantage, provided those personalities can be successfully transmitted.

Surely, if their underlying personalities were off-putting and alienating, there wouldn't be so many suggestions to use humor to better express those personalities. One would instead find dozens of articles suggesting librarians conceal their unpleasant selves and offering well-meaning advice on ways to fake more desirable personalities.

While an instructor's personality will establish itself over time on its own, "Humor may be even more important for librarians to use because we are only given a short time to make a good impression" (Brewerton, 2002, p. 29). Humor does not require more than a few seconds to work, and it conveys a tremendous amount of information in that short time, effectively compressing the amount of personal information delivered naturally over a period of days or weeks and delivering it in moments. It is further an effective teaching tool because it doesn't stop at conveying personal information but "carries the advantage of expressing the personality of the teacher as well as functioning as a method of communication" (MacAdam, 1985, p. 327). Humor, when used effectively, transmits information across multiple channels, simultaneously conveying social and subject-related data without cost to either channel.

If a significant portion of an instructor's personality is established during the first impression, and that the first impression produces ripples that affect future interactions and perceptions, then humor has value because it "helps ensure a positive 'first contact' and amplifies other desirable aspects of the learning process" (Petry, 1998, p. 82). Instead of waging an uphill battle to change the hearts and minds of students predisposed against the experience of library instruction, it is possible to begin an instruction session from a position of strength and use the goodwill created by that positive first impression to convince a room full of skeptical students that they should take the library and its resources seriously, if only for a 50-minute hour.

Establishing Trust

Surely trust between teacher and student is always helpful to the learning process, but for the instruction librarian it is crucial. Not only is there important information being passed along but students in the audience should feel comfortable seeking the instruction librarian's help on their own in the future. It is insufficient to be viewed as trustworthy but unapproachable. MacAdam (1985, p. 329) discusses "ingrained social barriers" that separate students and teachers and suggests they can be overcome with humor. Brewerton (2002) also discusses these barriers and recommends that the "use of self-deprecating humor by the presenter can help remove barriers and place the student and teacher-librarian on a more even footing" (p. 29). By cheerfully undercutting ourselves, we demonstrate that we are not insecure about ourselves and our message and earn goodwill by not emphasizing what educational or power differences might exist between us. That smoothing of differences through humor "reinforces camaraderie and just generally keeps morale up and stress down in the classroom" (Arnsan, 2000, p. 54). Of course, not all humor needs to be self-deprecating to be effective.

Laughing together involves everyone sharing a pleasant emotional experience. The collective experience of humor can "mold a collection of individuals into a group" (Trefts & Blakeslee, 2000, p. 370). If nothing else, the people in the classroom, both teacher and students, have the enjoyment of humor in common, and that enjoyment can serve as a foundation to establish a relationship with a connection that outlasts the hour or so allotted to an instruction session. Sultanoff (1993) reports that humor not only improves communication but also promotes personal connections between teachers and students, a finding echoed by Sarkodie-Mensah (1998): "A good sense of humor captures the attention of the students and brings them closer to the librarian giving the presentation" (p. 25). Laughter appears to act as a social glue, bringing otherwise unconnected people together and promoting mutual trust, provided that everyone is in on the joke. In the context of a college classroom, in which at least some of the humor might involve abstruse intellectual subject matter, there is significant risk that some students will miss the humor and feel resentful. "Misunderstood jokes—especially intellectual humour—can be perceived as 'cleverness', a form of mental one-upsmanship, producing a barrier—rather than a bond—between the group and the presenter" (Brewerton, 2002, p. 29). Even if the subject matter of the humor is not inherently obscure, it is especially important that everyone in the class be able to understand and appreciate the humor, lest it turn on its user and leave the instructor facing a now-hostile audience.

Even when it is perfectly understood, the appropriateness of humor is not perceived the same way by everyone, and college classrooms can be home to diverse audiences. In her seminal article, Barbara MacAdam (1985) explored the body of research regarding humor in the college classroom and applied it to library instruction. She found some conflicting reports. One report indicated that students see teachers as "more straightforward and honest when they use no humor of any sort" (p. 329). However, being perceived as "more straightforward" is something else entirely from being perceived as disingenuous. Another report found that "the ethos of the source who employed humorous content in a persuasive message will be regarded more favorably four weeks later than the ethos of the source who presented the serious persuasive message" (p. 331). To wit, teachers using humor risk their students perceiving them as less genuine than teachers who maintain a serious tone throughout. The risk comes with a reward, however. Students will remember the humorous teacher as being more trustworthy in the following weeks. For the instruction librarian, those following weeks are the time when students will most likely benefit from individual assistance, and that added feeling of trust generated by humor could be the difference between seeking help and not seeking help. MacAdam (1985) goes on to elegantly argue that the instruction librarian faces an unusual combination of challenges when standing up in front of an unfamiliar audience for the first time. Given that there is little or no time to build trust naturally, more aggressive methods, like humor, must be employed.

Delivery and Competence

Getting the audience to like the instructor (or at least to not actively *dis*like the instructor) and to feel comfortable are both important milestones to reach, but the audience must also believe that the instructor is competent and consequently worth paying attention to. Like everything else in library instruction, this must also be accomplished on an expedited timeline. Demonstrations of instructor competence in a subject area tend to naturally occur later in the session, such as while modeling search strategies or recalling relevant facts from memory. Waiting for these opportunities to occur naturally requires too much patience on the part of the audience, and artificially relocating them to the beginning of the presentation will only result in confusion. Instead of demonstrating competence through a show of skill in a subject-related area, it can be much more effective to demonstrate competence by proxy: by delivering an excellent presentation.

Public speaking skills are readily apparent to an audience and can serve as an ersatz demonstration of instructor competence. Warnken and Young (1991) argue:

More than anything, it is the delivery, the actual presentation in the classroom, that determines the ultimate success of any library instruction program. It is the delivery that convinces the instructor and students that the class session has fulfilled an identified need, and that library instruction does, indeed, have value. (p. 91)

Whether accurate or not, students view the degree of competence with which a presentation is given as a reliable indicator of the value of the message being presented. Consequently, an excellent presentation is perceived as conveying a superior message to a presentation that was poorly delivered. A high production value establishes trust, which manifests in students as a willingness to hear the message before passing judgment.

Humor is not necessary for a presentation to be excellent, but a presentation must be excellent in order for humor to be successful. If the class is laughing along with the instructor's humor, the instructor must be communicating with clarity, sufficient volume, and appropriate pacing, all of which are evidence of excellent public speaking skills. Moreover, humor makes a presentation more entertaining than it would otherwise be, and an entertaining presentation is likely to be judged a good presentation. Humor can also start playing a role within the opening seconds of a presentation, so using humor to demonstrate competence can help to begin the instruction session from a position of strength.

Reducing Student Anxiety

The library instruction classroom might not be the most pleasant place for a student to spend an hour or more. The room is unfamiliar, the teacher is unfamiliar, and the labyrinthine building everything is housed in could very well be an additional source of unease. Moreover, the visit was likely occasioned by an upcoming research assignment that students (rightly) fear will devour their free time, profoundly influence their final grades, and might even represent the first serious college-level research assignment in their careers. Whether or not the specter of library anxiety is to blame, there is a consensus that students in the library instruction classroom are prone to experience some kind of aversive emotional state, such as anxiety, stress, poor morale, or some combination thereof, and that humor is the antidote: "anxiety levels in [an] undergraduate class decreased by almost two standard deviations [when humor was used] (Berk & Nanda, 1988, p. 118). Additionally, Arnsan (2000), Fulton (1985), Trefts & Blakeslee (2000), Bryson (2008), Walker (2005), and Brewerton (2002) all claim that humor reduces stress or anxiety and advocate the use of humor in the classroom specifically to combat those emotions. If humor can make the library visit less aversive for students, then it warrants being used for that reason alone.

By reducing anxiety, other, more desirable emotional states can flourish. Arnsan (2000) notes that "Humor . . . just generally keeps morale up" (p. 54). Since students in library instruction often arrive "with a very low morale," tactics that can ameliorate low morale or even produce high morale deserve serious consideration (Sarkodie-Mensah, 1998). Putting students into a good mood seems worthwhile for its own sake, but it can have other benefits. Walker (2005) notes that "humor facilitated creativity in a classroom situation by reducing students' anxiety levels" (p. 118). While humor by itself does not promote creativity, it does seem capable of removing the obstacles to creativity that crop up during or before library instruction. The library instruction classroom might not be art class, but active learning techniques, not to mention effective research, benefits from a flexible, creative mindset.

Gaining and Maintaining Student Attention

Gaining and maintaining student attention has long been the bugbear of library instruction. Students who are paying attention are students who can be taught, but keeping a classroom distraction-free can prove challenging. Magnifying this problem (or at least not making it any better) is the often-tedious subject matter of library instruction, combined with the unfamiliar surroundings and unfamiliar presenter. Exacerbating an already bad situation is the commonly held notion that free online search engines have all of the answers, and the challenge of making library instruction appear meaningful becomes all that much harder.

Instead of trying to make the material spark interest and inspire students to pay attention, humor can be used. If the instructor is funny, students have an incentive to pay attention to the presentation, and it is an incentive that works. Humor is an effective tool that can be used to both piqué student attention and hold their interest (Sarkodie-Mensah, 1998; Walker, 2005; Fulton, 1985; Trefts & Blakeslee, 2000). In this context, humor is much like butter on lutefisk. Lutefisk, a gelatinous, protein-rich fish carcass preserved in lye and once eaten as a staple in northern Europe, now survives as a traditional dish enthusiastically served on holidays to acquaint young people of Nordic ancestry with their cultural traditions. It is quite nutritious, but requires a great deal of butter and pepper to render it even remotely palatable. Without grease and spice to mask its fishy odors and distract from its slimy, colloidal texture, it is repellent to modern palates. In the same way, a student who teeters at the brink of failure in a class might hang on the instruction librarian's every word, but it would be better if the student could be taught the relevant grade-preserving skills before the situation deteriorates to that point. Humor can play that role by masking the boring parts of library instruction and make the experience stimulating enough to promote student attention (Brewerton, 2002).

It is important to note that using humor to make library instruction more appealing does not and should not involve diminishing the educational content or making the instruction room into a comedy club. Humor does capture attention by virtue of being entertaining, but it is not entertaining in the way that a film is entertaining: The audience in a humorous library instruction session is not passive. On the contrary, the effort necessary to keep pace with a humorous presenter ensures that "this is not a mentally passive environment" (Brewerton, 2002, p. 29). Making sense of humor requires an alert mind, and laughter carries physiological effects that in turn promote alertness: "Laughter wakes up the classroom. More oxygen enters the blood during a good laugh and a variety of muscles react making your students more alert" (Arnsan, 2000, p. 54). Humor does not need to manifest as uproarious laughter to glean at least some of these effects, either: "Witticisms, word play, and erudite references also demand a type of flexible thinking" (Brewerton, 2002, p. 29). Humor captures and maintains student attention in large part because it is not intellectually predigested. The audience must make sense of each joke or humorous statement by making their own connections, and that effort cannot be switched on selectively to only interpret humorous remarks. It must be continued throughout the session in order to avoid missing humorous moments. Once students begin listening and thinking in this way, they cannot help but apply the same attention to the subject matter of the instruction session. The lutefisk has been buttered and peppered.

Fighting Instructor Burnout

Most of the discussion regarding humor has been on its effect on students and their often unflattering perceptions of library instruction, but students are not the only ones who can feel boredom. Instruction librarians teaching many similar groups of students the same material over and over are subject to "a sense of stressful tedium" (MacAdam, 1985, p. 328). While there are probably any number of creative measures that can be put in place to make the job of library instruction less tedious, adopting a humorous approach has been observed to effectively counteract this problem. Using humor in the classroom generally improves the "quality of teachers' lives" (Brewerton, 2002, p. 30). Students who are having fun will be more pleasant to teach, and humorous approaches can be readily changed to maintain a feeling of freshness and challenge. The advantages do not remain in the classroom, either: "People who have fun at work are more creative, more productive, get along better with co-workers, and are better decision makers. They also call in sick less often" (Bryson, 2008, p. 95). Even if humor fails to be the panacea that Bryson describes, integrating humor into library instruction offers a myriad of beneficial side effects for the instructor, any one of which would likely make the effort worthwhile.

Apart from the benefits imparted by experiencing humor in the library instruction setting, students stand to benefit from being taught by an instructor who enjoys humor: "Adding humor to the material helps keep the librarian interested. Bibliographic instruction can be repetitive; if the librarian is bored, why should the students be otherwise?" (Petry, 1998, p. 76). In answer to Petry, if the librarian is bored, there is no reason students should be anything other than bored. Emotional states can be contagious, and students will pick up on that immediately: "The tone and mood set by the teacher librarian's own demeanor will transfer to students. For example, if the instructor is smiling and laughing, then the students will react to the playful banter" (Walker, 2005, p. 122). On the other hand, if the instructor is emotionally compromised by stressful tedium, that is just as likely to transfer to students, so it pays for the instructor to be in a good mood. Although the students and the instructor are separate beings, they share an emotional state, to one degree or another, for the duration of the session, and the instructor has a great deal of influence on the quality of that emotional state. MacAdam (1985) sums the situation up: "of the many devices a teacher can employ to add interest, spontaneity, enjoyment, and warmth to the classroom, few are as widely palliative for both teacher and student as humor" (p. 328). In this respect, humor is remarkable for being a pedagogical technique that is at least as helpful to the instructor as it is to the student.

Promoting Comprehension and Information Retention

At the heart of the question about the value of humor in an educational setting are two questions. One: Does humor actually help students retain information? More specifically, will information presented in a humorous manner be remembered more accurately or for a longer time than information presented without humor? Two: Does humor promote comprehension? Can humor make a complex concept more readily understandable? For the purposes of library instruction, both retention and comprehension are of course necessary whether or not humor is involved. Memory without understanding has minimal value, and understanding without memory has even less. At best, the answer to both of these questions appears to be "maybe." This is an issue much of the literature avoids or only touches on briefly, and for good reason. Research on humor and pedagogy is relatively scarce, and what research exists is not especially conclusive (Berk, 2003). Humor does not appear to either hinder or assist the learning process in any way that is readily apparent or measurable, and there is ongoing scholarly debate regarding this issue.

Walker (2005) and Brewerton (2002) both assert that humor does indeed promote student learning, but they do so in passing, devoting at most just a few sentences to the issue. MacAdam (1985), in our opinion at any rate, conducted the most detailed analysis of humor in the college classroom and its relationship to library instruction, and her findings in this area were not encouraging. In general, humor in the classroom appeared to have little, if any, measurable effect on recall, with the possible exception of humorous examples: "use of specific humorous examples may actually increase retention for that particular material" (MacAdam, 1985, p. 332). This exception is also noted by Walker (2005): "studies also show that students learn more when concepts are illustrated with humor that is pertinent to the course material" (p. 120). In light of this information, it is perhaps not surprising that the literature on using humor in library instruction often recommends the use of humorous examples related to the subject matter over most other kinds of humor use.

Regardless of the research, it seems clear that at least some of the authors very much want to believe that humor aids retention and comprehension, and that belief deserves a moment of scrutiny. Although the research seems inconclusive, it does seem safe to say that humor shows no evidence of reducing either comprehension or retention, so at worst it is acting as a placebo, convincing the instructor that students are going to learn what is being taught. If that is the only effect humor can actually deliver, then it is a powerful effect indeed. Confident, enthusiastic instructors improve almost any classroom: they are the teachers who enjoy themselves and are consequently enjoyed by their students.

Undermining Negative Stereotypes

If librarianship is a profession that suffers from negative stereotypes, then humor is a tool that can be effective in combating those stereotypes, especially in the library instruction classroom. Students arrive in the library with the notion that both libraries and librarians are dull, as well as the belief that neither has anything valuable to offer. Using humor early in the session undermines those notions and suggests to the students that the coming session will have value (Sarkodie-Mensah, 1998). By virtue of delivering an experience that is the polar opposite of what the students expected to encounter in the library, the instruction librarian disrupts student expectations and opens them up to forming new perspectives about librarians and the library. Arnsan (2000) noted that:

When you [the instruction librarian] make your presentations come alive with humor, you help destroy those library stereotypes. Those English 100 students will remember the library/LRC as a welcome, pleasant place and even if they forget much of the content of your orientation, they are bound to remember the research possibilities and will return to you because your humor makes you approachable. (p. 55)

Being approachable in the future is perhaps even more important, and easier to achieve, than imparting all of the skills and information a student will need for successful academic research, especially in the limited context of an hour-long instruction session. There is no advantage in letting students' preconceived notions about the library persist any longer than necessary, especially since many of those notions are likely to be unflattering or inaccurate.

Conclusion

Students attending library instruction sessions are often taught by an instructor unfamiliar to them and find themselves sitting in a classroom environment that looks and feels rather different from the room where they usually meet. Often, they enter the classroom feeling either neutral or hostile towards the idea of library instruction and are inclined to make snap judgments about the instruction librarian using whatever evidence is readily on hand. If the librarian uses humor that expresses a distinct and likable personality early in the session, students become more open to paying attention to the librarian and the class material and might even reconsider previously held notions about libraries or librarians. By getting the class to laugh periodically, the instruction librarian can build on the initial goodwill created by the immediate use of humor to create feelings of comfort and trust with the class, while at the same time maintaining the students' attention on the subject matter being presented in that session. The challenge of creating and implementing humor in the library instruction classroom also helps the instructor remain excited about and engaged in what is otherwise fairly repetitive material. That excitement translates to the instructor having a livelier classroom presence, which energizes students and further improves the experience for everyone present.

Even if using humor in the classroom does little or nothing to augment students' memory of subject matter, it is worth using for the social benefits it offers. Retention of information is crucial, but without attention and some measure of trust, information won't be absorbed in the first place. Students can't retain what they refuse to pay attention to, and there is nothing like actually paying attention to something for learning about it.

WHO CAN USE HUMOR?

Can humor be learned, or is it something innate? Some scholars argue in favor of humor as a learned skill, and others see it as an innate ability. In order to better understand the issue, it is more productive to conceive of it in terms of a different dichotomy: skill versus aptitude. Skill is imparted by education and practice and can be acquired by anyone. Aptitude is the inborn capacity for excellence in any given skill, and that capacity cannot be increased. Two people with different degrees of aptitude can be given identical training and practice in a skill, but the one with superior aptitude will perform that skill with greater mastery than the one with inferior aptitude.

Humor, the ability to amuse others, is a skill. Like other skills, practice yields improvement. Because aptitude varies, some people, regardless of practice, possess a greater capacity for excellence than others. The common perception that humor is an inborn talent, something that cannot be acquired or improved through practice, discourages people from trying to learn to be funny. Sarkodie-Mensah (1998) notes that "the first major step in acquiring a sense of humor is to dispel the myth that a sense of humor is a gift for a selected few" (pp. 25–26). It might seem as if only a lucky few have the talent to make others laugh, but that might be because those people identified a high aptitude for humor relatively early in life and subsequently spent years and possibly even decades honing their skills and becoming funny people. While their abilities to make others laugh can seem almost magical, it really is just a high level of skill at work. Trefts and Blakeslee (2000) observed that " 'naturally funny' instructors actually creat[e] opportunities for their humor and spontaneity" (p. 375). Because a talent for humor often places them in the center of attention, these people are also especially visible; the many mildly funny people out there are eclipsed by those merry few. In combination, both that daunting excellence and high visibility conspire to propagate the myth Sarkodie-Mensah wishes to dispel.

This is not to say that anyone can decide to be funny and make it happen overnight. Although humor can be learned, not all kinds of humor are equally easy to implement. Some can be used right away, while others require experience to execute successfully. For example, Saunders (2002) discusses the challenge of using humorous banter with students and notes that it "demands a certain sort of person. The instructor must be very confident . . . to be successful with this type of humor" (p. 6). Using a technique such as humorous banter requires a great degree of confidence, which should ideally emerge from a high degree of skill, which in turn usually takes a lot of hard work. Fortunately, becoming a remarkably funny person is not a prerequisite for using humor in the classroom.

Being a funny person and being an instructor who uses humor are different things. Brewerton (2002) notes that "Humor doesn't come to everyone, but everyone can work to develop a humorous approach to teaching" (p. 30). It is not necessary to be hilarious in order to integrate humor into library instruction. The instruction classroom is a (relatively) controlled environment; it is possible to carefully plan ways to inject humor into the curriculum, and many kinds of humor can be used. Additionally, because curricula often remain the same from one class to the next, it is possible, and even desirable, to hone humorous techniques with the draft process, keeping whatever is funny and replacing the boring ones.

Apart from mastering the actual mechanisms of humor such as timing or delivery, the most important first step towards using humor in the classroom is to build comfort with being funny in front of an audience (Archibeque, 1987). Adding humor to one's repertoire does not happen overnight. There will be failures more often than there will be successes, especially at first (Brewerton, 2002; Petry, 1998). The beginning humorist must be able to accept a modicum (or even perhaps a heaping dose) of public embarrassment. It is through failure that much of the learning emerges, and being able to weather those setbacks is necessary to developing any level of skill with humor. Lack of comfort will translate to awkwardness in front of the classroom, and "the tone and mood set by the teacher librarian's own demeanor will transfer to students" (Walker, 2005, p. 122). The rubber chicken stretches both ways: if the instructor is anxious, that emotion will transfer just as readily as confidence and excitement will.

Anyone can learn to use humor, but it seems that not everyone using humor will be perceived in the same way by their audiences. The instructor's gender plays a role in the how students respond to humor. MacAdam (1985) cautions that "students judge men and women teachers differently" (p. 329). Students do not check their cultural backgrounds at the door; they carry with them the unconscious expectations for how they think instructors for each gender should behave. For librarianship, a field predominantly occupied by women, MacAdam (1985) notes a troubling finding:

For male teachers, use of humor was related to higher positive teacher evaluations than those using no humor, regardless of the particular type of humor employed (hostile, nonhostile, sexual, nonsense, etc.) Female teachers who used humor, however, generally received lower evaluation scores on competence and delivery as well as on the measure of overall teaching effectiveness. (p. 331)

It is perhaps worth noting that a college-aged student in 1985, the time of the writing of MacAdam's article, would now be in their 40s, and that attitudes toward how each gender ought to behave shift at least a little from generation to generation. At the time of the writing of this book, the students attending library instruction are the children of those college students described by MacAdam, and their evaluations of the behavior befitting each gender might be more egalitarian than their parents'. Then again, maybe those attitudes remain unchanged. Since the idea that women are less funny than men is ludicrous, it is tempting to speculate that, at least with the students in MacAdam's (1985) sample, students might perceive humor as a trait suitable and desirable for males but inappropriate for females. A female exhibiting a behavior associated with males might then be viewed through a more hostile lens. A rough analog for this situation might be body building: A male with large, well-developed muscles is likely to be viewed as virile or powerful. A heavily muscled female might be less likely to garner similar approval and might very well earn disdain for her efforts.

Using sexual or hostile humor can further compound this situation: "student perception of tendentious or hostile humor is especially negative when the instructor is a woman" (MacAdam, 1985, p. 330). To continue speculating, hostility is a trait often associated with masculinity, so when it is combined with humor, the gender-related expectations take effect. Further reinforcing the idea that humor is entwined with gender and sexuality, MacAdam (1985) reported that "teachers using sexual humor were found to be less appealing to members of the same sex but more appealing to students of the opposite sex" (p. 331). This last finding seems especially counterintuitive. Surely female students would react poorly to a male teacher making sexually charged jokes, or sexually charged statements of any kind for that matter. The opposite appears to be the case: teachers can more easily bond with opposite-sex students through the use of sexually charged humor. Used judiciously, this knowledge could prove useful for instruction librarians teaching in single-sex institutions or who find themselves in classrooms filled predominantly with a single sex. At the very least, it should be taken into account that a female instruction librarian could have a steeper road ahead of her when it comes to integrating humor into her classroom than her male colleagues face and that she should be especially careful before making any jokes of a hostile or sexually charged nature. However, female comedians have found success; there is no reason why female instruction librarians should be any different.

DELIVERY: SPONTANEOUS VERSUS PLANNED HUMOR

What is the best way to go about it bringing humor into the classroom? For people who don't consider themselves funny, it might seem reasonable to think up a joke related to the material in advance and deliver it when the time comes. MacAdam (1985) cautions against planning humor in advance, advocating instead a more free-form approach: "spontaneous rather than belabored or artificial use of humor appears to be a significant element in creating a positive communicative climate" (p. 330). This claim probably makes intuitive sense to anyone who has ever been subject to a clumsy attempt at humor. Walker (2005) agrees: "traditional age college students prefer anecdotes and spontaneous humor to memorized jokes" (p. 121). MacAdam and Walker are both describing the current audience's rejection of formulaic or planned humor in favor of the more informal or spontaneous humor featured in contemporary stand-up comedy acts or comedic films. The division between spontaneous and planned is not quite that simple, however. Walker (2005) observes that "even humor that seems spontaneous can be planned" (p. 121). Contemporary humor takes pains to appear conversational and spontaneous despite actually being carefully planned and scripted. This presentation promotes misconceptions about how effective humor is produced. Spontaneous humor is not inherently any better than planned humor at earning laughs. On the contrary, as we discuss in Chapter 5, one of the key behaviors of successful comics is their extensive planning.

The division between spontaneous and planned humor is like the myth of the natural comedian: incorrect, but an easy mistake for an observer to make. The act of planning does not drain humor of its vigor and comedic potential. Really funny material does not occur naturally in abundance. It must be gathered over time. It also does not come into being fully formed. Revision is required, as is practice delivering it out loud in a manner that feels natural and spontaneous to an audience. Thus, it is only through careful planning that humor can appear spontaneous. Even humor that appears completely free form, such as when a comedian banters with the audience, is usually the result of extensive preparation and practice.

A great dancer rarely performs without choreography and cannot perform at all without years of practice. It is only through exhaustive training and repetition that difficult movements can be made to appear effortless. The same rule applies to humor. This misconception that successful humor happens spontaneously and unsuccessful humor arises from planning demoralizes those who might seek to develop their senses of humor. If planned humor is terrible and unfunny and spontaneous humor happens on its own in the spur of the moment, then nothing is to be done. This would lead to the fallacious belief that one is either funny or one is not. Thankfully, this is a false dichotomy, just as the idea of the naturally funny comedian is a myth.

Instead of dividing humor into the flawed categories of either planned or spontaneous, it is more productive to make the division between types of humor as humor that has been delivered well and humor that has been delivered poorly. One of the traits that separate good humor from bad is how well it is delivered. When researchers describe situations in which "planned" humor fails, they are describing situations in which the audience figured out how the presenter was going to try to make them laugh in advance of the attempt. The problem did not originate from the humor being planned or scripted; it originated from the planning being insufficient for the task. In order to find a statement funny, the audience must be surprised, it must be caught off guard. A clumsy attempt at humor telegraphs the presenter's intention too far in advance of the humor, giving the audience time to duck down and warily peer out of their foxholes.

Such a fuss is made about the success of spontaneous humor and the failure of planned humor because the stakes are so high. Any attempt at humor creates a crisis: the audience will either laugh, or they will not. Each outcome carries social consequences. Making the audience laugh earns goodwill and any number of the other rewards discussed earlier in this chapter. Failing to make the audience laugh, on the other hand, can be destructive. In the library instruction classroom, students are not only critical of the failure to make them laugh; they can become resentful.

MacAdam (1985) offers a theory explaining this resentment: "students have the perception that 'deliberate humor is a sign of a teacher's intent to control the classroom' " (p. 329). Unsurprisingly, that intent is resented. Presumably, most students are aware that teachers want to be in control of their classrooms. It is likely the ham-handed way in which it is attempted, not the desired outcome, that is what the students resent. This same phenomenon can be observed in critical responses to films as well. Films that succeed in skillfully manipulating our emotions are often celebrated, while films that attempt but fail to do so are decried. Audiences keep going to the movies, though, so it appears audiences do not wish to avoid being manipulated. More likely, they do not mind emotional manipulation, provided it is done skillfully, with such facility that the manipulation goes unnoticed.

When the manipulation is obvious, as with a bad movie or a comedically inexperienced instructor, the audience not only sits immune to the desired effect, but they turn: "the use of obviously planned jokes or attempts at levity may have precisely the opposite effect upon a classroom climate" (MacAdam, 1985, p. 329). The audience now resents the attempt at manipulation and by extension the instructor, who must now be punished. They have banished the willingness to be manipulated, even skillfully, and set themselves to sullenly resisting further efforts to amuse or even possibly to educate them.

FREQUENCY OF HUMOR USE

Humor confers advantages in a library instruction session, but it is not donuts. In moderate, therapeutic doses, both can be effective and pleasant. Used excessively, however, they can cause harm or, in the case of donuts, bloating. In the same way that we all have differing tolerances for pastry, there is no hard-and-fast rule regarding the frequency with which humor should occur during a typical instruction session. The consensus, however, is that it should not be overused: "turning your classroom into a comedy shop with students rolling in the aisles certainly isn't conducive to learning" (Arnsan, 2000, p. 54). Given the generally low opinion students have regarding library instruction, it can be tempting to sacrifice some learning in exchange for a happier and consequently more pleasant group of students, but students are not the only audience for the typical session. The faculty members who requested the sessions often have their own expectations for what should transpire while their students are in the library, and those expectations usually include serious instruction on the subject of research. They might perceive excessive use of humor as "as a sideshow act without substance" (MacAdam, 1985, p. 332). The use of humor must not please students while displeasing faculty, or else those displeased faculty might not bring their classes back.

Nobody, not faculty, not students, should ever get the impression that the primary goal of an instruction session is anything but learning: "it is absolutely essential that the humorous instructor place bibliographic instruction goals over entertainment goals" (Archibeque, 1987, p. 28). Humor ought to be used as a tool to support the instruction effort, not the other way around. Students rarely show enthusiasm for research methods, but it is important not to think that this lack of enthusiasm is limited to the library classroom. Much can be done to make dry subjects more appealing, but serious education inevitably involves tedium. The library instructor can and should take steps to make the classroom environment stimulating, but the students must meet the instructor at least halfway and be willing to engage the material and put forth an honest effort to learn. Not everything must be funny in order to be effective. Use humor judiciously to break up the presentation, as a tool in support of your instructional goals.

Walker (2005) surveyed librarians about humor use and found that while "15 percent [of librarians] responded to only using humor occasionally, a great deal more (44 percent) admitted to using it one to two times per library instruction session" (p. 119). Given that the typical instruction session is at least 50 minutes and is traditionally lecture-heavy, this does not represent very much humor at all. Walker (2005) later argues that "three or four jokes per session [is] the optimum dose" (p. 120). Others, such as Archibeque (1987), take a more relative approach: "One funny example for one serious example is a good rule of thumb" (p. 28). At the heart of the matter is the idea that humor should never exceed educational content in either quantity or emphasis. More time should be spent covering class material, and students should walk out of the class armed with a useful skill or two, not just funny stories about their librarian.

TECHNIQUES AND APPROACHES TO USE

The literature tends to focus on the broader topic of humor's value in the classroom at the expense of discussing specific humorous techniques. Humorous examples, analogies, and one-liners are foremost among the few techniques that are specifically discussed. Humorous examples used in the place of nonhumorous, informational examples are fairly popular. They are relatively easy to implement and do not detract from class time, since an informational example was needed anyway. Their simplicity makes it so that "almost anyone can integrate into sessions without much risk of failure" (Saunders, 2002, p. 6). For all of these reasons, "the librarian who is trying to interject humor should seek out humorous examples" (Walker, 2005, p. 122). Examples can be actual, physical documents that have humorous titles or subjects or may be purely verbal, such as funny search terms (Fulton, 1985). Analogy is another form of the humorous example, which can be effective as an instructional tool in addition to being funny. Humorous analogies "have been used successfully for decades, however, to aid understanding in other fields" (Sutherland & Winters, 2001, p. 307). Illustrating an unfamiliar concept using a funny analogy connects the idea being taught with an entertaining and memorable concept. It is like attaching a keychain, which could be easily lost, to a moose, which is nearly impossible to lose. You just need to make sure you like that moose, because once you get him inside the house, chances are he's not going anywhere. Once your students hear an analogy, they can't unhear it even if they want to. The analogy needs to be apt as well as humorous; just being funny is insufficient.

Brief humorous statements such as one-liners and jokes "are a great way to break tension in a class and to help the students feel more relaxed" (Trefts & Blakeslee, 2000, p. 374). This kind of humor is not as on-topic as examples or analogies and might be of the most value early in the class as an icebreaker or scattered throughout the session to maintain a fun atmosphere. Jokes and one-liners are most effective live, but for instructors who are not comfortable with humorous delivery, canned material is an option: "humorous short videos can also be used to start off an instruction session" (Trefts & Blakeslee, 2000, p. 375). Although this approach carries the drawback of letting another voice into the classroom that might set a precedent of entertainment value that is difficult to live up to, it can be effective if it is well-chosen and brief.

In terms of content, it is usually best to avoid aggressive, hostile, or sexual humor, but these are only guidelines. Hostile humor can be of value if directed against something collectively feared or disliked (Brewerton, 2002, p. 29). Mocking the complexity of a research project or the size of the library (or anything else that gives rise to fear or anxiety) can help portray the instructor in the light of an ally and even defuse feelings of anxiety or fear. Sexual humor can work in the same way, "as long as it is not intended to harm or victimize: [while] telling nursing students to 'do a database search for Viagra to see what comes up' may not threaten Oscar Wilde's position in the top Ten of Wits . . . [it] will probably put your class at ease" (Brewerton, 2002, p. 29). Almost any kind of humor can be effective in the classroom, but it is imperative that risqué or hostile humor never be directed at students.

Fulton (1985) suggests instructors use humor they personally find amusing instead of guessing what students might enjoy. Humor should communicate the personality of the instructor. Comedians have their own preferred styles; certain methods just work better for some people than others. The final arbiter of whether a given technique should be used by a particular instructor is that instructor's ability to make that technique work in the classroom. If students are laughing and professors or colleagues are not complaining, victory may be declared.

TECHNIQUES AND APPROACHES TO AVOID

Avoiding humor that demeans students is probably the warning most often expressed in the literature. While it is impossible to argue with the sentiment, it is difficult to believe that many professionals, librarians, or educators, would deliberately use humor to demean students. Fulton (1985) suggests, with a note of understatement, that "sarcastic or aggressive humor directed at students is normally not an effective means of getting attention and establishing rapport" (p. 7). While a certain amount of jocular hostility is acceptable and even pleasant amongst close-knit friends, it is unwelcome coming from a stranger. Hostile humor directed at students creates an adversarial environment and will reflect poorly on the librarian. Walker (2005) echoes this sentiment: "Divisive humor, such as sarcasm, irony, insults, and parody tends to be biting and can often leave a student embarrassed. These types of humor can be extremely detrimental and should be avoided in the classroom" (p. 119).

The instructor should use their personal senses of humor, in conjunction with professional judgment, as a guide. This rule of thumb has limits, however, especially if the instructor is significantly older than the audience or possessed of esoteric tastes or interests. A very funny joke referencing *Citizen Kane* might send some audiences into hysterics, and could be a truly fine gem of comic wit, but might be misunderstood by someone under the age of 20. Misunderstandings are often harmless, but they can act counter to the purpose intended. Differences in age, education, and life experience all conspire to render an instructor's humor impenetrable to students if care is not exercised. An honest attempt at humor that goes over the audience's collective head is not likely to be ignored but rather interpreted as a demonstration of their ignorance, meant to be viewed in contrast to the instructor's wisdom. The audience knows they have missed the joke, and they can resent the instructor for putting them in that position. Alternatively, the audience might miss the joke but latch onto some aspect of it and misapprehend it, assuming the instructor meant to make a joke about something else entirely. Invariably, it seems, the audience chooses the most awkward possible interpretation.

Misunderstandings have the potential to be explained away, but making statements in poor taste can leave a room filled with disgusted silence and must be avoided

(Sarkodie-Mensah, 1998). Unlike hostile humor, which can be readily identified for what it is and avoided, taste is subjective. There are any number of possible topics that seem harmless but can inadvertently lead to offense. Consequently, while avoiding humor in poor taste is desirable, it can prove to be a challenge. In an effort to minimize the danger, it is best to avoid making jokes relating to politics, religion, and illness.

It is not possible to account for the ethnic background of every student, but when possible care should be taken to avoid culture-specific humor that excludes a significant portion of the audience: "although international students appreciated humor in instruction, the students felt frustration and confusion when the humor was culture-based" (Walker, 2005, p. 119). It is not necessary to scrub all culture-specific humor from one's repertoire as a preventative measure, but discretion should be exercised when planning for an instruction session known to include many international students or any other group unlikely to be able to share in the humor (Sarkodie-Mensah, 1998). The professor should always aim to use humor as a unifying agent, and as such it must be adapted to suit the audience and situation. Esoteric humor can be detrimentally misunderstood by students despite sharing the same culture background as the instructor.

Esoteric humor highlights different ways of thinking as well as unequal knowledge. Different cultural backgrounds can operate the same way. Sharing a similar worldview is necessary for the appreciation of some jokes. Cultivating an awareness of audience and flexibility to adapt to varying tastes can only improve one's use of humor.

Finally, apart from all of the serious dangers that can arise from confusion, hostility, cultural misunderstanding, and poor taste, there is an occupational hazard that comes with being a librarian: as a group, instruction librarians can be unintentionally funny, either in aspect or manner (Fulton, 1985). Allowing library jargon to intrude into an explanation, dressing in outdated or ill-fitting clothes, and speaking quietly or too quickly can make the instruction librarian into a spectacle, and it must be avoided. It is best to be funny only when one chooses to be funny. It is arguably better for students to laugh at the instructor than for the instructor to laugh at students, but really it would be for the best if nobody laughed directly *at* anyone else in the instruction classroom, and everyone instead laughed *with* one another.

2

Education and Humor

"[E]very teacher somewhat blushingly knows how easy it is to get a laugh from bored, restless—and restrained—students" (Holland, 1982, p. 43). It is possible that psychological theory explains why it is so easy for faculty and perhaps, by extension, librarians to make students laugh. Professor Daniel E. Berlyne published an essay in which he discussed "anticipatory arousal," in which the individual anticipated or forecast what was going to happen to him or her (whether good or bad), with a concomitant increase of arousal in readiness for whatever might befall. However, if the forecast was incorrect, the increased level of arousal could be dissipated in laughter (Haig, 1988, p. 26). For more on Berlyne's theory see Chapter 3.

Assuming that the students in the classroom are anticipating either a dull lecture or a boring class, then, applying Berlyne's theory, one would easily be able to get a laugh out of them. Once one told a joke, causing the lesson to be not dull, the students would laugh, according to Berlyne, so as to dissipate the feeling of anticipation that the class would be tedious.

This rest of this chapter will look at the didactic function of humor in relation to educating students with respect to information literacy. However, prior to actually discussing humor and education, first information literacy will be examined as an instructive part of the curriculum.

Information literacy fulfills a pedagogical function in that it teaches students how to find, use, and interpret information. Therefore, it is more than helpful to examine the use of humor in it not only from a librarian's point of view but, as stated, also from the point of view of the field of education. Just as a regular classroom lesson has learning outcomes, goals, and objectives, so too do "exemplary information literacy programs for undergraduate students at four-year and two-year institutions" (American Library Association, 2003). In the majority of the college library programs in the United States, these outcomes are based upon the American Library Associations' Association of College and Research Libraries (2000), *Information Literacy Competency Standards for Higher*

Education. In that document the learning outcomes for an information literate individual are given as the ability to:

- Determine the extent of information needed;
- Access the needed information effectively and efficiently;
- Evaluate information and its sources critically;
- Incorporate selected information into one's knowledge base;
- Use information effectively to accomplish a specific purpose;
- Understand the economic, legal, and social issues surrounding the use of information, and access and use [that] information ethically and legally. (American Library Association, 2000).

Prior to library instruction being termed information literacy, it was named bibliographic instruction. Even when it was bibliographic instruction the occasional article about humor would appear (MacAdam, 1985). The actual history of information literacy does not begin until the late 1980s (Grassian & Kaplowitz, 2009). It was then that the American Library Association issued its Presidential Committee on Information Literacy's final report (American Library Association, 1989). The difference between information literacy and bibliographic instruction is that bibliographic instruction tends to teach how to use a library and its accouterments, for example how to search the catalog (MacAdam, 1985), and "information literacy consists of recognizing when information is needed and having the ability to locate, evaluate, and use it effectively when the information is needed" (Walker, 2005, p. 118) with the additional goal of reaching the outcomes listed above.

In terms of humor being used in education, there are two points of view that explain why college teaching has been normatively a very serious, nonhumorous undertaking. The first of these is based upon the history of colleges and universities and could be called a *historical* viewpoint. The second is related to how people understand what colleges, universities, and faculty do and could be termed a *sociological* viewpoint.

Bryant, Comisky, and Zillman (1979) were the researchers who, in the authors' opinion, best laid out what is being referred to here as the historical point of view. They noted that when universities and colleges were first established in the Middle Ages, those schools that were most influential were "student universities" where students were able to control the "academic conduct of their professors." Because the students exercised fiscal control over the university, the students could control both the faculties' conduct and their teaching. In such schools the students made certain that the faculty was bound by their contract with the students to "adhere to tightly defined governance doctrines which guaranteed the students a substantial yield for their investment [by forcing] the professors [to] strictly follow the text, explain difficult problems, and cover a specified amount of material during each term [of the academic year]" (Bryant et al., 1979, p. 110). These very strict regulations as to what could and could not be taught precluded the use of humor, which was essentially seen as a time waster. According to Bryant et al. (1979) it took until the mid-twentieth century for this tradition to begin to loosen up and for humor to start appearing as a teaching technique in the college classroom. In the twenty-first century, "[i]f teachers want students to learn, then they should consider making learning more palatable, even enjoyable" (Torok, McMorris, and Lin, 2004, p. 14). "However, not all teachers should be encouraged to use humor. Some, because of personality, believe that humor may present a danger or are embarrassed by it (Ziv, 1984), in which case they had better not use it at all" (Ziv, 1988, p. 14) Additionally,

Torok et al. (2004) observe that by the time that their article was published, humor was seen as an acceptable part of teaching at every level of education from kindergarten to graduate school.

Korobkin (1988) explains the point of view that is being called the sociological point of view in this book. She observes that

[After the third century, at which time Rabbah, in Talmudic Tractate Shabbath 30a, was noted using humor by beginning all of his lectures with a joke (Swidler, 2010), but prior to the twentieth century], it was considered unscholarly to use humor as a teaching strategy or even [for teachers or professors] to show a sense of humor as a personality trait. Traditional subject matter and lessons were supposed to keep students interested [by themselves] (Wandersee[,] 1982). To entertain was not to educate. Thus humor was viewed as an unnecessary and undignified embellishment of the serious, classic educational experience [which school was historically meant to provide]. . . .

Collectively, teachers [who were] perceived [as] instructing with a sense of humor [were seen] as unprofessional, uncontrolled, and undignified. [Therefore, t]hey avoided using humor . . . for fear of being thought of as trivial, foolish, or ignorant. . . . [C]ollege instructors made a[n additional] conscious decision to be humorless because "serious professionals" conduct serious business. (Korobkin, 1988, p. 154)

Bryant et al.'s (1979) and Korobkin's (1988) points of view are not contradictory. It is possible that the aforementioned seriousness in education began in the Middle Ages due to the fiscal, contractual pressures mentioned above. It may have continued through to the twentieth century based upon the inarguable fact that the academy tends to be very conservative in its traditions. One need only think of the caps and gowns, hoods, robes, and other garb worn in most Western schools at their commencement ceremonies for an example of this conservatism. Perhaps, eventually, teachers maintained this seriousness of instruction due to the peer pressure mentioned in Korobkin's (1988) article. Humor was also seen as distracting students from learning and as lowering class enthusiasm (Torok et al., 2004).

Whether this hypothesis is true or not, both Bryant et al. (1979) and Korobkin (1988) agree on when instructors finally began to use humor in the classroom on a more regular basis. According to them it started during the major cultural shifts in the West of the late 1950s and the early 1960s when long-accepted traditions began to be challenged in American society. Therefore it may be an accurate guess that humor began to be used less when the social pendulum started to swing conservatively during the early 1980s. Nonetheless, by the early 1990s researchers felt that humor was being used at all levels of education from primary school to college (Rareshide, 1993). Humor had saturated education, so much so at that point in time that by 1999 even the venerable *Times of London* suggested using humor in the classroom. However, they were talking about both primary and secondary schools (Haigh, 1999).

Empirical research on humor in education started in the early 1970s when Hauck and Thomas (1972) first researched humor and learning in the fourth, fifth, and sixth grades. Since their article concerns students in primary school it is not relevant to this book. Nonetheless, it has a feature that the researchers of this book noted nowhere else and, as such, should be mentioned. Hauk and Thomas (1972) analyzed their data, not only by type of humor but also by IQ of the subjects. They found that "sense of humor correlated highly with both creativity ($r = .89$) and intelligence ($r = .91$)" (Hauk & Thomas, 1972, p. 52). Then, as will be discussed in greater detail in Chapter 3, in

1976 Ziv studied secondary students, and finally in 1977 Kaplan and Pascoe examined college-age students. For more on Kaplan and Pascoe's study see below.

According to Korobkin's (1988) overview of research on humor until 1988, when her article was published, more research on college-aged students was needed. She observed that

Some of the alleged benefits of humor to learners include *increased*:

retention of material;
student-teacher rapport;
attentiveness and interest;
motivation towards and satisfaction with learning;
playfulness and positive attitude;
individual and group task productivity;
class discussion and animation;
creativity, idea generation, and divergent thinking.

Other benefits to learners include *decreased*:

academic stress;
anxiety toward subject matter;
dogmatism;
class monotony. (Korobkin, 1988, p. 155, emphasis in original)

As the word "alleged" in this quote indicates, these were suppositions on the part of educators. After Ziv first published his empirical research on learning and humor among secondary school students in the 1970s (see Chapter 3), he was cited in literature reviews found in many education articles written on humor in every decade forward (Ziv, 1976; Korobkin, 1988; Dickmeyer, 1993; White, 2001).

There are at least two other uses of humor in the classroom that should be noted. The first is to help develop "a repertoire of stimulus-variation skills to gain and maintain student attention [a form of classroom control]. These skills include voice inflection, silence, [and] teacher physical movement" (Russo, 1992, p. 181). See Chapter 4 for suggestions on how to be funny in the classroom.

The second issue is the use of humor to help control the classroom by reducing tension (Millard, 1999). An out-of-control classroom is quite obviously one in which no learning is able to occur. Millard (1999) wrote about the use of humor in a middle school in Nebraska and described using humor to create a quick time-out in order to allow two fighting students to stop and think about school rules and thereby lower tension; this helped stop a fight.

Professor Sheidlower uses humor in the library classroom to create a time-out to allow students to control themselves, thereby getting back control of the classroom. Sheidlower's information literacy classroom is physically quite small. It only has 18 seats and computer stations. Cell phones are not allowed in the York College library. If one goes off during an information literacy class that Sheidlower is teaching, he stops teaching and doesn't say anything but just starts dancing to the music of the ringtone. Since he cannot dance, the class quickly gets the point, giggles, and asks the student with the offending ringtone to please turn it off (anything rather than having to watch Sheidlower, who can't dance, dance).

The rest of this chapter will deal with reviews of some of the major articles and studies concerning humor and education at a tertiary level. There are many places humor can be used at the tertiary level. It can be used in lectures, in tests, and in textbooks. Since the subject of this book concentrates on library one-shots, the librarian/teacher/professor is not using textbooks. Tests also would not be given. Therefore, the results of work on using humor in tests and in textbooks will be mentioned only in passing here and then not looked at again. Torok et al. (2004) concluded that while many students liked the use of humor in lectures, most students were opposed to its use in tests. This might be because students were afraid of accidentally picking the joke answer or question and appearing stupid. There is a definite need for further research on this.

Students' reactions to the use of humor in textbooks are the opposite of this. They like it and feel that it helps them focus their attention. Adult learners require the humor to be related to the text they are studying while children learn better regardless of the relationship of the humor to the text (Bryant, Brown, Silberberg, & Elliot, 1980).

The year after Ziv published his study, Kaplan and Pascoe (1977) conducted and published the first research work on using humor in teaching on a tertiary level. Ziv's (1976) research had been interested in examining whether humor expanded the ability of the learner to think creatively. On the other hand, Kaplan and Pascoe (1977) approached the issue differently and measured if, when humor was used and it was it related to a concept being taught or was out of context in relationship to the concepts being taught, how well or how poorly the humor increased retention of information. After using humor to teach this way, they then measured how each time humor was used it affected learning.

They measured this by teaching the same items in two classes. One class used humor in relation to some of the subject matter, and one class did not use humor. The investigators then gave an 11-item quiz to the students from each of the classes, the one where humor was used and the one where humor was not used. Kaplan and Pascoe (1977) discovered that the concepts taught in the class where humor had been used were not remembered much better shortly after they were taught than the concepts that had been taught without any humor at all. Six weeks after that first quiz had been given they gave the same quiz a second time. This time they discovered that the ideas taught with humor were better remembered six weeks later than those ideas taught without humor.

This comparison of these two articles (Ziv, 1976; Kaplan and Pascoe, 1977) demonstrates one of the problems in measuring humor and learning. What is learning? To Ziv it was thinking creatively, and to Kaplan and Pascoe it was facts being remembered after the lesson.

Three years after Ziv's groundbreaking article, Bryant et al. (1979) did a study of humor in the college classroom. They did not look at the outcome as Professor Ziv had, but rather they looked at the types of humor used, the frequency of humor used, and whether the sex of the faculty member affected the students' acceptance of humor in the classroom. Bryant et al. (1979) found that in a 50-minute academic hour, faculty used humor a mean of 3.34 times and that humor tended to be used more often by male faculty than by female faculty, an observation which they felt was normative in the broader nonacademic society. They additionally asked whether as societal sex roles changed this would also change. That is a study that needs to be redone in the twenty-first century to discover if indeed sex roles and humor use have changed. The types of humor that Bryant et al. (1979) found used in the classroom were jokes, riddles, puns, funny stories, and funny comments, among other types of humor. The three researchers recommended that the humor used in a classroom should be closely related to the topic being taught.

One problem with this study that was identified by the researchers is that there was a major difference between the number of female faculty studied versus the number of male faculty, with males numbering 49 and females numbering 21. Another problem is that although they identified the type of humor used they did not identify what percentage of students found the humor to be funny. This last item is an issue in most studies.

Humor is successfully used in many subjects, curricula, lessons, and other contexts. Its use in these is more than likely more closely related to a faculty member's teaching style than to a student's learning style. Its use in teaching style is more than likely related to a study of learning styles and teaching styles that was reported on by David Glenn (2009), which noted that teaching styles should closely match the material being taught. This would explain why humor cuts across subject matter and curriculum. It has been used to teach, among other subjects, accounting (Romal, 2008); communication (Hashem, 1994); foreign languages, specifically French (Berwald, 1992); law (Gordon, 1992); library science (for example, Marshall, 2002); nursing (Kuhrik, Kuhrik, and Berry, 1997); physical education (Check, 1997; Conkell, Imwold, & Ratliffe, 1999); statistics (Friedman, Halpern, & Salb, 1999; Berk, 2003); and writing (Goebel, 2009). Additionally it is an excellent teaching tool to use in general when dealing with "dread" courses (Kher, Molstad, & Donahue, 1999).

In the study of humor, education, and psychology (see Chapter 3), there is no set agreement whether humor helps students learn. Some researchers thinks it does (Ziv, 1976, for example) and some researchers think it does not (LoSchiavo & Shatz, 2005, for example). While looking at the literature of education, the authors found that this literature favored the idea that humor helps teachers teach and therefore it helps students learn (Check, 1986). In 1979 Check surveyed 929 students: 791 in college, 62 in senior high school, and 76 in eighth grade in order to determine what student's feelings were about the use of humor in the classroom. Check (1986) reported more than 99 percent of the students wanted the faculty to use humor during lessons and only .25 percent of the students wanted no humor used in class. One of the problems with this study is that Check was comparing apples with oranges. He did not compare similar students. For example, the needs of a college freshman who is from a very socially conservative country, such as, for example, Yemen, who has problems speaking English and is studying in a public community college, are very different from those of a native-born American latchkey eighth grader who is studying in a private school and whose native language is English.

Check tried to minimize the difference between respondents. The question he was asking was, "What qualities make a good teacher?" Many things showed up, including proper dress and grooming. What is of interest here is that "93 per cent [of all respondents] viewed humor as an essential ingredient in teaching. College students consider this element important to a greater extent than either grade school or high school students" (Check, 1986, p. 330). It would be interesting to see if all of Check's respondents in each of the grades had the same grade quotient and learning quotient discussed by Frymier and Weser (2001) and reported on in Chapter 3.

Since it would appear that in the field of education there is a strong belief that humor is a preferred teaching technique, it is important to identify how the literature explains the way that teachers should use this humor. The reader should keep in mind that this is from the literature of education that covers 15-week courses with traditional subjects such as English, mathematics, psychology, and so forth and not from the literature of library science that could include one-shot classes.

Some of the research, such as Kaplan and Pascoe (1977) looked at different types of humor. Kaplan and Pascoe (1977) weren't interested in different kinds of humor, such as puns versus cartoons versus physical humor. As explained both above and in Chapter 3, they were more interested in humor related to concepts that were delivered in the lecture being studied as opposed to humor that had nothing to do with the contents of the lecture. Once again, they discovered that if the humor was related to what was being taught in the lecture it was better recalled several weeks later.

Bryant et al. (1979) studied 70 undergraduate students in 70 different courses at the University of Massachusetts. They were interested in the frequency of humor used in the course and the types of humor used. Even though some professors did not use any humor, enough professors used enough humor that the average use of humor in the lectures they studied worked out to be approximately once every quarter hour. They also scrutinized their data according to the faculty member's age and ascertained that age did not matter. Older faculty used humor as often as younger faculty did. When it was broken down by gender, Bryant et al.'s (1979) data indicated that female faculty humor tended to be more aggressive and more spontaneous than male faculty humor. Finally, in this 1979 study, at least one-half of the humor was found to be either hostile or sexual. This was in opposition to a 1974 dissertation by Wells which surveyed elementary school teachers and found the humor used by the teachers at that level to be more "pleasant and playful" (Bryant et al., 1979, p. 116).

Even though Romal (2008) observed that studies from the 1990s and the early part of the second millennium identified humor as a desirable trait in effective teachers more than it was identified as such in studies from the 1980s, nonetheless to better understand this topic in the field of education these earlier studies will also be looked at. It should first be noted that empirical studies from the 1980s were fewer in number than in the following decade (Powell & Andresen, 1985).

An example of an uncertain result is in a study done by Bryant et al. (1980) and presented to the Speech Communication Convention. They looked at how humorous illustrations affected learning and reached conflicting conclusions. They discovered, after observing 180 college students, some of whom were given a textbook with humorous illustrations and some of whom received a textbook with just straight facts, that the humor, first, had no effect on learning or student motivation; second, positively affected the appeal of the textbook to the student; and third, decreased the student's belief in the truthfulness and credibility of the text. In spite of these findings, Bryant et al. (1980) also concluded that humor does not distract from the student's entire education. When one looks at this paper, one must question how deeply rooted it is in its time. For example, the paper's concluding sentence is "[t]hose hurt by humor use are teachers who desire to be influential agents of educational change" (Bryant et al., 1980, p. 24). While not a poorly written sentence, this desire to be an "influential agent of educational change," while a noble one, doesn't sound as if it was written in the second decade of the second millennium, but rather, as it was, closer to the more "hippified" counterculture of the second half of the twentieth century.

Powell and Andresen (1985) reported on a study done in 1983 of undergraduates that showed that humor had no effect on "knowledge acquisition" (p. 84).

In 1988 Korobkin published an article that presented an overview of how and why to use humor in the college classroom. Korobkin (1988) identified how humor reduces anxiety in a classroom (and we assume a library and its classrooms) by quoting Norman Dixon:

Norman Dixon (1973) describes the anxiety reducing role of humor as threefold. First, humorists broadcast a message that they can joke and be unafraid [unanxious]. Second, humorists clearly demonstrate their humanness and fallibility; and, third, the humor helps to diminish the perceived threat or fear. (p. 155)

Ziv, in 1988, did a new experiment and published a study on two experiments he conducted. In the first experiment, 161 students in an Introduction to Statistics course were divided in half. Half were taught the material using humor and the second half, a control group, were taught the course without humor. Ziv found that the group that had used humor did better on their final exams than the control group did. As the reader knows, one of the proofs that something is scientifically correct is that it can be replicated. Therefore, Ziv replicated his own study in this article. He did the experiment a second time, and this time he did it with 132 students in a Tel Aviv teachers' college. Again there was an experimental group that used humor and a control group that didn't use humor. Once more the experimental group did better on their final exams. This led Ziv (1988) to conclude that humor helps in the learning process.

In the 1990s several articles appeared discussing how to use humor in several specific fields of the curriculum (see above). A survey by Nancy Seale Osborne (1992) of 70 librarians who were members of the State University of New York's Librarian Association (SUNYLA) showed that although they had no concrete proof that humor helped students learn, both in the classroom and at the reference desk, nonetheless the 43 librarians who answered the survey believed that humor worked and helped students learn. There is a need to redo this survey surveying both the librarians and the students in order to see if the results from the students match those from the librarians. As stated, at the moment this is only a survey of a group of librarians and their opinions.

Dickmeyer (1993) contended that humor must be used carefully because he felt that humor misused could be more dangerous to the student in the classroom than any advantages that might be gained by its proper use. By misusing humor, for example by denigrating someone culturally or even anatomically within a sexual context, the teacher is sending the message that the student is not respected and that the class is a hostile environment. Because of this Dickmeyer recommends that all humor should be planned and none of it should be spontaneous. One of our objections to Dickmeyer's article is he bases all his suggestions on reading academic articles and none on looking at performance theories or works. For a different approach to this, that is a combination of research using academic articles and performance theory, see Chapter 4. Using humor correctly, that is to say respectfully, could help create a safe classroom or library. It allows students and teachers to make mistakes, thereby reducing the pressure on the two groups and allowing them to concentrate on the combined tasks of learning and teaching.

White (2001) correlated teacher's understandings of humor with students' perceptions of it. White (2001) surveyed 365 professors in 14 universities in the state of

Arkansas. She also contacted more than 200 juniors and seniors at a further 65 completely different colleges and universities. This article reported her results (White, 2001). She found that most faculty in her survey agreed that humor was an effective and important teaching tool. The majority of the 206 students who responded to the survey agreed that humor was an acceptable tool for use in teaching. Of all the things humor can do, such as relieve anxiety, increase a student's awareness of something, reduce stress, and create a healthy learning environment, both faculty and students felt that it was of little to no use in teaching about other cultures and did not help students build a better self-image. While students accepted humor as a way to control a class at a college level, faculty did not. This is opposed to Millard (1999), who found that at least at the middle school level it is a good strategy for controlling students. Sheidlower has found humor to be a good way to help control classes Like White (2001) had done, Torok et al. (2004) surveyed both faculty and students. However, unlike White (2001), the vast majority of the respondents in Torok et al.'s survey were students. They used, for respondents, three faculty in three different fields: "biology, educational psychology, and theater" (Torok et al., 2004, p. 15). They also used 123 of these faculties' students. They found that 60 percent of the faculty felt they used humor and 70 percent of the students agreed. Most of the faculty, according to both the studied professors and their students, used both humorous stories and comments. Interestingly enough, over 70 percent of the faculty and students believed that humor is a good teaching tool. It would be enlightening to redo this study and see whether the fact that these students, assuming they were between 18 and 25 and therefore never knew a time when they weren't exposed to "edutainment" in the form of *Sesame Street* and all its progeny, might not prefer humor to older students, over 40, who grew up with the idea that education is a more serious endeavor (the sociological point of view discussed above).

Torok et al. found the following types of humor to be positive: "funny stories, funny comments, jokes and professional humor" (2004, p. 16). Even though sarcasm fell between positive and negative they decided that it was negative. The observation that sarcasm is negative is further enforced by Dickmeyer (1993), who also warned against using it; nonetheless Millard (1999) allowed sarcasm to be used carefully. While Torok et al. (2004) found faculty to be hesitant about the use of sarcasm, nonetheless it was students who favored its use. Torok et al. identified the following as negative forms of humor in the classroom (we have extracted sarcasm from this list): "sexual humor, ethnic humor, and aggressive or hostile humor" (2004, p. 16).

In an editorial in *College Teaching*, Layng (1991) especially warned against the use of sexism in humor that is used in pedagogy. He wrote that sexism in classroom humor continues the idea that women are inferior to men as well as the idea that sexism and sexual discrimination have a place in an enlightened society, such as the academy.

Shatz and Coil (2008) warned against using offensive humor because it would waste the class's time. Therefore, they suggested that the professor use "self-deprecating" humor because it offends no one and humanizes the instructor in the students' eyes. One can also use a campus joke. For example, if school A has a well-known rivalry with school B, then a professor at school A could use a program or team at school B as the butt of his or her joke. Sheidlower has found that if one doesn't have a rival school creating a made-up rivalry such as Nothingville College versus Harvard or the reader's school versus a local, national, or international powerhouse will also work.

Wanzer, Frymier, Wojtaszczyk, and Smith (2006) categorized the humor in their study of 284 undergraduates differently. They divided the humor they found in the classes they surveyed into four types. These were: " 'related humor,' 'humor unrelated to course material,' 'self-deprecating humor,' and 'unintentional humor' " (p. 184). Wanzer et al. (2006) determined that the best humor used in teaching was "related humor" or humor related to the subject matter being taught. Once again, Kaplan and Pascoe (1977) had already determined this (see above). Wanzer et al. (2006) defined inappropriate humor as humor used to offend students, for example calling a student an "idiot." They defined appropriateness to be related to social norms and students' expectations of those standards.

Based on [Wanzer et al.'s 2006] study, instructors should avoid using humor targeting a particular student or group of students and joking about a student's intelligence, personal life/interests, appearance, gender, or religion. Additionally instructors should refrain from using humor targeting student's in-groups or using sexual or vulgar types of humor. . . . Instructors should keep in mind that 47% of the appropriate examples [of humor in this study] were related to course content. Students viewed this type of humor as appropriate because it helped them relate to the material and recall information. Such humor also served to make the class interesting and improve the classroom climate. (p. 193)

While there is more research to be done about how to use humor in the classroom, obviously the next question is, should it even be used? Torok et al. (2004) asked if it should be used. They came up with the answer that it should be used, that both students and teachers liked its use. Garner (2006) surveyed students to try to determine the link between humor and learning. Garner, a professor at Sam Houston State University in Texas, noted that his own experience confirms what Torok et al. (2004) and other researchers identified as concerns concerning the use of humor in the classroom (see above). Garner, in the literature review in his article, noted four problems in much of the research in humor and education. Garner (2006) found these to be:

1. a limited number of participants;
2. a weak methodology;
3. [the research is] primarily limited to elementary-aged children; or
4. [it] is [mainly] anecdotal in nature. (p. 178)

In his survey of humor and education, Garner (2006) surveyed 117 undergraduates who listened to three distance-education lectures about research methodology in statistics. "The results support the notion that humor can have a positive impact on content retention" (p. 179). It is important to note that these results are based upon humor used in context, that is, the humor was related to the subject matter used in the lectures. Since this study was done using a distance-education format with a member of the faculty the students did not know personally, it would be interesting to know how or if the outcome would differ if the students knew the faculty member and could be influenced by his or her body language, tone of voice, or by any "history" the faculty member had with the students, such as "in" jokes. One of the unusual things that this study did was to conduct follow-up interviews to make certain that the conclusions of the study were correct.

Romal's (2008) aforementioned study was not a survey but rather a meta-analysis of the literature of education and humor. She used nine studies of this topic. Many of the studies (for example, Ziv 1988) were reviewed in this chapter. She further asserted that humor aided in the retention of facts and concepts and that its importance in the field of education had increased over the past 20 years.

Gute and Gute (2008) did a study of two sections of a writing class and found that an instructor using humor and being funny helped the students concentrate on the class-work, enjoy it more, and be more engaged in it. Their study may not be accurate because they had surveyed a total of only 25 students and were able to work with results from just 18 of them. They were also not researching humor and learning but rather dis-engagement in the classroom.

Besides trying to figure out whether or not humor helps with learning, researchers also have looked at the question of whether or not humor helps by increasing immediacy in the classroom. Baker (2010) has defined immediacy in education in the following manner:

Communication immediacy, a concept proposed by Mehrabian (1971), refers to physical and verbal behaviors that reduce the psychological and physical distance between individuals. Nonverbal immediacy behaviors include physical behaviors (e.g., leaning forward, touching another, looking at another's eyes etc.), while verbal immediate behaviors are nonphysical behav-iors (e.g., giving praise, using humor, using self-disclosure, etc.). (p. 4)

In 1990 Gorham and Christophel researched two things. First, they studied how humor affects immediacy in the classroom. Additionally, they looked at how the profes-sor's and the student's gender affected or did not affect the use of humor (Gorham & Christophel, 1990). They surveyed the same 206 undergraduates twice over the course of about one month starting in week 10 of a regular 16-week course. First, they asked them about the professor's behavior vis-à-vis immediacy, looking at the teacher's immediacy behaviors such as using student's names, speaking with individual students before and after class, praising students, and so on. In the second phase, Gorham and Christophel (1990) requested that the students observe if the instructor used humor while teaching over five sessions. The results of this survey showed that a teacher's use of humor increased the student's feelings of immediacy especially among male pro-fessors and male students. Female professors and female students were less successful in using humor to increase immediacy. While the surveyed students might have enjoyed a female teacher's humor, it was found to undermine the teacher's credibility. This is in opposition to the findings a decade earlier of "Bryant, Comisky, Crane and Zillman (1980) [which found that] female teachers' use of humor did not appear to have a neg-ative effect" (Gorham & Christophel, 1990, p. 59) Gorham and Christophel's study also agreed with other studies (for example, Romal 2008) that showed that humor used in relationship to what is being taught in a class worked better than humor used out of con-text. Gorham and Christophel's final conclusion (1990) is that humor increases immediacy and immediacy increases learning.

Crump (1996) also reported that immediacy increases the three types of learning set out in Bloom's taxonomy: cognitive learning, affective learning, and behavioral learn-ing. Of the 12 immediacy behaviors surveyed in this study, humor was the most suc-cessful in increasing learning. She came to this conclusion by surveying 70 students taking a basic communication course in a community college (Crump, 1996). Immediacy increases learning, according to Crump (1996), by heightening students' motivation. Lack of motivation on the part of students leads to them being bored and distracted and unable to see the connectivity between the various things they learn. Just as "[immediacy behaviors on the part of the teacher enhances] teacher-student relationships" (Crump, 1996, p. 7), so it is reasonable to conclude that it also enhances librarian–student relationships. In other words, it reduces both the psychological distance between the librarian and the student and reduces the librarian's "psychological size" (Fulton, 1985, p. 13). This type of enhancement is something that is most definitely needed in the student–librarian relationship.

Besides immediacy, Downs, Javidi, and Nussbaum (1988) concluded that "a dramatic teacher (i.e., a teacher that utilizes dramatic style behaviors such as *humor* [italics mine], self-disclosure, and narratives) provides the student with an emphasis on course content which can help students organize their ideas, focus their thoughts, and sort the trivial information from that which is relevant to course content" (p. 138).

Shatz and Coil (2008) noted another excellent using for humor in pedagogy. They realized it permits the entire class, both students and professors, a short intellectual break that might be refreshing to the entire class. This is the break from boredom that is discussed above, and it also permits a transition to another topic, "allowing the brain a 'breather' to process and integrate lesson material (Loomans & Kolberg, 1993)" (Kher et al., 1999).

Powell and Andresen (1985) suggested that use of humor should be part of the teacher's training and professional development. Expanding upon this thought, there is no reason that humor training should not be part of the coursework in library school and other fields of study. In fact, it has been recommended that humor should be included in the curriculum of college counselors-in-training (Vereen, Butler, Williams, Dang, & Downing, 2006). In the field of education, the literature in learning how to teach at a college level is already changing to include tricks and techniques for teaching online courses. This literature additionally recommends using humor to teach online (James, 2004). It is not a large jump to suggest that the field of literature in education concerned with training college faculty in general should also include teaching the future college professor how to be humorous in the classroom. Some suggestions for how to be humorous in the classroom are laid out in Chapter 4.

In this chapter, with the brief discussions of both immediacy and how the brain uses humor (see above), we have skirted around the field of psychology. In the following chapter, theories of humor will be looked at from the point of view of psychology.

3

Psychology and Humor

Educational theory and psychology are closely related. Educational theory deals with studies of theories as to the manner in which one can teach the mind, and psychology deals with the study of the theories and facts of how the mind learns, acts, and reacts. This chapter combines psychology and communication theory to try to present a survey that will review how humor is studied in the field of psychology in relationship to the field of education. However, not all articles, books, and other materials written about psychology and humor are written vis-à-vis education. Some psychologists, such as Holland (1982), are concerned only with the psychological study of humor and its relationship to laughter; in other words, what causes us to laugh. Holland (1982) noted that there is no simple trigger that will cause someone to laugh, except, of course, for tickling and laughing gas. Therefore, according to him, responses to humor must have a psychological foundation. Exactly what this is he is unable to state, but he believes it has to do with taking humor and mentally recreating it in such a way that it affects the psyche of the listener by recreating that psyche (Holland, 1982).

Other psychologists, as well as some sociologists, have noted the fact that since laughter is present in babies and does not seem to have to be taught, unlike language, it could possibly be a vestigial trait of something. These psychologists and sociologists research what it might be a vestige of by studying indigenous peoples and babies to better understand laughter and humor's workings (Holland, 1982). Sociologists do the same type of study from a Darwinian point of view. To them, laughter and all other emotions are evolutionary survivals of primitive actions which had some practical use to man in earlier times. However, what laughter derives from they cannot tell us (Eastman, 1921/1972, p. 206–207). This research falls outside of the purview of this book and as such will not be presented here in any further detail.

In addition, psychologists can use humor as a diagnostic tool or a therapeutic strategy (for example, Haig, 1988). However, as already specified, this chapter will mainly deal with psychology in relationship to both humor and education, and so these uses will not be dealt with here. Before beginning to present information about the psychological relationship of humor and education, in order to give a fuller picture of psychology in connection to humor, the various nonsociological Western theories, with the exception of theories in literary criticism, of what causes people to laugh will be presented.

A generally agreed upon theory of laughter does not exist. In the late 1890s G. Stanley Hall tried to locate one and sent out a questionnaire to discover it. In spite of receiving three or four thousand responses he was only able to conclude that " 'all current theories [of humor and laughter] are utterly inadequate and speculative' " (Eastman, 1921/1972, pp. 132–133). No wonder researchers have stated that there are over 100 theories of humor and laughter in many and diverse fields (Haig, 1988, p. 9). For those interested in identifying more of them, Haig (1988, p. 11) suggests that the researcher turn to Ralph Piddington's book *The Psychology of Laughter: A Study in Social Adaptation*, first published in London in 1933 and then republished as a second edition in New York in 1963, Nonetheless, the majority of psychologists base their understanding of humor and laughter upon one of three separate categories of theory. These three types of theories are:

1. Superiority/disparagement theories
2. Incongruity theories
3. Psychoanalytic theories (Martin, 2000, p. 202).

The superiority/disparagement theory is most probably the oldest theory of humor in the West. It goes back to the great ancient Greek philosophers Plato and Aristotle. Plato presented it in *Philebus*, and Aristotle wrote about it in two of his works: the *Nichomachean Ethics* and the *Poetics* (Greig, 1969, 225–226). The superiority/disparagement theory hypothesizes that humor arises out of a feeling of superiority that the laugher has over the comic situation. For example, "We laugh at the misfortunes of our friends, and our feeling is mixed pleasure and pain" (Greig, 1969, 225). Specifically, Plato, in the following snippet of dialogue from *Philebus*, put it as follows: "You remember . . . how at the sight of tragedies the spectators smile through their tears? Certainly, I do. And are you aware that even at a comedy the soul feels a mixed feeling of pain and pleasure?" (Eastman, 1921/1972, p. 123).

It is important to remember that although there is an element of meanness and harm in this theory, it is "something harmful presented harmlessly" (Holland, 1982, p. 24). In this sense it is the opposite of Aristotle's "tragic flaw," and thus we may understand it as a "comic flaw" (Holland, 1982). If we feel too sorry for whomever we feel superior to then there is no comedy, but there is tragedy. The following is an illustration of the difference between comedy and tragedy: if we see an old lady fall and break her hip and we feel bad for her, that is tragedy; whereas if we see a clown slip on a banana peel, fly through the air 25 feet, land on his back, dust himself off and stand up with a smile, we do not feel sorry for him, so that is comedy. In other words, as a feeling comedy contains elements of Schadenfreude.

In the seventeenth century, in his book *Leviathan*, Thomas Hobbes, in Part I, Chapter VI, which is entitled "Of the interiour [sic] beginnings of voluntary motions, commonly called the passions, and the speeches by which they are expressed," also presented a very nasty version of a superiority theory under the heading of "Sudden Glory" (Haig, 1988, p. 15). It reads as follows:

Sudden Glory is the passion which maketh those *Grimaces* called LAUGHTER and is caused either by some sudden act of their own, that pleaseth them; or by the apprehension of some *deformed thing in another, by comparison whereof they suddenly applaud themselves* [italics mine]. And it is incident most to them, that are conscious of the fewest abilities in themselves; who are forced to keep themselves in their own favor, by observing the imperfections of other men. *And therefore much laughter at the defects of others, is a signe [sic] of Pusillanimity* [italics mine]. For of great minds, one of the proper workes [sic] is, to help and free others from scorn; and compare themselves onely [sic] with the most able. (Hobbes, 1651)

Alexander Bain, in the middle of the nineteenth century, based his theory of humor on Hobbes and so presented yet another restatement of the superiority theory. Bain wrote, "not in physical effect alone, but in everything where a man can achieve a stroke of superiority, in surpassing or discomforting a rival, is the disposition to laughter apparent" (Greig, 1923/1969, p. 255).

The next theory, known as the incongruity theory, can be traced back to the late eighteenth- and early nineteenth–century German philosophers Immanuel Kant and Arthur Schopenhauer (Martin, 2000, 203). Kant wrote about laughter in *The Critique of Judgment* (*Kritik der Urteilskraft*) (Greig, 1969, p. 247), and Schopenhauer presented his views on humor in *The World as Will and Idea* (*Die Welt als wille und vorstellung*) (Greig, 1969, p. 253). This theory supposes that when two incongruous ideas are juxtaposed or, as Arthur Koestler termed it in 1964, are *bisociated*, then this causes humor and subsequently laughter. The punch line of a joke is the ultimate resolution of both of these juxtaposed or bisociated ideas (Martin, 2000, p. 203).

Before getting to modern psychological theories on humor, the "official" German psychological theory on humor, dating from 1886, will be presented. It was written down by Emil Kraeplin in the fourth edition of Wilhelm Max's *Grundzüge der Physiologischen Psychologie*, and in translation it reads in Eastman's book (1921/1972) as follows:

In the comic the separate ideas which enter into a totality of perception or of thought are partly harmonious and partly contradictory either to each other or to the manner in which they are united. Thus arises an oscillation of feelings, in which, however, the positive side, the pleasure, not only prevails but gains the mastery in a particularly strong way, because it is likely all feelings elevated through the immediate contrast.

With all respect to the official psychology, we may dismiss this "oscillation of feelings" as an interesting myth. But the fact remains—and it seems to have been the special German contribution to insist upon it—that in the adult and artistic forms of humor an apparent combination of pain with a source of pleasure produces a more pleasant feeling than would arise from the pleasure-source alone. (p. 221–222)

Obviously this mixture of pain and pleasure hearkens back to Plato and the superiority/disparagement category of theory.

The final species of theory, the psychoanalytic theory, has two subtheories, one of which includes the work of Sigmund Freud (Greig, 1969, p. 273). These two subtheories are arousal theories and incongruity theories (Lefcourt & Martin 1986, pp. 4–9). Because Freud used the word *humor* to mean something specific, in this in this and the following two paragraphs and whenever discussing Freud, the word *levity* will be used for the whole field of humor and the word *humor* will be used in the specific context with which Freud used it in his writings. Freud laid out the first modern psychological theory of levity in 1905 with the publication of his book *Der Witz und seine Beziehung zum*

Unbewussten, which had been translated by 1916 into English. It is known in English as either *Wit and its relation to the unconscious*, *Jokes and their relation to the Unconscious*, or *The joke and its relation to the unconscious*, with the last title being the more modern translation, the middle title being the official translation (Holland, 1982), and the first title being the most accurate one of the three.

1905 was also the year of the first empirical study concerning humor and psychology (Eastman, 1921/1972). It was conducted by Lillien Jane Martin, one of the first women to study psychology in Germany (Fenton, 1943). Martin's (1905) study was less about what causes humor and more about which theories of humor were correct. In this it was similar to Hall's aforementioned 1890s survey. In her study, Martin took various humorous pictures from comic magazines of the day and showed them to various subjects ranging from a group of German students of psychology to 119 students studying psychology at Stanford to a 13-year-old boy and a 17-year-old boy. She also showed some to a Catholic, a Protestant, and a Jew and studied their reactions.

The psychology students and professional psychologists involved in this study then analyzed the reactions to the pictures and determined that the following theories were applicable in the following numerations: "Schopenhauer's theory was named fifteen times, [Herbert] Spencer's [he added nervousness to humor theories (Haig, 1988)] eleven [times], Hobbes's eleven, [Ewald] Hecker's nine, [Alexander] Bain's seven, [Emil] Kraepelin's five, [Karl] Groos's [who wrote about ticklishness (Greig 1923/1969)] five, Aristotle's four, [Professor Harald] Hoeffding's three [who added feelings versus only intellect to theories of humor (Greig, 1923/1969)], Kant's two, [Dr. Wilhelm] Wundt's [who is also known as "the father of experimental psychology (Mandler, 2007)] two, and several others once" (Martin, 1905, p. 111). It can be reasonably speculated that Freud's theory of humor was not mentioned either because his article had not yet come out or was just being published as Martin's study was being conducted, and so his theory was not yet widely known.

In his 1905 work *Jokes and their relation to the unconscious*, Freud explained levity by analyzing it as a relief of tension between the conscious and the unconscious. He also noted its relationship to dreams, a conclusion he drew based upon their shared elements. These elements are "aggressive, satirical, defensive, and sexual elements" (Haig, 1988, p. viii). In this book Freud explains levity by dividing it into three categories: jokes (which he also terms wit), the comic, and humor.

Jokes or wit use repressed feelings and allow the individual to release both aggression and sexual impulses. This first subcategory, jokes or wit, is further divided into two types, tendency wit and harmless wit. Tendency wit ridicules or demeans some person or group. Therefore it is related in some manner to the superiority/disparagement theory. Harmless wit does not ridicule or demean. "It is interesting to note . . . that Martin Grotjahn, in his book *Beyond Laughter*, points out that Freud himself was patently *unable to supply a single example* of 'harmless wit' which did not also have some 'tendency' " (Gruner, 1978, p. 9). The second subcategory, the comic, includes all nonverbal forms of levity, such as slapstick. Humor, the third subcategory, is a defense mechanism that converts negative emotions such as sadness into pleasant, positive feelings (Martin, 2000, p. 203). For example, if you are in an accident you might think of something funny, which will help deflect the pain of the mishap.

Hence, levity is related to both the ego and the id (Holland, 1982). Therefore, because of this relief of tension, Freud's theory is often considered an arousal theory. In an arousal theory, levity is seen as something that relieves stress. Another way of looking at it is "in jokes [an] economy of effort [results] from a comparison of reality with an idea processed rapidly by the unconscious" (Haig, 1988, p. 21), whereas the comic is based upon an exaggeration and humor is more mature, "transforming pain into pleasure" (Haig, 1988, p. 21). Humor also does not always produce a laugh. Sometimes it only produces a smile (Haig, 1988, p. 21).

If this explanation of Freud's work appears unclear it is because, as Eastman (1921/ 1972) noted,

The scientific world is . . . aware that Sigmund Freud . . . made an important contribution to the understanding of wit and humor. But just what that contribution is, nobody seems to know. One [reason for this] is that Freud himself has not a clear conception of it, and the other [reason] is that he has chosen a method of exposition which would leave his reader in a state of refined doubt and madness, even were his own thoughts the clearest in the world. [Freud's] method is to coax and allure us with original and apparently fertile ideas continually up to the verge of some point or conclusion, only to dodge away at the last moment, intimating that the matter must wait in suspense until "later on," and then never explicitly to mention it again. (p. 190)

In the 1960s, D. E. Berlyne theorized that levity is based upon the concept of an arousal boost and an arousal jag. The arousal boosts happiness during the telling of a joke. Due to the properties of the joke, anticipation, and other factors, the listener's arousal mechanism increases beyond a pleasurable level. At the punch line the arousal jag occurs reducing the listener's feelings back to a pleasurable level. This causes laughter (Lefcourt & Martin, 1986, p. 7).

From this point forward, since we are through with explaining Freud's 1905 book, we will once again use *humor* for the general field of humor and not *levity*. Ziv (1984) notes that according to an article Freud wrote in 1928 entitled "Humor," humor is also a defense mechanism. It helps us to successfully deal with such feelings as tension and anxiety by releasing these feelings (p. 48). Therefore, even though it needs to be formally studied more, Malvasi, Rudowsky, and Valencia (2009) in their monograph on library anxiety mention humor as a way to reduce library anxiety (p. 62). However, it is not one of the dimensions of their statistical study, and they recommend that someone should do an empirical study to verify that it can reduce library anxiety. Although this hypothesis is mentioned here, this book is not such a study, and it still needs to be done.

None of these theoreticians or philosophers dealt with humor as a teaching tool. Nonetheless, in writing about his work with patients, Sigmund Freud modeled it (Oring, 1984, p. 118). He would discuss a theory or a case and then give a humorous example. According to Oring (1984) this use of humor was cultural. It had to do with Freud's background as an Eastern European Jew. The authors of this book cannot verify the following explanation one way or the other, but it is possible, in the opinion of Oring (1984), that Freud used humor to reduce his own anxiety when presenting his revolutionary theories to his contemporaries. While Oring's case about why Freud used humor is strong, especially from a Freudian psychological point of view, nonetheless, from a larger cultural point of view we need to remember that when Freud presented his theories in the late nineteenth or in the early twentieth centuries he was more than likely anxious that the readers of his time might not accept them. The jokes could have been put in his writing as examples either to make them appear more innocuous to the reader, thus making them seem less revolutionary and dangerous and thereby reducing the reader's anxiety and raising their willingness to accept Freud's ideas, or perhaps they were inserted to reduce Freud's own anxiety when presenting such new concepts to a possibly hostile public.

Freud's is not the only arousal theory. Another arousal theory that explains humor psychologically is known as reversal theory. M. J. Apter first hypothesized it in the 1970s. Apter's theory hypothesizes that people are in one of two states at all times, either the *telic* state or the *paratelic* state. The telic state could be defined as an adult, serious state. The paratelic state could be explained as a more childlike, funloving state. In this theory laughter is supposed to "increase arousal" and transform one from the telic state to the paratelic state. "In the paratelic state arousal is experienced as pleasurable and exciting because it enhances one's experience of the current activity [humor, jokes, wit, etc.]" (Lefcourt & Martin, 1986, pp. 8). This increase is in direct opposition to Freudian theory, where laughter's goal is a decrease, and laughter is used to "decrease (unpleasant) arousal" (Lefcourt & Martin, 1986, 8–9).

Before moving on to either physical explanations of humor or humor as a coping mechanism, it should be at least noted, although it will not be discussed here, that there are literary theories of humor that have been put forth by authors such as Max Beerbohm and John Dewey, among others (see for example Gregg, 1969; Holland, 1982). Lefcourt and Martin (1982, p. 13) concluded that the various psychological theories hereunto mentioned should not be seen as contradicting each other but rather as complimenting each other for the most part. According to Martin (2000, p. 203), prior to the 1970s much research in psychology focused on Freud's theories, but after the 1970s much of this research examined humor as a coping mechanism. This is mainly because of the work of Norman Cousins (1979).

In 1964, Cousins was part of a cultural mission to the then Soviet Union. Shortly after he returned from abroad he was diagnosed with a severe collagen illness. He decided to battle it using vitamin C and humor. He was successful in doing so. While medical literature at the time recognized the efficacy of vitamin C for fighting various illnesses, there was little to no writing about the use of humor to fight illness. Cousins attributed the remission of his collagen illness to both the humor and the vitamin C. He had used these treatments against the advice of his doctors. Various psychological studies after this instance tried to determine whether the humor was truly a part of Cousin's recovery. As Cousins wrote, "If negative emotions produce negative chemical changes in the body, wouldn't the positive emotions produce positive chemical changes? Is it possible that love, hope, faith, laughter, confidence and the will to live have therapeutic value? Do chemical changes occur only on the downside?" (Cousins, 1979, pp. 34–35).

Obviously for Cousins the answer was yes. Many professional researchers in psychiatry and medicine in addition to Cousins, an amateur, have found the answer to be yes as well (Strean, 2009; Hoare, 2004). If the answer we are to accept is that that humor does reduce stress, then humor more than likely would also help to reduce library anxiety, making it possible for students to learn more effectively in the library both in a reference session and in an information literacy class.

Once Cousins had found a physiological link between the body and health, logically it was only a matter of time before scientists began trying to understand how humor and laughter affect the human body in ways other than the obvious ways, namely an increased pulse rate while laughing and taking in more air during a good, hearty laugh. Indeed, neuroscientists have discovered, by using a functional MRI to measure brain waves while subjects were enjoying humor, that jokes that are based upon incongruity resolution are " 'a product of humans' ability to make rapid, intuitive judgments' about a situation, followed by 'slower, deliberate assessments' which resolve [the] incongruities [in the joke]" (Elkan, 2010). Joseph Moran, then at Dartmouth, found that the brain became particularly active in the left posterior temporal gyrus and left inferior frontal gyrus, areas related to language and attention focus, while resolving a joke's incongruity (Elkan, 2010). Dean Mobbs, who was working at Stanford at that time, found increased activity in the limbic system of the brain once one has resolved the joke's incongruity. The limbic system is related to reward processing by dopamine release. This has led Mobbs to observe that "[h]umor thus taps into basic rewards [such as sex or our favorite music] that are important to our survival" (Elkan, 2010).

Since humor also activates both our frontal and our cingulated cortex, specifically the frontoinsular cortex and the anterior cingulated cortex, areas related to learning and decision making that have only evolved in the human species, it would appear that humor is only a human feature (Elkan, 2010). However, research also indicates that personality and gender affect how humor is perceived. Women seem to take longer to process humor. Although both sexes seem to find about the same number of jokes funny, because women process more humor in their left prefrontal cortex it takes them longer to respond to the joke than it takes men to do so. In terms of personality,

Mobbs has shown that people who are classed as extrovert and emotionally stable have increased activity in rewards areas of the brain during exposure to funny stimuli. Neurotic people, in contrast, have less of a reward compared with the average person (*Proceedings of the National Academy of Sciences*, vol 102, p 16502). "This suggests that personality style may be important in how we process humor," Mobbs says. (Elkan, 2010)

All of this research has shown that understanding humor is much more complicated than it seems at first glance. "As Andrea Samson[, a researcher] at the University of Fribourg in Switzerland [has observed] getting a joke would seem—on the surface—to be a very trivial, intuitive process. But brain imaging is showing us that there is more going on than we might think" (Elkan, 2010). It is possible that in the various studies of humor that follow, one of the reasons that many of them do not agree in their conclusions and findings is that while some take into account the gender of the participants, very few look at the participants' personalities. Perhaps researchers need to begin including personality type as one of the variables they include in their research.

Even so, humor is currently an unremarkable subject for research in the field of psychology. Currently, the conjoined field of study of psychology and humor even has its own journal. This journal is entitled *Humor: The International Journal of Humor Research* [ISSN (Print) 0933-1719; ISSN (Online) 1613-3722] and is published by Walter de Gruyter GmbH & Co. KG in Berlin under the auspices of the International Society for Humor Studies, which, according to the Society's web page (Holy Name University, n.d.) is based on the campus of Holy Name University in Oakland, California. This commonplaceness of the psychological study of humor was not always the norm. According to Ziv (1976), at least through the middle 1970s scientific studies on humor in the field of psychology were extremely rare, possibly because, as already discussed, humor and laughter are very complex psychological phenomena. According to Cousins (1979) such studies were also rare in the field of medicine.

In the late 1970s, according to Holland (1982), studies on laughter began to increase to the point where "[t]he most recent 'big' book [about humor and psychology]

contain[ed] 96 articles and a bibliography of 1,135 items" (p. 62). This "big" book was Chapman and Foot (1977), and according to both its cataloging record and its preface was the "reports of papers presented at the International Conference on Humour and Laughter held in Cardiff, [Wales, on] July 13th–17th, 1976 and organized by the Welsh Branch of [the] British Psychological Society" (p. xi). The articles in Chapman and Foot (1977) were the conference papers, and the bibliography was a major, stand-alone chapter (Goldstein, McGhee, Smith, Chapman, & Foot, 1977).

Many of the papers in Chapman and Foot (1977) dealt with laughter and humor in children. Some of the key questions in the research of children and humor are whether humor and laughter are taught; whether they are genetically programmed, and if, programmed, what antediluvian purpose they served.

Ziv's work may have helped give a boost to the study of humor, especially in education. He is mentioned in many literature reviews found in education and psychology articles on humor in every decade written since the 1970s (Korobkin, 1988; Dickmeyer, 1993; White, 2001). This leads us to conclude that Ziv was an important figure and a catalyst in research on the psychology of humor in relation to learning. He wrote not only in English (Ziv, 1976) but also in Hebrew (Ziv, 1981) and French (Ziv, 1979).

Professor Ziv's work was very important because, as already noted, it is among the first studies of humor and learning to be an empirical study as opposed to being based solely upon observation or guesswork like the work of the psychologists preceding him. Because Ziv was an academic psychologist, he taught at Tel Aviv University and Bar Ilan University in Israel, and he was a visiting professor at Boston University and the University of Quebec in Montreal (Ziv, 1984), it is not surprising that he approached humor in the most professional, scientific manner he knew—empirically.

Ziv (1976) noted that the number of such studies began to increase around that time (the mid 1970s) as new techniques to study humor were created and as new theories about the subject started to be articulated. In the same article he further observed that the research being done on humor could be divided into three types of research: developmental studies, correlational studies, and causal studies.

Developmental studies focus on the various phases children pass through and how they understand humor at each phase. In these studies the researcher is looking at "cognitive aspects [of the] . . . children's appreciation of humor" (Ziv, 1976, p. 318). The correlational studies mostly research humor's relation to negative feelings. For example, they research how humor both relates to and relieves anxiety. Causal studies concentrate on how humor causes attitude changes to occur (Ziv, 1976).

As stated, one of the earliest empirical articles on humor and learning, if not the earliest, was the aforementioned article by Ziv (1976). In this article, Ziv (1976) looked at a statistically valid group of 282 tenth graders (138 boys and 144 girls) in Israel and used humor in order "to investigate the causal relationship between humor enjoyment (i.e., laughter) and creativity in the educational setting, [Ziv's] hypothesis being that listening to humor would increase, at least temporarily, the creative ability of those subjected to it." He used the Torrance Creativity Test to measure whether the subjects' creative thinking increased after listening to humor, stayed the same, or decreased. He found that it increased. In his conclusions he warns that the findings are not necessarily transferable to other groups. He concluded that the use of humor helped to bring out more creative thinking in the test subjects. However, he warned that they do not become more creative people. They just are able to show more creative thinking as "defined operationally as scores on a creativity test" (Ziv, 1976, p. 320). He further noted that "many of the original responses [on the test] are humorous responses. This could account for the fact that the highest sub-scores for the[se] subjects were in originality" (Ziv, 1976, p. 320). This may be due to the fact that the humor either increased group cohesiveness or reduced anxiety, allowing the subjects to feel it was more acceptable to be original (Ziv, 1976).

One of the problems with Ziv's study is that he never tested the humor vis-à-vis the subjects. He assumed that they all found the same things funny in the same way. As we all have experienced, everyone approaches humor differently. You might show up one day at work and tell your colleagues about the most unfunny movie or comedian that you saw during the previous weekend, only to be greeted by another colleague who saw a very funny movie or comedian. After discussing it both speakers realize that you were talking about the same film or performer!

Nonetheless, there have been various attempts in the field of communication theory to measure humor through various scales. Booth-Butterfield and Booth-Butterfield (1991) list these scales as going back to 1925, and if the scale they created is included in their list, then their list of seven scales goes from 1925 to 1991. The 1991 scale, which had been created by them, is called the Humor Orientation Scale. It is a 17-item Likert scale that measures how respondents perceive how funny they themselves are. However, as pointed out, these are not a set of psychological scales but rather a set of scales found in the field of communication theory. There are, however, two psychological tests that measure humor which will concern us here. These two scales or tests are the Situational Humor Response Questionnaire (SHRQ) and the Humor Perceptiveness Test–Revised (HPT-R). These will both be explained later in this chapter. In addition, Holland (1982) mentions three more tests that will not be further discussed. These are the Wit and Humor Appreciation Test (WHAT), the Mirth Response Test (MRT), and the Institute for Personality and Ability Testing Humor Test of Personality (IPAT Humor Test of Personality). There are also the Sense of Humor Questionnaire (SHQ), the Sensitivity to Humor Scale, and the Coping of Humor Scale, all three of which were used by McDowell and Yosuyanagi (1995) in their study. These scales and tests are, in our opinion, probably very important to use, especially in a diverse, multicultural classroom, since studies have shown that humor is not necessarily understood cross-culturally (McDowell & Yosuyanagi, 1995). Hence these allow the researcher to verify whether the subjects perceive the humor as funny or not.

McDowell and Yosuyanagi (1995) did an exploratory survey of 110 American undergraduates and compared them to 108 Japanese undergraduates. Both sets of students were given the aforementioned self-reporting questionnaire, and the results indicated that the Japanese students were more sensitive to the humor than the American students were. Does this mean that humor works better in Japan in relieving anxiety, in focusing the student's attention, in relieving boredom, and in helping the students learn? A future study is needed to further explain how humor works within a cross-cultural context. This would probably be of concern to college counselors as well. Vereen et al. (2006) warned that college counselors must be culturally sensitive when using humor with African American students, especially when counseling across racial lines.

From another point of view, Kaplan and Pascoe (1977) realized that not only did researchers have to make certain that the subjects all found the humor used to be funny but that the investigators had to "determin[e] the nature of the humor [used] and make certain that all researchers used the same type of humor, [i.e. all used jokes and defined them in the same manner or all used puns in the same manner]" (Kaplan & Pascoe, 1977, p. 61).

There was, after 1976, a definite need to continue doing empirical studies to look at how humor worked in the classroom; did it increase learning or memory, did it in fact reduce anxiety, and did the demographics of the students or the gender of the teachers matter to each study's outcome? There was also a need to check whether humor worked on the tertiary level as well as on the secondary level studied by Ziv (1976).

Additionally, empirical studies of humor, psychology, and learning after Ziv further parsed the study of the use of humor in education by changing the variables in the question, "How does humor affect student learning?" These later studies analyzed humor and different curricula; for example, physical education on the secondary level (Conkell, Imwold, & Ratliffe, 1999), and they changed the variables and switched the emphasis in the question to "How does humor affect faculty teaching?" An example of this final type of study is found in Wanzer, Frymier, Wojtaszczyk, and Smith (2006). Additionally, studies on education were parsed into even smaller slivers of the educational process, such as educational testing. An example of this sort of study is the comparative review of educational testing written by McMorris, Boothroyd, and Pietrangelo (1997). On a general note, as an aside, Holland (1982) noted that in the latter part of the twentieth century the majority of the research on psychology and humor had to do with when and why babies smile and laugh.

In their literature review of studies of humor and education up until that year, Chapman and Crompton (1988) noted that most empirical studies on this topic on the tertiary level had been done using large college lecture classes with the humor contained in the lecture. According to these two researchers, this meant that the "studies have been characteristically poorly controlled" (Chapman & Crompton, 1978, p. 85).

Another strong need for further empirical studies of humor and education was due to the fact that while Ziv's research indicated a strong correlation between learning and humor, especially in increasing both creative thinking and divergent thinking (Ziv, 1976, p. 320), other researchers found only a small correlation (Frymier & Weser, 2001, p. 325). This naturally led researchers to want to find out who was correct, Ziv or Frymier and Weser. No absolute conclusion based upon empirical research has ever been reached.

It should be pointed out that Chapman and Crompton's (1988) research was done with five- and six-year-old children and so is not germane to this work and will not be further investigated. In 1977, Kaplan and Pascoe had done a study of undergraduates enrolled in 16 sections of an introductory psychology course in a large public university. The students watched a videotaped lecture concerning Freud's theory of the personality. There were four different versions of the lecture, with one being serious and three humorous. Students were tested immediately after the lecture and then six weeks later to check on retention. The results of the test taken shortly after the lecture were approximately the same for all groups, both those groups that had viewed a humorous lecture and those that had seen the serious lecture. However, the posttest, administered six weeks later, showed that the students who had been in the humorous lecture remembered the facts that had been presented humorously better than those who had had the facts presented in a nonhumorous manner.

Kaplan and Pascoe (1977) concluded that one reason that studies were showing that humor was not a strong teaching tool was that the researchers were not looking at information retention after time, and those who did retest were not using questions on the test relating to information that had been presented in the lecture with humor. The earlier research, which will not be discussed here as it only relates to retention after public speeches and not retention vis-à-vis learning, was conducted by C. R. Gruner in 1967 and 1970 and can be found in Kaplan and Pascoe's (1977) reference list. Nonetheless, one of the studies about the relationship between humor and retention, conducted by Markiewicz (1974), also concluded that humor had no significant increase on retention of facts. Markiewicz (1974) had done a bibliometric study of humor and persuasion. Writing prior to Kaplan and Pascoe (1977), she did not have their data which helped show that humor helped retention after a longer period of time, especially if it had been used in the context of the lectures, that is, not just a joke thrown into the lecture but rather humor which was related to the facts of the lecture. Studies done after Markiewicz (1974) and Kaplan and Pascoe (1977) confirmed that for humor to work it needs to be used in context so that it is either "relevant to course content [or used to] clarify course material" (Downs, Javidi, and Nussbaum, 1988, p. 137).

In the 1990s, one of the questions that was asked was what effect, if any, humor had upon testing results (McMorris et al., 1997; Newton & Dowd, 1990). Newton and Dowd (1990) looked at whether humor and having a good sense of humor helped students to overcome test anxiety (the anxiety felt by students prior to taking a test), thereby helping the students to do better on a test. They concluded that it did not help.

The researchers used the two previously mentioned tests, the SHRQ and the HPT-R, to measure humor in their study. The SHRQ uses 21 items to measure an individual's qualitative sense of humor. The HPT-R is a quantified test measuring joke memory (recall of jokes) and humor-reasoning skills (these can be used to create jokes) (Newton and Dowd, 1990, p. 669). Since, as mentioned, the test was negative, it seems to this book's authors that this makes the need for an empirical study of library anxiety even more interesting and compelling. These tests are important because they allow there to be norms against which all research can be contrasted. This lack of norms in humor research was first discussed by Brophy (1979). Because Brophy only discussed the creation of norms at an elementary school level, his work falls outside the boundaries of this book and is only being mentioned in passing.

McMorris et al. (1997) did another study of humor and testing. Their article was basically a literature review. One of the points they noted that should be brought to the fore here is that most researchers they looked at only did one study about humor. While there is no inalterable conclusion as to why this is true, the authors have two suggestions. The first is that in some academic cultures humor is not seen as a serious topic. The second reason could be that while you can test for a subject's sense of humor (see above), it is impossible to define humor scientifically, and this makes writing and studying about it difficult.

In 2001 Frymier and Weser (2001) did a study in the field of communication that is very closely related to work done in education. They looked at the relationship between student expectations and instructor behavior with reference to humor. They based their study upon the idea that "from a transactional view of communication, all interactants contribute to the communication process and influence the meaning that is created between interactants" (Frymier & Weser, 2001, p. 314). For Frymier and Weser (2001) the interactants were college students and professors. This study was done using 249 university students as subjects. The researchers looked at four items that are thought to increase learning ability. These were their communication apprehension, or their fear of and lack of comfortability in communicating with others; their learning orientation; their grade orientation; and their humor orientation. Learning orientation is the idea that a student is there to learn new ideas and concepts; grade orientation is the idea that a student is there to get a grade and to be certified in something; and humor orientation is the idea that some people have a better sense of humor than others.

Since this book is only concerned with humor, only the results concerning humor orientation in this study will be reported here. When researching humor, Frymier and Weser (2001) were only interested in the following hypothesis: "Students' humor orientation will be positively associated with expectations for teachers' use of verbal and nonverbal immediacy and humor behaviors" (p. 318). They concluded that students with a high grade orientation, that is, a strong motivation to get good grades with the strong goal of receiving a diploma or certification at the end, but without a strong motivation to learn for learning's sake, are helped by the addition of humor to a lesson.

The first decade of the second millennium also saw research done concentrating on specialized groups of college students (McMorris & Kim, 2003; Vereen et al., 2006). These two articles are covered in Chapter 2. That decade Torok, McMorris, & Lin (2004) studied what types of humor—riddles, cartoons, sexual humor, puns, and so forth—were the best to use during teaching. Their results are discussed in Chapter 2.

A study done in 2003 (McMorris & Kim, 2003) looked at both graduate and undergraduate foreign students studying in the United States at the State University of New York (SUNY) at Albany. The researchers sent out 410 questionnaires out and received 93 questionnaires back. Of the 93 respondents, 62 percent were Asian and 38 percent came from other continents. The gender split was approximately 50–50. The respondents were all comfortable with English (86% were comfortable writers of English and 99% were comfortable readers of English). They were all also comfortable with humor. "The percentage of students who agreed or strongly agreed to enjoying *telling* jokes was 80%, to *reading* jokes was 89%, and to *being told* jokes was 94%. Most (84%) reported having a good *sense of humor*" (McMorris & Kim, 2003, p. 132).

These students found funny comments and stories, professional humor and cartoons, puns, and sarcasm as the most acceptable forms of humor. They found sexual humor, ethnic humor, and aggressive or hostile humor as the most unacceptable forms of humor (McMorris & Kim, 2003). One of the problems noted by these students is that humor is culturally based, so that when they understood the joke it worked well, but when they didn't understand the language or the cultural references they were extremely confused. In spite of this, like the American students in their classes, they supported the use of humor in the classroom, but these students added one caveat. "They appreciated and desired humor *if* they could understand it" (McMorris & Kim, 2003, p. 141). "It is imperative to recognize that when used inappropriately, humor can cause international students to feel uneasy, separated from the group, and frustrated in their learning" (McMorris & Kim, 2003, p. 143). Therefore it is important to first practice using humor prior to actually using it in class (see Chapter 4).

As the technology used in education changed, so too did what was researched. LoSchiavo and Shatz (2005) researched the use of humor and online instruction. They studied 44 randomly chosen students in an online general psychology course. They determined that while "[h]umor significantly influenced student interest and participation [it] had no effect on overall course performance" (LoSchiavo & Shatz, 2005, p. 246).

Obviously, since there is no generalized agreement as to whether or not humor works within an educational setting, either from a psychological point of view or from an educational point of view, more research must be done.

4

Stand-up Comedy and Information Literacy Instruction

Can only naturally funny librarians use comedy in the classroom? Evidently not, according to experts on comedy in the classroom. Although making groups of people laugh seems to come easier to some than to others, it is nonetheless a learned skill (Hill, 1988). More importantly, it is much easier to be a very funny teacher than it is to be a very funny professional comic. Teachers are not expected to be especially funny, and that goes double for instruction librarians. Unlike a comedian, the instruction librarian's audience doesn't usually show up with the expectation (or demand) of being entertained; if anything, just the opposite—students arrive expecting to be bored into unconsciousness (Fulton, 1985). Simply making an instruction session marginally less boring than the audience expects can be counted as a success. Furthermore, nobody is expecting the students to be howling with laughter, and in order to learn much of anything, they probably shouldn't be laughing too much anyway (Archibeque, 1987; Arnsan, 2000; Petry, 1998). Students are required to attend library instruction in order to learn some research skills, not to be entertained. Humor should not occupy more than a tiny portion of the instruction session, amounting to perhaps three or four instances in many cases.

If the task of integrating humor into library instruction still seems daunting, consider this. Most instruction sessions cover the same basic material: some aspect or another of the Association of College and Research Library (ACRL)'s information literacy competency standards for higher education. Given that instruction sessions are also normally filled to overflowing with learning objectives, there is not much extraneous class time available, so there is little room for humor. A library instruction session that effectively integrates humor might only devote three or four minutes to the business of humor, spread out over 50 or 80 minutes. That's all. Three or four minutes of material is all that is necessary, most of which can be used and reused with every new batch of students. While it is true that four minutes of solid material can take many hours of work to produce, it is not any more work than creating learning objectives and designing a class around them. Like creating learning objectives, once that work has been finished, it is done. All that is needed afterwards is periodic polishing to maintain freshness. A few hours of work can improve years of teaching, both for you and for your students. It might even be fun, too.

PLAN

Even if you have never intentionally made another human being laugh in your entire life, you can learn to effectively incorporate humor into your instruction. It comes down to this: if you can plan, you can be funny. Although their acts are put together in such a way that they appear spontaneous, serious comedians rarely ad-lib. Almost every joke, gesture, or pause is scripted and practiced beforehand. They do not invent their material overnight, either.

Humorous ideas are gathered up over a period of weeks, months, or years. Think of those funny moments that happen from time to time, and imagine if you wrote them all down. Even if such moments only rarely occur for you, you would still eventually end up with dozens of funny ideas that could be developed into comedic material. While this means that pretty much anyone can develop comedic material, the process does not stop there. The performance aspect is at least as important as the development of comedic material. A good joke poorly delivered goes nowhere. The delivery must be planned and practiced as well, ensuring that each joke works as well as possible. This is a lot of work, but it also takes the pressure off of you when you are actually performing. With every joke scripted and practiced, being funny becomes much easier than it would be otherwise.

AVOID OBVIOUSLY FORMULAIC HUMOR

Although there are a myriad of ways to be funny or fail at being funny, there are a handful of comic rules that apply to the instruction librarian. Let's begin with what not to do. First off, don't tell jokes that are obviously formulaic—highly formalized comedic structures that might begin like this: "How many librarians does it take to write a book on humor?" This format is presently out of favor in stand-up comedy and is not likely to produce many laughs either there or in the classroom. Because it is so formalized, it is easy to spot a mile away, and modern audiences, especially college students, resent obvious attempts at using humor, which they interpret as a desire to manipulate them and control the classroom (Carter, 1989; Walker, 2005; MacAdam, 1985; Fulton, 1985). Jokes of this ilk carry further dangers as well. If they are complex or require the audience to have specialized background knowledge, not everyone will get it. Students who realize that a joke has been told but who fail to understand the joke can view the use of that joke as "mental one-upsmanship" and react poorly. Instead of breaking down barriers and creating rapport, the joke has now built up a new and possibly stronger barrier than was present before (Brewerton, 2002, p. 29). Sometimes this kind of joke can be interpreted in more than one way, opening up the possibility of misunderstandings. That is, some audience members will think they understood the joke when in fact they did not. Such a misunderstanding can lead to offended audience members.

AVOID STORIES

It is also best to avoid telling stories. For starters, too much time elapses between beginning the story and getting the payoff at the end. Stories involve too much time investment and not enough laughter. Moreover, stories require attention to detail.

Nightclub audiences are often drinking alcohol, which abbreviates their attention spans and makes it difficult for them to glean any enjoyment from a story that requires them to track details with any accuracy (Carter, 1989). Our students presumably are sober, but we still should not strain their capacity for maintaining attention, since we are already asking them to pay attention to the instructional aspects of our presentations. Because we are accustomed to getting laughs by telling our friends funny stories, it seems natural to cherry pick one or two of our best stories and relate them to our classes. Resist this temptation. The story might indeed be quite funny, but without the benefit of being your friend and knowing that if you are bothering to tell a story there is going to be a decent payoff, your audience has no reason to pay attention (Carter, 2001). They are already bored by the subject matter you are trying to teach them and are going to be reluctant to expend any effort paying attention to a story being told by someone they have probably already dismissed as irrelevant to their lives. Bear in mind that an unfamiliar class is a very different audience than a group of your friends. Treat them accordingly. If you must tell a story, make it brief, ensure that it requires no prior knowledge of you or your character in order to be funny, and make sure it pays off right from the beginning. Do not make the audience wait. In a library instruction classroom, students are already waiting for the period to be over, so they do not need anything else to wait for. One of the biggest reasons to integrate humor into library instruction is that the subject is so relentlessly dull (Walker, 2005; Fulton, 1985; Trefts & Blakeslee, 2000). We have already filled the tedium quotient for the day and should have zero tolerance of anything that adds to the tedium in our classrooms.

DON'T BE CAUGHT TRYING TO BE FUNNY

Have a plan in place and adhere to it. The literature on humor in college classrooms references the superiority of spontaneous humor over planned or contrived humor (Walker, 2005; MacAdam, 1985). Most audiences, not just college students, react poorly to contrived and obvious attempts at humor. But the humor does not actually need to be spontaneous to be successful. With the exception of ad-libbing, the great majority of successful humor is heavily revised and carefully rehearsed. It is so well-rehearsed, however, that it has the appearance of effortlessness and spontaneity (Trefts & Blakeslee, 2000; Berk, 2003). This is rather like ballet, except few people would watch a ballerina leap a yard into the air as if unaffected by gravity and assume that this is a skill she has always naturally possessed and that the 10 hours each day she spends training is just for fun. Even effective humorous ad-libbing is normally the result of years of practice. For humor to be successful it needs to sneak past the defenses of a sophisticated audience, which includes almost every American college student. This sophistication is another reason why stories and formulaic jokes tend to fall flat. The audience can tell you are attempting to be funny, evaluates the attempt as clumsy, and rejects both it and you. To be successful, humor needs to be delivered quickly, with no time for them to analyze your effort, and in a natural manner that keeps their attention on you and the joke, not on the joke's structure or the style of your delivery.

PAY ATTENTION TO PROFESSIONAL COMICS

Comics tend to deliver their routines with an air of seriousness. They are not trying to give a funny opinion; they are giving a serious opinion in a way that will be funny

(Ajaye, 2002). They are telling the truth, not saying something silly. They get laughs because humor arises from accurately reporting the different ways they see the world, by revealing a way of thinking that deviates from what is expected (Carter, 1989). An air of seriousness is also appropriate given that the subject of comedy is usually tragedy (Allen, 1998). For example, crying oneself to sleep is not usually pleasant and is certainly not funny. But to comment how much you enjoy crying yourself to sleep because you always get such a good night's rest when you do can be quite funny indeed.

DON'T USE PROPS

An instruction session involves enough logistical problems without adding further complications by introducing some object that you need to keep track of and flourish at just the right moment. While there are indeed comics who make excellent use of props, they are rare, and an instruction librarian should carefully consider the ramifications before adding props to a presentation. It is counterproductive to redirect student attention away from you and onto an object after devoting so much time and effort to getting them to focus on you in the first place. As a performer, you should be the center of attention. One of the reasons to use humor in the classroom is to get students to pay attention to you. By establishing that you are worth paying attention to because you occasionally say and do funny things, the class is more likely to maintain that attention while you teach. Your rubber chicken will not help you maintain their focus, so leave it out. Props also take away an excellent opportunity to be funny yourself. Carter (2001) suggests in the place of using a prop, you "describe and mime it" (p. 151). No real object can ever be as funny as a person's imagination will contrive, and the acts of description and miming are rife with possibilities for humor. They can also be a lot of fun to do. Describing and miming open you up to include anything you like in your act. Rubber chickens and fake severed limbs are very well and good, but what about Atlas carrying the world? Or Bigfoot? Or a peg-legged pirate? If you can imagine a way to describe or mime it, you can use it in your presentation. Imagination is also a lot more affordable than props, a lot harder to steal or lose, and easier to deploy at will.

Library instruction sometimes features examples of documents that can be found using library resources, many digital, some physical. While bringing in props can be a distraction from the presenter and should be generally avoided, if you are using examples as part of instruction, making some of those examples humorous can be tempting. This is a somewhat popular approach among instruction librarians for bringing humor into the classroom. Berk (2003) categorizes humorous examples as "low risk" approaches to humor, but the only risk that is low is the risk to the presenter's ego. It might be easy to add humorous examples to an otherwise drab presentation and hope for the best, but there is no free lunch. The audience will get wise to the approach very quickly and will most likely view the effort as forced and not especially funny. There is also the danger of the humor in the examples mostly appealing to librarians. I (Vossler, throughout this chapter) find the title *What bird did that? A driver's guide to some common birds of North America* (Silver, 2004) utterly hilarious. It is a guidebook to bird droppings. Who wouldn't find it hilarious? Hundreds of my students, it turns out, do not find it even a little bit funny. A few expressed revulsion. I used that as an example of a book for a presentation I gave 30 or 40 times to the better part of 500 students. Apart from myself and some faculty members, nobody enjoyed it. This is just a single example, but the lesson learned was that students rarely enjoy humorous examples to the degree that I do. Because students are not expecting humor in their class materials, they are not looking for it, so they fail to notice it even when it is right in front of them. And if you have to point out that an example is funny, well, that is just really depressing.

One possible way to use humorous examples despite these problems is to orchestrate events so that the humorous example will appear to be a fortunate accident. This is especially easy when demonstrating a live search. In advance, figure out a seemingly innocuous search term related to the class material that returns one or more humorous results. When making a point about the free web being full of insanity, my favorite lead-in is asking students to search for the phrase "feline research," which in Google at the time I am writing this returns a link to the spoof article "Feline Reactions to Bearded Men" near the top of the results list. I certainly enjoy using this example in class, but in the interest of full disclosure, I do not think I have ever gotten much more than a chuckle from this example. It is amusing but is a shadow in comparison with the full-on laughs I have gotten while miming myself being crushed by the weight all of the madness that exists in the free web. In sum, humorous examples might be too much of a temptation to avoid, but they will never get the laughs that you can get through other methods. They are also a logistical nightmare: what happens the day "Feline Reactions to Bearded Men" vanishes? Or, as often happens, the local Internet connection is down? I will have to recover and find another way to make my point. But I can mime being crushed whether or not the network is active.

MANAGE YOUR FEAR

If you want to add humor to your instructional routine but are afraid that you are not funny or that your students will be bored by you and your jokes, then I have good news for you. Your students walk into the room convinced you are not funny, that they will be bored, and that the visit to the library will quite likely be a waste of time (Sarkodie-Mensah, 1998; Fulton, 1985; Petry, 1998; Trefts & Blakeslee, 2000). In our students' perception, we cannot sink all that much lower. They already think we are boring and as interesting as lint, albeit a lot stranger, so what is there to worry about? That they will think we are boring and weird and try to crack lame jokes? Perish the thought. In that respect, there's pretty much nowhere to go but up. Stand-up comics report facing stage fright all the time, but their audiences show up with the expectation that they will laugh, so they are facing real pressure to perform (Carter, 1989). In that context, failure is a real possibility. In the context of the instruction librarian, failing to be funny means you have met the audience's expectations (Fulton, 1985). Anything more stimulating than utter boredom will garner approval.

Making the class laugh is not the only criterion for success or only worthwhile goal. There are many skills that work in concert to make people laugh, and you cannot get them all right on the first try. Clear delivery, remembering your material, keeping a good pace, and pausing in the right places are all valuable skills to develop and will contribute to your superior performance if you take the time to get them all right. You can manage your nerves by setting specific and realistic expectations for yourself before each performance (Ajaye, 2002). Instead of judging yourself by the number and volume of laughs, decide to focus on pausing at the right times. Even if nobody laughs during that performance but you succeeded in inserting appropriate pauses, you will have succeeded. Over time, the various skills that support your goal will come together. It just might take a little while. Avoid black-and-white thinking about your performance. Good and bad are not the only options. Think in specifics: what part worked, how well, when? Also, judge your act, not yourself (Carter, 1989). Beating yourself up about an imperfect performance gets you nowhere.

Nervousness is nature's way of making sure you are alert and in command of your faculties. It is a beneficial feeling, a warning: "Nervousness alone will not make you fail, but if you're unprepared, it will" (Ajaye, 2002, p. 33). Creating a well-organized plan might go a long way to settle your nerves, and even if it does not some performance anxiety is nothing to be ashamed of. Most professional comics have it, as do performers of all kinds (Carter, 1989). One last thought on nervousness: It is not a static condition. It ebbs and flows. Even if you are very nervous before a performance, there is a good chance that you will probably start to relax as the performance goes along (Ajaye, 2002). The trick is to just go up there and do it.

PLAN FOR PROBLEMS

Three things can derail a performance, whether or not humor is involved. One, people in the audience can give you trouble. Two, the environment can give you trouble. Three, you can give yourself trouble. It is a good idea to have plans in place for each of these contingencies. Fortunately, all three problems can be opportunities for humor.

Comics routinely face hecklers and develop methods for dealing with them. In the library instruction classroom there will be the occasional heckler, such as the enlightened individual who will ask charming questions like, "Aren't libraries kind of pointless now that we have the Internet?" I actually quite relish these students, as they supply a nearly endless stream of teachable moments. While on the surface appearing hostile, those questions are some of the most honest and useful questions that can be asked during a session, and I am always glad they were voiced and dealt with directly instead of being allowed to fester quietly in the background. For this kind of heckler, one need only answer the question honestly and without a trace of annoyance, and the heckler will either quiet down or become an ally for the rest of the class. But there is another, more insidious heckler that is a lot more common: the student who flagrantly ignores the presentation, often in favor of poking and prodding a piece of mobile communications technology. Whether these problem people are heckling actively or passively, they must be dealt with. In a nightclub, a heckler is someone, often drunk, who wants attention (Carter, 1989). In a library instruction classroom, sometimes the heckling student is only seeking attention, but just as likely is acting out because he or she does not want to be there in the first place and is looking for someone to punish. Students in a library instruction session usually are not in attendance by choice. They have been required to attend by their teacher and feel more trapped than a voluntary audience in a nightclub ever would, because they can come and go at will. When a comic at a nightclub deals with a heckler, it is vital to shut the heckler down without losing rapport with the rest of the audience (Ajaye, 2002). Rapport is lost when the comic overreacts to a heckler, or worse, loses his temper. The reaction needs to suit the situation. The same goes for the instruction librarian. This is where preparation becomes helpful. Any experienced comic or instruction librarian can rattle off at least a handful of statements commonly uttered by hecklers. The next step is to think up clever rejoinders to those statements. Often, the best rejoinders will occur to you in the spur of the moment, but brilliance is not always necessary. Just slowly repeating back a provocative comment can be effective, although this is only recommended for useless color commentary. A question, even an obvious confrontational one, should never be mocked. When you come up with a useful rejoinder in the heat of the moment, be sure to write it down so it can be reused.

So far, I have been recommending that hecklers be dealt with publicly, meeting fire with fire. This approach is effective so long as the heckler is relatively tame. If the heckler is egregious in any way or persists in disrupting your class, it is best to remove them before the situation escalates into something awkward. Ejecting a student has potential to damage your rapport with the rest of the class, but it is not nearly as dangerous as letting the disruptive student push you into showing anger or allowing the student to derail the lesson. Whether dealing directly with hecklers or ejecting them from your class, do so with kindness. If a heckler is bothering you and persists after being responded to once or twice, you can just ask him or her to please stop interrupting or to leave. On the next infraction, tell him or her to leave. Do not hesitate to take this step in the uncommon event a student persists in heckling. It is best for everyone present. Finally, do not let a heckler ruin your day. Hecklers are not representative of the entire audience; in fact, they are usually rather disliked by the rest of the audience (Ajaye, 2002). There have been times when I have removed hecklers from my class and had students come up to me and thank me afterwards. I have even had the heckler come up to me after being ejected to apologize.

Although I devoted a lot of space discussing how to deal with hecklers, you are likely to have far more problems from classroom and presentation technology than you will ever have with students. It makes sense to prepare reactions in the event of technological breakdown. For common occurrences like slow data speeds during a database demo, you will want to have readymade clever comments. Not only will this give you something to say instead of cursing at the offending technology, it will also allow you to acknowledge the problem elegantly. Do not try to move along without publicly recognizing the problem. The students are certainly going to realize something is wrong, and any effort spent trying to hide or ignore it will be met with the same kind of derision bald men who wear combovers receive. Everyone can see the problem, so attempts to hide it appear rather foolish. Problems that occur in the classroom can actually be opportunities in disguise: facing up to a problem creates trust and intimacy with your audience (Ajaye, 2002). After all, you are not alone in the room. The audience is just as frustrated by the hold-up as you are, so you are actually all sharing an irritating experience and can use that shared experience to bond, even if just a little. The same advice applies when you make an error, forget the next segment, or do anything embarrassing. Trying to ignore or explain away a mistake or taking any steps to defend yourself only undermine your goals. Do not belabor the failure. Acknowledge your error, maybe try to find something funny to say about it, and move on (Berk, 2003). I cannot imagine that anyone who walks into a library instruction session expects an ideal performance. They are too busy dreading the coming hour of boredom (Carter, 1989; Walker, 2005; Fulton, 1985; Trefts & Blakeslee, 2000).

LEARN TO PAUSE AT THE RIGHT TIMES

Being funny is clearly a complicated business, and timing is a crucial component. Pausing at the right moment, and for the right amount of time, creates tension that fuels humor (Berk, 2003; Ajaye, 2002). A pause also creates a silent moment that focuses the audience's attention and helps to ensure they clearly hear your next statement. With the potential for misunderstanding being one of the main drawbacks to using humor, steps that maximize the audience's understanding become important. Once you have paused for effect a few times, the audience will be trained to listen intently to whatever occurs after the pause. In the library instruction setting, this Pavlovian response can be used to sneak in important information, not just to draw attention to a punch line. Pausing is also important after you get a laugh, whether on purpose or by a fortunate accident. Let the audience finish laughing and settle down before you try to press forward in your presentation (Ajaye, 2002). You went to all of the trouble to make the audience laugh; you might as well let them finish. Pauses also give you time to think about what comes next and to reflect on your performance.

ADOPT A PERSONA THAT REFLECTS WHO YOU REALLY ARE

The instruction librarian faces unfamiliar classes with the goal, among other things, of fostering a personal connection. Delivering content is not sufficient by itself. That content must be delivered to an audience that has been made receptive to listening and disposed to like the speaker. As it turns out, this is precisely the same goal pursued by stand-up comics. Their solution is to carefully and deliberately craft a persona. Although topics and attitudes can shift throughout the performance, the persona is the one thing that remains unchanging. It is the unique perspective behind all of the observations and statements that lends a backbone of continuity to the dog- and-pony show of library instruction.

While we all have personalities, those personalities shine through with varying degrees of clarity and consistency. In general, it is a good idea to project a consistent persona to students and even colleagues, but in the short time frame library instruction typically offers, projecting a clear and consistent persona is paramount if you hope to develop any significant amount of intimacy with a strange audience. Before you can be funny, you need to decide to express who you are and take steps to clearly communicate that to the audience. Please note that I did not suggest you decide who you want to be. This is not a costume contest. People are perceptive and will know if you are presenting a persona that is not grounded in an honest appraisal of who you really are. Steve Allen (1998) gives two reasons why who you are on stage should be very close to who you are off stage. One, the audience will be less likely to detect anything phony about you, which makes you easier to like and trust. Two, since you don't have to put effort into being someone other than yourself, you will feel more comfortable on stage and will be more likely to perform up to your full potential. A relaxed performer sets the audience at ease and has an easier time making them laugh or learn. Ajaye (2002) supplies a third compelling reason to use a persona that closely resembles who you are: "that will enable you to bring the full weight of your feelings and thoughts (a.k.a. your point of view) to the matter" (p. 26). Instead of having to imagine how someone else might think or feel about something on the fly, which takes time and energy, you can simply consult your own opinions and react instinctively. So be yourself, only more so: "On stage, you are you plus fifteen percent" (Ajaye, 2002, p. 36). A little exaggeration is fine, and even rather desirable, provided the exaggeration is based on real personality traits.

In order for your persona to be clearly transmitted, the audience needs some evidence to work with. You need to open up and share true things about yourself. Stand-up comics rely heavily on sharing negative personality traits, as they tend to be a lot more entertaining (and less off-putting) than hearing about how successful, wealthy, and happy someone is. Instruction librarians are not entirely free to follow this model, however, as we must balance positive and negative traits. We want to be entertaining, but that is only one part of the job at hand. We must also appear competent at our jobs if our message is to be taken seriously. Fortunately, appearing competent does not mean appearing to be perfect. Mostly, it just means that it is a good idea to avoid any personal foibles that reflect poorly on your education, your intelligence, or your skills as they relate to the subject matter for whatever class you are teaching. Pretty much everything else is fair game.

EXPLOIT YOUR WEAKNESSES

When it comes to choosing what to share with a class, some of your best options include negative traits that are truthfully described and possibly even painful to talk about. As Carter (1989) points out, "The more miserable your life, the better your act" (p. 5). There are two primary areas to draw from when looking for material to share with an unfamiliar audience: Your physical appearance and your psychological traits. Susan Carter provides an excellent step-by-step guide to building a comedy act that I will not do the disservice of reproducing in short form here, but I will briefly summarize the approach and reasoning behind it, along with some thoughts from other comic experts.

The first step, physical appearance, is a valuable trait for a comedian or instruction librarian to take advantage of (Allen, 1998). Most of us have some physical trait that stands out or is likely to be noticed by a person meeting us for the first time. This might be especially the case with librarians. Fulton (1985) notes that librarians have been known for being unintentionally humorous in appearance or demeanor. Extraordinary ridiculousness of any kind can be used as raw material for quality comedy. Are you overweight, underweight, have funny hair, a big nose, or are tall or short? Do you make your own clothing out of used book jackets or braid your facial hair? Whatever it is, the audience is certain to notice it, even if they make no mention of it. For example, I have Tourette syndrome, which gives me uncontrollable facial twitches. I am also quite bald. Both of these traits are impossible for me to conceal for any length of time. Neither trait is especially desirable, either. By making jokes about these things soon after they have been noticed, I am releasing tension, both in myself and my audience. I am also publicly facing up to some uncomfortable truths, which builds rapport with everyone in the room: "Use of self-deprecating humor by the presenter can help remove barriers and place the student and teacher-librarian on a more even footing" (Brewerton, 2002, p. 29). It makes me less of a stranger, and quickly. Self-deprecating humor not only helps make a connection with the audience, it is also useful in that making fun of yourself harms nobody. You are a safe target, since the only person you can offend with that kind of humor is yourself (Berk, 2003). Furthermore, as an instructor, there is a natural gulf between you and your students created at least in part by the power differential—you are a teacher, the person in charge in the room; they are the students, and they are relatively powerless. Mocking yourself takes you down a notch and can humanize your presence. By now I hope to have sold you on the value of self-effacing humor, but if you are not lucky enough to have obvious genetic and neurological impairments like mine, do not despair. Ask a friend to tell you, or perhaps a stranger or a class you have just taught. Once you decide on the trait, find a way to make humorous mention of it in the future.

The second area to draw from is from inside of you: your psychological traits. In the same way obvious and undesirable physical traits supply the best comedy fodder, your inner foibles and flaws make for excellent material. As Judy Carter (1989) notes, "Material based in truth helps establish a personal relationship with an audience" (p. 24). Provided you do not seriously undermine your competence by disparaging your intelligence or other traits that enable you to hold a professional position, revealing your flaws in a humorous manner should help not only to get laughs but also help build bridges between you and your students. Unlike physical traits, psychological traits are rarely obvious and usually require some form of explanation. Since explanations take time, it is helpful to choose traits that relate to the subject matter at hand. For example, maybe you are extremely detail oriented, possibly to a degree others might consider pathological. Introduce that trait while discussing citation, noting how working on citations reminds you of all those Friday nights you spent cleaning your floor with a toothbrush. Any negative trait can work, provided you can connect it to class-related subject matter. Of course, making such a connection is not absolutely necessary, but it is easiest to build a case for using humor if that humor directly supports your pedagogical goals.

USE A HUMOROUS OPENER

Whether or not an instructor intends on using humor, the opening is one of the most important parts of the entire presentation (Carter, 1989; Hill, 1988; Berk, 2003). In this respect, the instruction librarian and the stand-up comedian face a similar challenge. In Judy Carter's experience, "Your opening is the most important part of your act. Within ten seconds an audience will decide whether or not they like you. If you create a bad first impression, you will spend the rest of your act on damage control" (Carter, 1989, p. 103). While the classroom is not a comedy club, and university students are, one hopes, more alert and forgiving than a group of nightclub patrons, both situations share rather a lot in common. Both involve giving a presentation in front of a group of strangers, and both have a myriad of goals that need to be accomplished in a short period of time and that must be done before the rest of the presentation can have a reasonable chance of success. These goals include rapidly creating rapport, demonstrating competence, establishing a persona, and shaping the atmosphere into something conducive to laughter and, in the case of the instruction librarian, learning. Fortunately, these goals interrelate, so any given technique meant to achieve one of these goals will likely also work toward one or two of the others. While some of these goals clearly are not directly humor related, they all contribute to the successful integration of humor in the classroom.

Creating rapport with a group of unfamiliar students can be a challenge because library instructors so rarely have the luxury of time to allow students to gradually get to know who they are, so steps must be taken in order to help the process along at a faster pace than usual. Rapport is vital to humor because the comic is inviting the audience to share his or her worldview for the duration of the presentation. The audience needs to identify with the comic, at least to a degree, if they are going to fully enjoy the humor. The same goes for the instruction librarian, but even more so: the instruction librarian wants the audience to laugh but also wants them to feel comfortable seeking his or her assistance on a one-on-one basis in the future (Arnsan, 2000). Additionally, the audience should like and trust him or her enough to value, and want to remember, the nonhumorous parts of the presentation. Rapport must be sought and established early so it will have time to grow over the remainder of the presentation. In the opener, this can be achieved by consciously taking steps to make yourself appear friendly but also in charge of the room. Make a special effort to project friendly nonverbal signals like smiling or making eye contact. Greet students as they enter the classroom, and move around the entire room so everyone has a chance to see you up close (Berk, 2003). These actions break down the emotional barriers created by distance before they have the opportunity to form. When the time comes to begin speaking to the entire room, be sure to "speak to the audience, not at the audience" (Ajaye, 2002, p. 13). If students get the impression you are reading from a mental script, just going through the motions of communicating with them, they will get the impression you do not care about them and will react poorly to any attempts to build rapport. Even if you teach 300 sessions each year, students in each session must feel like the session they are in is unique and important to you and that you really value connecting with them on a personal level.

It is also important to be consistent about how you project your persona and be aware that any deviation from that persona will impede your progress towards establishing rapport. One other serious impediment is the use of humor at the expense of anyone in the classroom (apart from yourself) or the expense of anyone or anything collectively valued by anyone in the classroom (Allen, 1998). There are many ridicule-worthy aspects of popular culture, but chances are good that at least a few of your students are fond of whatever it is you want to make fun of and will resent you for it. Hostile humor has its uses, but not in an opener. Now is the time to maintain a positive, upbeat attitude. Finally, although creating rapport with the classroom is crucial to a successful instruction session, it is important to note that "you can't and won't be able to make everyone love you" (Carter, 1989, p. 2). Provided that the majority of the class is on your side, or at least is not trying to undermine your efforts, the opener can probably be considered a success, at least in that respect.

Demonstrating competence is especially important for the instruction librarian who uses humor, since one of the biggest potential drawbacks of using humor in the classroom is being dismissed as being silly and lacking substance (MacAdam, 1985). For an instruction librarian, competence can be quickly demonstrated by proxy, through a display of public speaking skills. Students are much like any other audience in this respect. When they lack criteria by which to judge competence in a subject area (How exactly is one to determine how good a librarian is at his or her job by looking at him or her?), they naturally rely on other channels of information. In the case of a college classroom, this can be the instructor's public speaking ability. A polished and confident speaker is clearly competent at being a public speaker, and it seems reasonable to assume that a person who is competent at one thing is likely to be competent at another; admirable attributes correlate. It follows, then, that in order to be an effective comic, it is necessary to be a good public speaker (Ajaye, 2002). Specifically, feeling (or at least appearing) comfortable and in command while on stage, projecting your voice, maintaining control of your speed and intonation, and omitting useless filler words and sounds (*uh, um, like, you know,* etc.) from your speech are essential (Carter, 1989; Ajaye, 2002; Allen, 1998; Berk, 2003). Although a comic or library instructor may employ visual elements as part of a presentation, it is through verbal communication that the great majority of information is delivered. Public speaking skills, then, serve the dual purposes of rendering the instructor easy to understand as well as demonstrating competence in a primary job skill that is valued by students who sit through lectures on a routine basis. They are a sophisticated audience in that respect and know the difference between good and bad public speakers.

Once you have worked out your persona, who you are and how you want to come across on stage, the next step is to determine how to establish that persona to an unfamiliar audience. During your opening, when you are already trying to do a lot of things, it is especially important to display a consistent persona, since this will introduce the audience to who you are and prepare them for what the rest of the presentation will be like. Since an effective opener for an instruction librarian who plans to use humor needs to be at least somewhat funny, this is an opportunity to establish your persona while getting a laugh or two. Choose one or two traits about your persona that strike you as especially revealing about who you are and that represent the kind of humor you plan to use throughout the presentation, and share them during your opener. That should provide enough laughs to get you into the meat of your presentation. Also, whatever your physical style might be, introduce it here. If you are a peripatetic sort of instructor, start moving around during your opening. The same goes for whatever presentational idiosyncrasies are likely to recur throughout the duration of the class: voice volume, intonation, speed, and so forth. Let your behavior and overall presence in the first few moments be the guide for your behavior and presence for the remainder of the class. Maintaining a consistent persona will pay off later in the presentation when students begin to trust you.

Creating an atmosphere in which both learning and laughter can more easily occur boils down to broadcasting social cues to the audience that they have entered a safe, constructive environment (Brewerton, 2002). Walker (2005) suggests that "the tone and mood set by the teacher librarian's own demeanor will transfer to students. For example, if the instructor is smiling and laughing, then the students will react to the playful banter" (p. 122). To reinforce the feeling of energy and play, get up and move around (Ajaye, 2002, p. 15). Being a moving target helps keep the audience engaged. If nothing else, they have to track your position, which requires a modicum of alertness. Being active also adds energy to the performance and helps keep you awake and alert. "Bibliographic instruction can be repetitive; if the librarian is bored, why should the students be otherwise?" (Petry, 1998, p. 76). Even if you are not feeling excited about teaching the same material for the 87th time this semester, forcing yourself into motion will energize you whether you are in the mood to teach or not. Because we are not stand-up comics, however, there must also be social cues indicating that while laughter and fun are welcome here, the primary purpose remains education. This can be accomplished by nothing more complicated than returning to the instructional topic immediately after laughter has naturally dissipated. While it is possible to get laughs using deadpan, low-energy styles, this approach is not recommended. Classes tend to mimic or even adopt the teacher's emotional state, and enthusiasm contributes as much to instruction as it does to humor. Finally, humor is built around contrasts. It is hard to find a better contrast than showing glee for something that has taken root in our culture as the epitome of tediousness.

Judy Carter (1989) suggests that comics open with material that sets the stage and teaches the audience what the comic will be like for the rest of the performance: "A good opening defines who you are and lets the audience know what to expect" (Carter, 1989, p. 104). On the other hand, a poor opening also teaches an audience what to expect: a poor presentation. Creating or failing to create rapport, demonstrating competence or incompetence, establishing a consistent or inconsistent persona, and shaping the atmosphere for good or ill occurs in every class, whether or not any effort is made to consciously take control of them. If there is a single argument for creating a well-organized opener for library instruction, it is this: either way, you are making an impression. Only you can decide whether that impression will be constructive and helpful to the educational process or haphazard and possibly harmful to your efforts to educate and bond with each audience.

When choosing material for the opener, useful topics to focus on are your personal appearance, your character defects, something that happened to you very recently, something about the audience (keep this positive and polite), or something about the immediate environment that is noteworthy (Carter, 1989, pp. 104–105), but avoid clichés like asking the audience how they are doing. An effective opener for a 50- or 80-minute instruction session is short, not more than a few minutes long. It sets the stage for what is to come, which in an instruction session should be learning first and foremost, with entertainment second. It establishes the instructor as a reasonably competent and likable individual with a well-defined persona and infuses the room with energy. There is no single way to do this. Each instructor must find an approach that suits his or her personality and individual style. What works beautifully for one person can, and most likely will, fall flat for someone else. The purpose is to reveal yourself to your audience in a constructive manner that will pave the way for everything else that follows. This is also why it is important to be careful about choosing what to reveal about yourself in the opener. Although the purpose is to reveal yourself to your audience, it is important not to move too quickly. Just like when you are on a first date, revealing too much too fast can make you appear creepy and alienate your audience. In general, self-revelation should be paced to increase as time progresses, so that the more intimate personal details come after more superficial ones.

For example, in my opener, I share the highlights of my education, make some self-deprecating comments about studying instead of dating, and stress my role as a resource both during and after the session. It takes a couple of minutes to get through, and it usually gets three rounds of modest chuckles. More importantly, however, it communicates who I am, both in terms of credentials (it's amazing how many students think librarians are people who just answered an ad in the local paper and were previously roofers and bar backs—no wonder some of them walk in not wanting to listen to us), and persona, which in my case is something akin to a mad scientist crossed with a rhesus monkey. I poke a little fun at my shiny, bald head but also speak highly of my educational accomplishments as they pertain to my ability to provide valuable assistance. It is far from perfect, and I spend a fair amount of time revising it and trying alternative approaches. By the time this book has been published, my introduction will probably have evolved into something rather different. In general, though, it and its various incarnations have worked for me rather well. In a very nonscientific study, I tracked the number of student requests for private appointments for six months before I started using a deliberate opener (I simply introduced myself as Joshua, an information literacy librarian), and compared it to the number of requests I received in six months of using it. I went from getting an average of five requests per month to more than 20. Students seemed to respond more favorably to me in class, and I felt more comfortable and connected to them than ever before.

USE HUMOROUS ANALOGIES TO EXPLAIN DIFFICULT CONCEPTS

Humorous analogies are one of the more convenient and effective techniques for integrating humor into the body of a library instruction session. In the introduction, the primary goals involve creating an atmosphere and establishing your personality, so you are rather free to deliver humorous material based on yourself or pretty much anything else you like, as long as it works in concert with those primary goals. The body of the instruction session, however, is crowded with educational material. Injecting humor into that mix can be difficult, since there is little time to spend setting up a joke, so the path of least resistance is using humor directly related to the subject matter of the class. Conveniently, in an instructional setting, using humor related to the subject matter tends to be received better than unrelated material (Walker, 2005). That makes for two rather compelling reasons to come up with humorous material related to library instruction. It would be natural to think that there is very little inherently funny about libraries or library instruction. You would also be correct, with the exception of those times when librarians end up being unintentionally humorous in manner or appearance (Fulton, 1985). It is this lack of inherent humor, however, that makes library instruction relatively easy to write jokes about. In general, the more serious and devoid of humor something is, the more potential it has to fuel comedic fires (Allen 1998). If libraries were funny, silly places and librarians widely noted for being wildly entertaining people, it would be very challenging to try to write jokes about them.

There are an effectively limitless number of ways to be funny, but humorous analogies lend themselves especially well to generating humor related to educational topics. Library instruction often involves explaining or demonstrating processes: searching databases, generating keywords, locating books. Any time you find yourself explaining how something works you have an opportunity for an analogy. Analogies are useful for explaining or illustrating concepts in an instructional setting, so chances are good they already occupy space in your curriculum. By replacing at least a few of them with humorous versions, you can introduce on-topic humor to your session with little or no additional time cost. I would like to be able to say that they will definitely make your instruction more effective, but the research on the pedagogical efficacy of analogies is inconclusive (Berk, 2003). Regardless of their educational impact, analogies are ripe for humor. Pairing a unfamiliar concept with a familiar concept to show how they relate is really a tiny step away from humor. For example, take the concept of locating a book using the Library of Congress (LC) classification system. For many beginning university students, this is unfamiliar territory. An instruction librarian might employ an analogy to explain how the LC system works. Maybe finding a book using the LC classification system is like the address of a building. It tells someone who knows how a city is laid out where to find that building. Like navigating a city, paying attention to where you are right now gives you clues about where you need to go. Seventh Avenue is going to be next to Eighth Avenue, in the same way that PR is pretty close to PS in the stacks. This analogy works pretty well, but it is deadly dull. Accurate and helpful though the analogy might be, it may have the unintended effect of putting the class to sleep.

To convert this practical but unfunny analogy into something entertaining, the key is to consult your persona and look for inspiration. My persona is that of a mad scientist, a high-energy individual who might be at least a little bit crazy and consequently has trouble getting dates. One day I was about to relate the address analogy, when an idea came to me. I explained that books were a lot like people: they both have names and addresses, which makes finding a book in the library a lot like stalking someone you have just met—you will not get very far if you do not have the person's name, but what you really want to know is where that person lives, so you can dig through his or her garbage. This new humorous analogy is a lot more fun to than the original one, but it is not very likely to work for other librarians. That analogy worked because it unfolded naturally from the persona I had been cultivating since the beginning of that class. Instead of borrowing from someone else, create your own unique analogies. Make a list of the analogies you use for instruction and reexamine them through the lens of your persona. Take that reexamination to extremes and see what you come up with. The new versions will match your persona and help lend continuity and individuality to your presentation, as well as humor.

EDUCATE YOUR FUNNY BONE

Writing humorous material is a creative process, which can make it seem like a slippery thing indeed. However, there is nothing magical about it, and there are a number of practical steps you can take to help the process on its way. For starters, if you want to get more in touch with the funny side of yourself, expose yourself to comedy on a regular basis. The presentation format does not matter. Songs, live performances, and videos are all good, provided they contain humor. Spend more time laughing, and you will become more attuned to humor in the world around you. You will also develop a better sense of how you want to perform and be funny. Football players watch games; boxers watch famous bouts. Exposure to the professionals will help you learn and improve (Allen, 1998).

Once you have steeped yourself in comedy, make a short list of the comics you admire. Go over their performances and analytically study them, especially the ones that seem to be funny in some of the same ways you fancy yourself to be. Try to tease out how they do what they do. Afterward, emulate their styles and study them in order to better express your own (Ajaye, 2002). The key here, as always, is to unlock your own unique comic persona and to develop the tools to communicate it to your audience, not to learn to mimic George Carlin.

Your own personal taste in comedy is extremely important, but you are not going to be performing in a vacuum. As an instructional librarian, you are performing for students in a classroom. Their tastes must also be taken into account, though you do not need to pander to them. It can be helpful to view currently popular comics, even ones you do not think you will enjoy, to see what kinds of humor are currently in favor (Hill, 1988). Most of our students are young and might have different tastes than we do. If you want your students to laugh, you will need to present comic material they can appreciate and in a manner they can recognize as comedy.

COLLABORATE FOR BETTER RESULTS

In front of the classroom, you will usually be the lone presenter. When it comes to actually generating original material for your routine, however, working with a partner can be a really good idea. Professional comedians often work in collaboration with others. Working with someone else allows you to develop good ideas faster than working alone. The other person acts as an advance audience as well as a writing partner. Choose this partner well and you will both be a lot funnier together than you ever are alone (Carter, 2001). Instead of sitting quietly and trying to think up funny things as you might do when working alone, with a partner you can run with a topic and try to make each other laugh. Working with a partner is also just a whole lot more fun than working alone. Furthermore, spending time with a person who is funny will almost certainly help you become funnier (Allen, 1998). It can also help you avoid stagnation. That other person will bring different experiences and attitudes to the table and will probably see any given topic in at least a slightly different light.

Even with a partner, sometimes the comic juices will not flow. When this happens, do not try to force the process (Carter, 2001). Some days you will feel, and be, funnier than others. Developing good material simply takes a lot of time. It can also happen by surprise. Pay attention to the funny things that occur to you in the course of your daily life and be prepared to write them down. Some of your best material might come when you are not expecting it. Not everything you write down will be useful, but daily life is a constant resource for humor; mine it. Alternatively, when having trouble coming up with ideas, ceasing work and hoping for inspiration to come to you is not always an effective approach. Sometimes you just need to focus on whatever idea has been giving you trouble until you find a solution (Ajaye, 2002).

Finally, if writing comedy seems hard and frustrating at times, that is because it is. Ajaye adroitly points out that "one of the greatest misconceptions about being an artist is that the creative process is always supposed to feel good" (p. 27). The payoff is not in the process; it is in the product.

END ON A STRONG NOTE

For a stand-up comic, the conclusion is extremely important, as it will dominate the overall impression the audience takes away. For this reason, Ajaye (2002) recommends comics place their best material last: "A strong ending can save a weak beginning, but not vice versa" (p. 32). This is sensible advice for an entertainer, but what about the instruction librarian? As long as the material held in reserve is not done so to the detriment of the opener, ending the session on a high note will do for you what it does for the stand-up comic. The audience will walk away with the strongest positive impression you are capable of leaving them with. It also makes sense to place your best material at the end because you will relax as the performance goes along, so your best material will have the greatest chance of succeeding by the time you get to it (Ajaye, 2002).

Because the session is at its end, the need to create humor directly related to the subject matter of the class diminishes. At that point, your last remaining goal is to leave the students positively disposed to both yourself and the library. Carter (1989) suggests that comics arrange material according to escalating intimacy. It is best not to open by talking about highly personal subjects. At the end of the session, once the audience has grown as comfortable with you as they can in 50 or 80 minutes, you should also be free to make jokes about nearly any subject, no matter how intimate, provided it is appropriate to a classroom environment. To wit: The conclusion is the time to deliver your best joke, even if it might be a bit risqué (although it certainly does not need to be).

If you do not know what your best joke is, figure it out. You can record your sessions and play them back with an ear for the biggest laugh, or you can ask a colleague to unobtrusively observe a session and pay attention to where the audience laughs the hardest. Then find a way to relocate the material to the end of the session, or write something new that does the job. The closing joke does not need to be anything huge or elaborate. Scott Sheidlower ends his sessions with "If you have any further questions feel free to ask me, or you can ask one of the other librarians. They're sane."

Part II

INTRODUCTION

As helpful as research and theory can be to understanding how and why humor works in a classroom environment, it is only one side of the equation. Practical, hands-on experience is the other side. The following five chapters contain 50 techniques for using humor to teach information literacy. A few of the techniques came from the authors, but most were contributed by professional librarians who responded to our solicitations. Some are readily implemented into almost any classroom with almost no adjustment; others require a custom-made lesson plan and extensive practice and preparation. However, the real purpose of providing them here is to supply you with examples of how others are using humor in the hope that you will find inspiration to create your own approaches or to adapt elements you think will suit your curriculum.

The techniques reproduced here reveal a broad range of approaches to using humor in the classroom as well as a broad definition of just what humor actually means. Many techniques are meant to be laugh-out-loud funny and demonstrate a straightforward conception of what humor is, but others are more subtle. Those techniques reveal a definition of humor that might better be described as warmth of personality and genuine interest in others. In light of that definition, you do not have to make students laugh in order to be successfully using humor in the classroom. At the heart of every technique found here is the idea that we as teachers should be revealing ourselves to our students and take steps to make them feel welcome, comfortable, and safe.

Contributions were solicited through listservs, email, and word of mouth. We put together a submission form and distributed it three times, each time three or more months apart, over the space of a year. Contributors were encouraged to submit as many techniques as they wished, and many of our contributors submitted multiple techniques. It was interesting to note how people who use humor in the classroom rarely seem to use only a single technique. Unfortunately, there was only room to include 50 techniques, so a number of the submissions had to be omitted due to space considerations.

STRUCTURE OF PART II

The techniques in Part II fall roughly into five categories: ad-libbing in the classroom, connecting with students, evaluating sources with humor, searching with humor, and making jokes. Each of these categories was given a chapter. Each chapter begins with a brief introduction that characterizes the techniques found in that chapter along with their advantages and drawbacks. The entries for each technique are divided into two parts: technique and commentary. Entry length varies greatly, depending on the complexity of the technique and the amount of detail the contributor chose to include.

Entries are all written by the people whose names are listed at the top of each entry, and their original language was retained, with the exception of minor alterations that were limited to clarifications of meaning and editing.

DISCLAIMER

As we mentioned in the Introduction to this book, if you choose to use any of these techniques, it is crucial that they suit your in-class persona, your learning objectives, and your audience. The techniques in this book are meant to serve as raw material for you to work with. Just like buying a fine piece of fresh fish from the market, important precautions and steps must be taken to transform that slab of raw flesh into a healthy, flavorful dinner. You do not leave that fish out in the trunk of your car all day and then drop it on the dinner table. These techniques, just like a piece of fish, have the potential to be harmful or helpful. You need to supply the judgment and insight necessary to integrate humor into your lesson plans.

5

Ad-libbing and Spontaneous Humor

INTRODUCTION

Of all the techniques in this book, the ones in this chapter share perhaps the most in common. All of the other chapters in Part II contain what are essentially scripts for implementing humor. The people who wrote them discovered specific combinations of words and ideas that have specific effects on specific audiences. The techniques in those other chapters also rely on the model of instructor as performer and students as audience. The three techniques that make up this chapter still rely on the instructor to take a central role, but that role has less of an emphasis on being a performer to be appreciated by the audience and more of an emphasis on being a facilitator. The instructor acts as both actor and director, guiding the audience to actively participate in the session and contributing when appropriate. This shift in roles reassigns the focus away from the instructor as performer and onto the performance, which emerges from the interactions between the instructor and the students and between the students and each other.

PURPOSE

Laugh-out-loud humor, when it occurs, happens by accident, is always the product of two or more people collaborating, and does not necessarily revolve around the instructor. Laugh-out-loud humor, however, is not the point of these techniques. Humor in this context does not necessarily involve laughter, although that is certainly a possibility. In this context, humor refers to a light-hearted, creative atmosphere in the classroom. The purpose of these techniques, then, is to keep both you and your students mentally alert and engaged. A feature common to these techniques is not rejecting anyone's comments or questions, whether or not they are constructive. By welcoming what everyone adds, you demonstrate that your class is a safe place to open their mouths. We will never know how many questions students choose not to ask because they are not comfortable opening up.

ADVANTAGES

From the perspective of instructor burnout caused by tedious repetition, ad lib is extremely effective. No two classes will ever unfold the same way. Ad lib elements can also be applied as desired to pretty much any subject or audience. Unlike canned humor, which relies on having prior knowledge of your audience's tastes and can be useless if you find yourself facing an unexpected audience, ad lib adjusts to suit any group without conscious effort on your part. It is also especially useful in promoting participation from students who tend to hold back. Done well, it is also a powerful tool for building rapport and gaining insight into your students' needs.

DRAWBACKS

Planning for using ad lib in the classroom is just as rigorous, if not more so, than planning for more traditional approaches to humor. A set list of jokes can be memorized and mastered, but ad-libbing results in a different experience every time through, so the amount of energy and attention it demands will never diminish. Experience will make you more comfortable with the process and more efficient in how you proceed, but you can never go on autopilot at the end of a long day and expect things to work out. To ad-lib effectively requires you to be alert, energetic, and gregarious. These techniques place a lot of demands on your ability to inspire your audience to participate. Ad lib can also be risky. There will be times when a class is hungry, tired, or just in a bad mood, and nothing you try will get them going.

Yes, and Library Instruction

John Watts, outreach and reference librarian, Kimbel Library,
Coastal Carolina University

In professional improv, saying no, or failing to address something that has just happened are both very bad things. This is because in improvisational theatre, there is no script. If you say no, ignore what people say, or contradict them, the scene loses its momentum and inevitably crashes and burns. There is even an exercise meant to train actors to never say no. It is called the "Yes, And" game. It goes like this: Two or more people build a scene by making back and forth statements, each statement addressing and adding to the previous statement. For example:

Person A: "Boy, it's really sunny outside."

Person B: "Yes, and me without my sunscreen. Do you have any?"

Person A: "Yes, and it's a special sunscreen that is made from the brains of dolphins. It's even safe to apply to your pets, unless they're dolphins."

Person B: "Yes, and I hear tell it tastes good on pancakes."

No matter how odd, unexpected, or difficult a statement might be to follow, each participant must address it and do their best to build on it. Improvisational techniques are applicable to library instruction because we face class clowns, hecklers, willful ignorance, and god knows what else. We usually have a script to follow, but with the ever-increasing emphasis on active learning, we find ourselves interacting more and more with students in a free-form environment. When you are going from a fairly regimented script, it is possible (though, I submit, not the best idea) to ignore irrelevant or unhelpful student comments. In an active learning environment, however, the structure of the class becomes less rigid. Student questions and interests need to take a front seat. Sometimes the questions or responses you get from a class will be on-topic and helpful. Much of the time they will not be. The trick is not to evaluate those responses and only dignify the best ones with a response, as that will alienate the class and reduce the likelihood of future participation. Respond to every response with the same amount of attention and respect, and never say no. The class will end up going in some surprising directions, but all it takes is a little creativity to bring it back where it needs to be. At the heart of the matter, this is about walking into the classroom in the right frame of mind and approaching student interactions with the intention to allow them to move the session forward, even if it goes in a direction you did not expect. Most of the time students offer constructive responses and questions, but many of the librarians I've spoken with expressed concern over what do to when a student heckles.

As an example, here's a hostile response I encountered from a student while explaining library resources:

Me: We have online chat service available through our web site.

Student: Do people actually use the chat service?

Me: Yes, my mom does and she's thrilled with it. We actually keep statistics on how often students use our resources, and around 250 students use the service each semester. That's about 5% of our student population. It's best for quick questions that can be answered with a sentence or two. More complex questions you should save for meeting with a librarian in person.

"Yes, And" promotes participation from the entire class. By never shutting anyone down or ignoring anything, you create an egalitarian environment for communication. You want students to not self-censor, since that kind of behavior will preclude as many valuable questions as it will off-topic comments. Off-topic comments or even heckling can actually be desirable as long as you make sure to build in a positive way off of the exchange. It is also important to take each interaction with a student seriously, to focus on the person you are interacting with and the content of his or her responses to the exclusion of the overall goals of the class. Each person's comment or question is not an obstacle to be dealt with before returning to the lesson plan. It is a valuable addition to the lesson that will alter how the lesson plays itself out. Along those same lines, do not make an effort to be funny or clever; just be honest. Reply to everything sent your way with equal focus and enthusiasm. The key to this, and to "Yes, And" in general, is the ability to think quickly on your feet and have no fear of your audience. Being relaxed in front of groups is a big advantage. The more relaxed you are, the easier you will find that clever responses come to you. Although some natural talent undoubtedly comes into play, ad-libbing skills can be developed. Spending time practicing "Yes, And" will help you develop these skills.

Reactions from students certainly vary, but this approach builds a positive energy in the room and turns mundane subject matter into a more free-flowing and fun experience for everyone. This is technique designed to augment the social environment of the class. It encourages a wider variety of students to offer questions and responses than might usually speak up. These responses do tend to run the gamut of quality, and the time required to address each one can put the squeeze on your lesson plan. But those are too packed in general anyway, so this is a good excuse to cut it down into something more reasonable. I find that this technique often takes the class is directions I did not expect, and sometimes those directions are really productive. Finally, it seems to reduce teacher burnout, as no class will ever be the same. The constant mental challenge of responding to student responses keeps me alert and prevents boredom from ever setting in.

Joking with the Jokers

Sara D. Miller, assistant library instruction coordinator,
Michigan State University Libraries

Rather than plan humor or jokes into my class, I try to keep an eye out for funny things that present themselves as a result of discussion or examples of websites that the students find as a group. It's much easier for me to capitalize on something that the students are already laughing about than to plan to say something that I think is funny and get blank stares in return. I always try to keep a light, informal tone with my classes in order to encourage the class jokers to emerge. There always seems to be at least one in every class. My classes are heavily discussion based, and I will ask the students open-ended questions to which the joker will sometimes provide a humorous answer. Some past examples are: Me: "Why don't you think your professors want you to use Wikipedia?" Joker's answers: "Because it's awesome," or "because it's too easy and they want to torture us." If a student provides a funny answer, or uses a humorous website, topic, or resource as an example, I tend to expand on the response with a smile on my face, at the same time asking them more questions that get to the point. "Why is it so awesome?"

I also occasionally find humor when leading students through an evaluative process. I have them present Web sites that they have searched for as a group, and then we look at the sites as a class using evaluative criteria. Often trying to find information about authors provides humorous results, particularly when I have asked the students to find evidence of the qualifications of the author, and the only author information is some sort of silly bio about how much they love cats, or how they are a stark raving environmentalist, etc.

There are three attributes necessary for getting this approach to work. The first is a sense of humor, which involves the ability to see humor in others' comments as much or more than being able to make funny comments yourself. The second is a high degree of awareness of the audience's mood, which must be constantly maintained, as the emotional landscape changes rapidly. What would have been funny or appropriate five minutes or even five seconds ago might not be funny now. The third is sensitivity to the audience's attitudes, especially to what might be offensive. Rub too many people the wrong way, and a class can become unproductive, unresponsive, and unsalvageable.

This approach works because it makes library instruction more lighthearted and counteracts students' expectations of tedium or excessive seriousness in the library. By making yourself more approachable to students, you can by extension make research more approachable and less of a punishment. Being approachable and friendly is not the only advantage to this approach. Some of the more important messages we want to relay, such as the necessity of effective source evaluation, are deadly dull and even seem condescending. Using humor while covering such a topic can make the experience more tolerable for students, and maybe make them less likely to tune us out. Although it is not the primary goal, students laugh, and their written feedback suggests that they both enjoy the approach used and feel less put off by the library as a building and the complexity of its resources as a result. Students are more inclined to interact upon discovering their comments and even jokes will be tolerated or lauded. Accepting their commentary regardless of content seems to make them feel more comfortable during the session and more inclined to share their thoughts and questions. Their attention to the class, as opposed to their mobile devices, seems to improve when there is the possibility of something funny happening.

When You're Smiling

Anonymous

Being funny is not an aim in itself. The aim in using humour in a library session is quite simple—you are trying engage your students, sure, but most importantly you are trying to put them at ease so they are in a better mental state to learn something. You can't seriously hope that deeper learning will occur while students are bored, disengaged or anxious. Judicious use of humour also puts you, the instructor, in a position where students will feel more comfortable asking questions. As someone who is capable of smiling, you are seen as more approachable. With humour, barriers are broken down and inter-communication can occur more freely.

My technique is not to crack jokes, but simply to make the odd quip here and there, to lighten the mood from the outset. To students filing into a lecture theatre: "plenty of good seats down the front; this isn't a stand-up routine, you won't be made to participate. Or hypnotised. I won't hypnotise you. I'll try not to, anyway". It's difficult really to provide concrete examples as it really is best off-the-cuff and natural.

Slightly humorous images often work well—"think of your search results as an enormous block of ice; adding further search terms or using limiters will hack away at this big block. Like an ice sculpture, something beautiful will emerge . . . but don't over-do things—too narrow a search and you'll end up with an ice-cube . . . or a puddle of water". This isn't a "joke", but delivered light-heartedly (and responsively—do the students follow what you are saying?) it can make a point that might otherwise be missed.

Remembering moderately humorous examples from previous teaching sessions can be useful to illustrate points. I use "the seagull guy" a lot. He was a PhD researcher looking at the public health implications of over-wintering seagull populations in Britain. He knew a great deal about public health at the outset of his doctoral research but was unfamiliar with the biology/ecology literature (migration and nesting patterns and so on). I use this as an example of cross-disciplinarity in the literature review process, and the need to look at different 'literatures' at doctoral level when I'm conducting researcher training. It's not funny per se; there are no jokes. But seagulls are just amusing. People smile.

It is important not to force or belabor this approach. Any obvious attempts to do so will preclude its success as assuredly as not trying it in the first place. The goal is for the students to relax and have fun with the class, and this is done by setting the example yourself. You must appear relaxed, comfortable, and open to communicating. Never come across as scripted or overprepared. That can make students feel railroaded and stifled. Even if you are a naturally friendly person, make a point to amplify your outgoing traits: be a friendlier, warmer, chattier version of yourself. People respond in kind to friendliness and become more open to new ideas.

The aim is to put the students at their ease. If they are relaxed, they will be much better able to learn and benefit from the session. Laughter is always enjoyable, but it is a rare occurrence with this technique and is not the point for using it. Mostly, students react well. Smiles are a good indicator of success, as is an overall class mood that feels relaxed and shows evidence of students interacting with the instructor and with each other. However, things do not always work out. When this happens, it is best to accept the failure and move on. Adding humor to your presentation comes with the risk of appearing foolish. Just be sure not to make yourself into such a caricature that your students cease to respect you as a trustworthy source of information.

6

Connecting with Students

INTRODUCTION

Using humor in the classroom does not necessarily involve trying to make students laugh. This chapter focuses on techniques that use a more relaxed definition of humor, one that emphasizes friendliness and an informal atmosphere. The ideas here focus on sharing the instructor's personality and making the learning environment feel productive. They can be elaborate, involving activities in which students are given roles to play or avenues to help them engage with the subject matter of the class. In other cases, they are simple and brief, consisting of short speeches or demonstrations. Regardless of complexity, they all work to create memorable and pleasant classroom experiences that emphasize personal connection with the instructor over laughter or clever presentation of subject matter. It would probably be fair to say that instructors who prefer these techniques value forging lasting connections with students as much or more than transmitting specific information and skills through library instruction.

PURPOSE

Humor in the classroom serves a purpose: it helps to establish rapport between the students and the teacher and brings the students together as a group. The techniques in this chapter take that idea to heart and are consequently less interested in making students laugh than they are in forging connections with students and creating a positive learning environment. Their goal is to generate positive energy and goodwill in the classroom. If laughter comes about in the process, that is well and good, but it is not sought after. Most of the techniques in this chapter can be counted as having been successfully implemented without so much as a single chuckle occurring, provided that students and teacher leave the room with a lasting connection. Instead of using laughter as a mechanism to promote rapport, these techniques rely on one of two approaches. The first is by creating personality showcasing opportunities: talking like a pirate, dressing oddly, and showing compromising home videos all find homes here. The second is by giving students interactive and (at least partly) entertaining tasks to complete over the course of the session. By working together and having fun, students forge a connection with the instructor and with each other.

ADVANTAGES

Once any of these techniques have been adapted to your needs, they can be deployed with minimal effort, even after sitting on a shelf for a year. Because they do not rely on laughter, they are more easily adapted to a variety of audiences, and their humor does not require as much practice or revision to be successful. Although not active learning per se, some of them get students involved and speaking up in class. Many of them are also brief, demanding only a few seconds or minutes each, and the ones that are longer are meant to integrate with your existing lesson plan, so there is relatively little time taken up by using any of them. If your goal is to encourage students to seek personal assistance from you in the future, these approaches warrant your attention.

DRAWBACKS

Few of these techniques are ready to go as they are; they need to be adapted to your particular lesson plans. Adapting many of these techniques will take time and effort; you cannot just try them out on a whim to see what works for you and what does not. Because instructor personality is such a focus for them, you need to be prepared for the spotlight. Your energy and personal warmth act as a kind of fuel for this category of techniques. If you are not comfortable bringing those traits to bear, the techniques will suffer. Finally, bear in mind a side effect of encouraging students to make connections with you, specifically, they become more likely to reject assistance from other avenues if you are not accessible. If you are one of only a small number of librarians available to provide individual assistance, this might not be a problem. If you are not present, then there is no assistance available anyway. However, if you work as part of a larger team, having students reject assistance entirely if they cannot get it from you while five perfectly competent colleagues are standing by would be unfortunate.

Pirates of the Cephalonian Method

Joshua Vossler, information literacy and reference librarian,
Coastal Carolina University

I first encountered the Cephalonian Method in 2008 at a conference presentation given by Nigel Morgan and Linda Davies. I was struck by how they got the audience to participate in a manner that was both constructive and fun. It also struck me that this was an approach I could readily adapt to my own instruction duties, albeit with my own spin. The Cephalonian Method is an approach to library instruction that features a question-and-answer format, but instead of relying on the audience to come up with their own questions the instructor hands out color-coded cards with questions printed on them. The colors correspond to sections of the presentation. For example, in my lesson plan, questions pertaining to Google's advanced search features are printed on yellow paper. During that section of the class, I direct the audience to ask only yellow questions. Other sections are coded green, orange, and so forth. For this particular lesson plan, I used two sizes of paper for my questions, half-size and full-size sheets. The sizes gave me more control over the order in which questions were asked. The full-size sheets (only one per color) contained questions designed to introduce each new topic, and the half-size sheets contained the follow-up questions that could be asked in any order.

In addition to the cards, the Cephalonian Method uses music and visual aids whenever possible. The idea is to provide a stimulating environment. For my adaptation, I chose to build the lesson plan around a central theme: pirates. I wrote all of the questions from the perspective of a pirate who is adjusting, often poorly, to life as a college student. To set the stage, I played the score from *Pirates of the Caribbean* during the first few minutes while students were filing into the classroom and finding their seats. I introduced myself and gave a quick overview of how the class was going to work. To make the class a little more fun, I exhorted the students to deliver their questions in their best pirate accent, if they felt comfortable. I also allowed students who felt uncomfortable asking questions to pass their questions off to someone else. Before beginning the question-and-answer portion of the class I wanted to introduce the audience to the fundamentals of pirate-speak, so I read aloud a letter, which I have included below, that I wrote several years ago to the Quaker Oats Company, with regard to Cap'n Crunch cereal. Where appropriate, I used my best pirate accent. Because it seemed fitting, I gave this lesson plan its debut on September 19, International Talk Like a Pirate Day.

I have provided more questions than there is time for in even an 80 minute class. I recommend picking and choosing the questions most appropriate to the needs of your class. The references to alcohol and other undesirable piratical behaviors might need to be edited out, depending on your institutional culture and the strength of your desire to retain your job. Although it can be a lot of fun to play along and use your own pirate accent, I had a lot of success responding to each question as if I was unfamiliar with pirate culture. Try playing the straight man: answer each question seriously, and throw in the occasional nervous laugh or awkward stare at each student who asks a pirate-themed question. Behave as if you are a normal person and the students are crazy people who scare you just a little and whom you are trying to placate. If pirates aren't your cup of rum but you like the interactive element that this approach provides, I recommend you create your own version. The Cephalonian Method lends itself to the use of overarching themes. Think of a theme that might resonate with you and your audience and make it happen.

Dear Quaker Oats Representative,

First let me say that Cap'n Crunch™ is the finest cereal I have ever eaten. I fill my cereal bowl very full, and yet I've never had to face the soggy last bite or two that so many other cereals leave you with.

This letter is concerning the box of Cap'n Crunch I purchased earlier this week. On the front and back of the box the phrase "Crunch-a-tize me Cap'n" appears. I'm confused by this phrase. At first, I thought it just lacked a comma after "me". After all, a single piece of punctuation is easily missed. I'm sure I've missed dozens, if not hundreds of little things like that in my own writing. Anyway, with the comma the phrase would have read "Crunch-a-tize me, Cap'n". Punctuated in this way, the phrase would seem to indicate that somebody wants the Cap'n to crunchtize them: an experience I highly recommend.

But sailors have their own way of speaking. When used by a sailor, the word "me" can function equivalently to "my", as we can see in such phrases as "Arr, me cereal be the crunchiest cereal thar be", or "Egad, me peg leg's a-burnin' ". If written by a sailor or pirate, then the phrase "Crunch-a-tize me Cap'n" makes sense as it is, and nobody would be at fault. I'd like that.

But since the phrase seems to be a demand that the Cap'n be crunchatized, I am left with a few questions.

1) Who is supposed to crunchatize the Cap'n, if he is supposed to be crunchatized? Is it me?

2) What exactly is crunchatization? I thought it revolved around eating Cap'n Crunch cereal. But doesn't the Cap'n eat it all the time? If it means something else, I would sure like to know.

3) Which captain is the "Cap'n" in the phrase referring to? If this captain needs to be crunchatized, that makes me think that maybe the cereal box has some other captain in mind. I'm certain that there is nobody in the world less in need of crunchatization than the Cap'n. But if it is the Cap'n, then why would anybody say he needs crunchatization? That's like saying the pope isn't holy enough.

In closing, I hope there is only a minor typographical error to blame for me confusion and anxiety, and that something more malevolent is not at work. I wish the Cap'n good health, long life, and that his powers of crunchatization wax gloriously for all time, illuminating breakfasts everywhere with his crunchy radiance.

Best,

Joshua Vossler

There are six categories in this lesson plan: books and library services, EBSCO databases, Points of View Reference Center, iPoll (a public opinion poll database), CQ Researcher, and Google advanced search. As written, this lesson plan was designed to introduce second-semester English composition students to a wide variety of resources in support of a researched argument essay focused on current events. Emphasis was placed on covering as many relevant databases as possible in the allotted time. The category and color are listed at the top of each set of questions. The big question, which is meant to introduce each topic, comes first.

Blue (books and library services)
- Yar. I be needin' something full of information and heavy enough to smash bilge rats. How do I find books?
- Be I mad from syphilis, or be thar other libraries on this campus?
- What be thar to do if some mutinous sea dog has checked out the book I want?
- Matey, ye have helped keep me feet toasty warm with your beard through many a northern night in our flea-infested bunk. What kinds of help can I find here in the library?

Orange (EBSCO databases, especially Academic Search Complete)
- When I want to find rum I go to the tavern. When I want to find a snack I check me beard for bits of fried manatee. I want to find articles for my research. Where do I go?
- Why be there as many search boxes as I have teeth? Avast, there must be as many as three of them!
- Ahoy! What be that scurvy box on port side of the results screen? (Prompt to discuss ways to filter or refine the search. Note: Port is left)
- How might I best strike terror into the heart of this database, that I might force it to cite articles for me?
- Rabid penguins reduced me carrier pigeons to useless mounds of flesh and feather. How can I email articles to myself?

- Being a pirate, I prefer lies over truth, liquor over love, and booty over everything else. Should I prefer PDFs over HTML documents?

Green (Points of View Reference Center or any viewpoint-centric database)
- As a pirate, I resolve quarrels with the plank or a knife. Lately, I've taken to wonderin' if there's more to life than killin' all who cross me. Where can I go to learn about different perspectives on pressing social issues?
- Be it just the fleas and lice infesting me clothes and hair that be drivin' me mad, or be thar different kinds of entries in this database?
- I've sailed the seven seas, pulled the still-beating heart from a man's chest, and eaten my weight in baby seals. Even so, I was hopin' you could tell me the best way to search this database.
- I found a useful article, but today I be in pursuit of a terrible white whale whom I must stab at from Hell's heart, so I don't have time to print it out. Can I email it to meself so I can work with it later?

Pink (iPoll, or any public opinion poll database)
- Me first mate feels peg legs be all the rage. Where do I find information about public opinion polls?
- By Poseidon's beard, I like what these salty dogs have to say, and wish to cite this opinion poll in me paper. How do I be makin' that happen?

White (CQ Researcher, or other current-events database)
- I've looked in the bellies of whales, at the bottom of bottles of rum, but I still haven't found a reliable source of information on current events. Where should I go?
- Ahoy. A kraken ate me cabin boy. Without him, research goes slowly. Can I use the Issue Tracker to help keep track of ocean-related issues?
- Yesterday thar were a minor misunderstandin' between me and the authorities over what's for show and what's for dinner at the aquarium. Might I be allowed to use this database from me bunk while I'm under house arrest?

Yellow (Google advanced search: limit domain to .gov and search for statistics)
- Mark Twain said there are three kinds of lies: Lies, damned lies, and statistics. As a pirate, I approve of lies. How can I be usin' Google to find government statistics?
- What has 8 arms, 8 legs, and 8 eyes? (8 pirates)
- Yarrr. Me mates and I disagree about which state has a higher percentage of lasses, Utah or New York. Is there any way to resolve this dispute without havin' to spill blood on me new boots?

For the actual Cephalonian Method component, colored paper is all that is absolutely necessary, if you want to do this on the cheap. If possible, I recommend laminating cards to discourage students from doodling on them and to make them more resistant to normal wear and tear. Bent and scuffed question cards can be demoralizing. It is also a good idea to make at least one spare copy of each card. Sometimes cards will vanish, and if you have three classes in a row a missing question can be a problem. It also helps to be comfortable with the idea of being silly in public, but I submit that's just a valuable life skill in general. A sound system and projector are helpful if you want to incorporate audio and video into the presentation.

The purpose for this technique is to engage the audience and take some of the burden off the instructor. Database introduction classes are boring to teach and boring to sit through. For the instructor, these classes can be downright soul killing. They also take a physical toll: three or four of these classes in a day can leave your voice weak and your throat ragged. The Cephalonian aspect of this technique lends energy to the class and makes it less taxing for the instructor. The pirate-themed aspect of this technique makes helps break up the serious tedium of database chitchat with humor, helping to reduce the tedium of repetition for the instructor. My experience creating the lesson is also worth mentioning. Writing all of those silly pirate-themed questions was fun. Really fun. It made the work of designing a new lesson plan feel like play, and I spent a lot of time laughing in the two or so weeks I spent putting everything together.

Students usually react warmly to this technique, as do their professors. The Cephalonian Method is less about getting the big laughs than it is about creating a pleasant, energetic learning environment. Some students lean into the opportunity to talk like a pirate and can be quite entertaining. The less extroverted students tend only to observe, but they are observing the class and the instructor, not their mobile phones. Faculty members tend to also get a kick from this lesson plan as well, sometimes much more than their students. Students also stay awake. I have observed that students with questions in their hands that they had not yet read aloud tended to remain quite alert and focused on me. They were waiting to be called on with a surprising intensity. The more theatrically oriented among them could be seen mentally working out their performances. Some of these students bought into the exercise with enthusiasm, doing their best to approximate a pirate's accent. The humorous aspects, while quite silly, remain separate from the content of the class, so the actual educational content never feels like it is being made light of. Instead, the humor creates a pleasing rhythm for the class. There is a funny question, a minute or three of serious explanation, followed by another funny question, and so forth. This rhythm seemed to help students maintain attention for the duration of the class, avoiding the usual drop-off of interest I have observed after the first 30 minutes of a typical instruction session. There are, of course, always a few students (and the occasional professor) who do not enjoy this lesson. The disapproving students usually just avoid participation and glower a bit, but rarely heckle.

As an approach intended to get everyone involved, it works well. I observe some of the least prevalence of mobile phones and social networking when using this lesson plan. While the pirate speech and general silliness in the questions can appear distracting, in practice students stay focused on the underlying purpose of the session: to learn about research. While this lesson plan is elaborate, it is also readily modified to suit classes of varying lengths and subject matter. The Cephalonian Method is suitable for any presentation in which a large amount of information must be delivered and there simply isn't much room for hands-on activities. This technique lends the atmosphere created by a hands-on environment to situations that would otherwise remain deadly dull.

I have not conducted any formal assessment of this technique and cannot comment on its influence on student learning. That said, the Pirate Cephalonian Method gets students engaged and keeps them alert and paying attention during the instruction session. Its cost in time is relatively minimal: the five or six minutes required to read my Cap'n Crunch letter aloud and explain how the question cards work is about all this technique takes from the session. It reduces the physical demands of teaching multiple sections in a row, which leaves the instructor more energy to devote to interacting with students. The reduction in tedium also leaves the instructor in a better mood, which translates to more positive emotional landscape in the classroom. It is probably best applied to undergraduates, as the frivolity might put off more advanced students.

REFERENCES

Morgan, N., & Davies, L. (2004). Innovative library induction: Introducing the 'Cephalonian Method.' *SCONUL Focus* 32, 4–8. Retrieved from http://www.sconul.ac.uk/publications/newsletter/32.

Our Mantra

Jan Turner, reference librarian and associate professor,
Regis University

I tell the students that I am giving them a mantra and ask them to repeat it. Their mantra is "Ask a Librarian." I also tell them that I don't expect them to remember everything from the class today but I do want them to remember their mantra. I have them repeat it again at the end of class.

Students seem to find the association of mantras with librarians comical, which is harmless enough if it helps them remember to ask for help when they encounter a research problem. It helps to take a humorous attitude to explaining their new mantra; adopting a faux-formal and grandiloquent vocal inflection can add a nice touch.

Audio and Video

Shea A. Taylor, chief of reference and psychology subject specialist,
Cohen Library, City College of New York

I use videos and commercials through YouTube, Hulu, or company websites to link everyday information needs to research/library needs. For example, I use a commercial for Bing that makes fun of information overload. I use this commercial to link this to what students experience when they have a research assignment and the first time they have to use the library. I've used the Old Spice Library commercial to promote humor and the importance of using the library. When I have a discussion on starting an assignment, I use the Procrastination video.

Bing Commercial: http://www.youtube.com/watch?v=6jMt6saTqq4
Old Spice Commercials: http://www.youtube.com/watch?v=2Arlj236UHs
Procrastination: http://www.youtube.com/watch?v=4P785j15Tzk

For this technique to work, you will require an audio/video system and a high-speed Internet connection. Commercials are often familiar to students and can be comforting as well as entertaining. Library instruction, especially when paired with a difficult research assignment, can be stressful, and these videos can help lighten the mood and add some fun to an otherwise dreary subject. They also serve as an introduction to the topic of research but with higher production values than would be practical for an academic library to produce. Students typically laugh along with the videos and ask more questions and generally interact more in the aftermath.

Play Ball

Professor Dale Vidmar, Southern Oregon University

I begin class, I tell them my name, email, and office phone number. Then I ask them to pull out their cell phones and program my number into their cell phone: 552-6842. As they program the number, I tell them in case you cannot remember my number, it is simple especially for those with a basic understanding of baseball. If they look at the keypads on their phone like a baseball diamond, my phone number is pitcher-pitcher-catcher-third base-second base-first base- and back to the catcher.

One day was when one student asked how do you figure in the area code, which is 541. I explained that the pitcher (5) checks the runner on first (4) then looks at the batter in the on deck circle (1). Knowing he needs to get out of the inning before having to face the on-deck batter, the pitcher (5) winds up and fires an inside fastball to the catcher (2). The ball is hit to third base (6) who throws the ball to second base (8) then on first base (4) for the double play. Then the ball is flipped over to the umpire standing at home (2).

To implement this technique, you will need students with mobile phones and a solid understanding of baseball. Since they already have the number and are programming it into their phones, the baseball metaphor serves as less of a mnemonic device and more as an icebreaker. To a baseball aficionado, however, the mnemonic aspect could also be useful. Demonstrating an interest in something other than research can have a humanizing effect as well. This technique leaves students with both a telephone number that they can use for research assistance and a positive impression of the instructor.

AHA/ONO!

Tamara Brathwaite, librarian II, Institute of International Relations,
University of the West Indies, St. Augustine Campus, St. Augustine

---

I have a course that I teach to Postgraduate students at the Institute of International Relations; it's called "Information Literacy". I teach a class every Monday afternoon for one and a half hours during the first semester. The students usually come in after having had two four-hour lectures, so that by the time my students sit in my class they are very saturated.

In my first lecture, I hand out index cards (actually they are old 3x5 catalog cards we still have in stock in the library that we don't use anymore). On one side of the card I put three letters, "AHA!", and an exclamation mark and on the other side of the card I put the letters "ONO", with a frowning emoticon.

I don't explain to them what the cards are about until ten minutes before the end of the lecture, at which time I ask them if they had any moments of learning or clarity, any ideas that struck them, any thoughts they want to share about the lecture. If so, please put them on the side of the card with "AHA!"—I call it an AHA! Moment. Usually you see their eyes light up, because the mystery of why I handed them the index card begins to make sense and they begin to smile and think and then scribble away a thought or an idea that they wish to share on the card. Three minutes later, I ask them to flip the card over to the "ONO" side and now I ask them to write anything on this side that was expressed during the lecture or in any of their classes today that they did not understand or would like clarified. After a few seconds of furrowed brows, they eagerly fill in the card. Then I ask them to pass all of the cards to the front of the class. I advise them that at the beginning of the next lecture I will address all of their "ONO" moments. I do this for every single lecture thereafter; with students identifying any "AHA!" or "ONO" moments on index cards which I then address at the start of all subsequent lectures.

You will require 3×5 index cards or something similar for students to write on. Recycling old cards from the card catalog can be a convenient and money-saving approach. This technique creates a forum for students to provide immediate feedback regarding the instruction session. Many students never feel comfortable enough to voice questions to the entire class, so this technique allows them to address whatever is troubling them without having to admit ignorance or confusion publically. There tend to be more responses on the "AHA!" side than the "ONO" side, but the comments are usually either helpful or at least entertaining and provide some insight into what the students are thinking about.

Riding the Mechanical Bull with Carrot Top

Monique Delatte, librarian—acquisitions and adjunct librarian,
Fullerton College Library, Rio Hondo College Library

Query: What is funny in academia?
Time: Opening morning.
Place: Rio Hondo College Library classroom.
In spite of an overwhelming desire to kill, my experience with inspiring humor in the sober and barely awake student body was so limited, that dying seemed more likely. The Apollo Theater's Sandman did not tap dance out and hook the librarian with his shepherd's crook, but crickets did chirp softly somewhere in the nosebleed. Employing Jerry Seinfeld's advice that finding one's comedic voice requires seven years of performance practice,[1] my endeavor evolved into a marathon. Notes would be taken. Hours of stand-up would be scrutinized. Inspiration came from unexpected sources, namely, the much-maligned prop comic, Carrot Top. I'd once sipped borscht next to the orange-haired beefcake at the Barney's Greengrass bar in Bev Hills, unaware that his act would someday teach me that when a joke flops, move on swiftly, offering up novel material until the audience breaks. As soon as the crowd rewards you with a chuckle, reveal only props closely related to the line that got the giggle. Classical conditioning is pivotal to comedic success. Watching live local acts prompted the awareness

that the bit that works with the 7a.m. class might not impress the 11:30ers; thus, I kept vigorous mental notes re: snicker variability.

Scenario: Speech 101 showed up before noon with four class clowns, providing the challenge of outperforming these established jokers. The solution was to use them as an opening act to loosen up their stone-faced peers, and willfully step on/steal their laughs.

Research: In the name of good humor science, a librarian bull-riding film was staged the night prior to be integrated into the standard issue Speech 101 info lit class as a comedic device. Necessary supplies included a mechanical bull,[2] a librarian/jockey, and a video recording device.

Reactions: 7a.m. students noticeably perked up, 11:30a.m. group—the class of four clowns —was so enthralled by 3 seconds of video that the clip was briefly considered for banishment from all future lessons.

Observations: Two days later, a student inquired, "You're the bull-riding librarian, right? Can you help me find data about the duranguense?" This represented the first time a student had ever approached me referencing a previous Info Lit class, and it felt like victory. That rodeo-inspired video and my face stuck. The purpose of the reference desk adhered, too. The comedic attempt wasn't a total loss. In fact, I'd become a bull-surfing barnacle on the brains of freshmen. Very Carrot Top.

Assessment: The pre- and post-test did not betray significantly improved results for the level of information literacy achieved by the class. However, informal interviews with the speech instructor and pupils revealed that the effort was appreciated, and indeed no student remained in slumber through the duration of the film clip—re-engagement goal achieved.

Showing students a video of their librarian behaving in a fashion incongruous with their expectations creates a compelling image that makes the encounter memorable and increases the likelihood of students remembering the librarian and (hopefully) asking for help in the future. The use of a video is especially helpful for this purpose, as it allows the effort of creating a memorable scenario to be expended only once but reused indefinitely. The video format supplies two additional advantages: one, a video provides the same experience again and again, regardless of how tired the instructor is; two, it shifts the focus briefly away from the instructor. Each time focus is shifted, attention is usually renewed. Also, students enjoy funny videos.

"Yippee"

Linda J. Goff, head of instructional services,
California State University, Sacramento

I teach a 2-hour research seminar to new MSW grad students in the summer before they start the program. When talking about published bibliographies, which can be extremely useful to those doing their literature reviews, I make the class say "Yippee" every time I mention the word "bibliography." (They have to say it twice if I say "annotated bibliography"). Usually the first effort is really half-hearted so I give them a chance to do it again with a smile and they sit up and say it louder and with more conviction. Then as I keep using the "bib" word they catch on and I get a few yippees throughout the class.

I do something similar with the SFX "FIND IT" button in our databases. This button links to full-text in articles in other databases. I make them repeat after me: "FIND IT IS MY FRIEND" and show them that by following the link they can be rewarded with a full-text article from another source.

This technique offers two advantages. One, it gives students a canned response they can holler out at various points throughout the class. This method creates the impression of interaction and can encourage students to interact in other ways as well. Two, it focuses student attention on the presentation better than a regular passive lecture environment. Students are given an immediate reason to pay attention and have the added pressure of not wanting appearing foolish in front of their classmates by missing the cue. This approach is also helpful for making a lasting impression on the students; it is not likely that many of their other instructors demand they yell "Yippee" during class.

Information Literacy Is the Fashion!

Joshua McKain, college librarian, Fisher College

I was teaching a session about fashion designers for a Fashion Merchandising class, and I was sporting a pair of Lilly Pulitzer pants and an Izod shirt, using the former as an example while searching Google, the online catalog, and a variety of databases. Although the vast majority of the young adults had not heard of Lilly Pulitzer, they were amused by my outlandish attire, and they paid attention to the lesson that I had prepared for them, which I handed out as well upon completion.

Coordinating the lesson plan with the presentation makes the entire endeavor appear well thought out and cohesive. In this case, the eyecatching clothing served the dual purposes of coordinating the presentation with the lesson and making the instructor harder to ignore. The clothing provided a natural segue into database search techniques using familiar concepts and terms to make the experience less aversive.

Physical Comedy in the Classroom

Joshua Vossler, information literacy and reference librarian,
Coastal Carolina University

I've always been a squirrely guy. Back in high school I used to do flips in the hallway between classes, and in college my best friend and I spent hours practicing how we would collapse if we were puppets whose strings were suddenly cut. In retrospect I pity his downstairs neighbors. As a teacher, I've brought that joy of movement into the classroom with me. The following are a handful of physical techniques I've had success with over the years.

1. *Cartwheels.* The phrase "head over heels" never made much sense to me, since that's the position in which I spend most of my days. However, if the occasion calls for that phrase, or an expression of excitement over anything, it's fun to turn a quick cartwheel. I prefer one-handed, since two-handed cartwheels cover too much distance, and walkovers (cartwheels with no hands) require more oomph than I like to put into any given class. Assuming you are trained in how to do a cartwheel and physically capable of performing them without danger of injury, I recommend finding a space at least 6 feet wide and 10 feet long. Do the cartwheel in the direction of the long end of your space. For maximum effect, do not make a production out of this. Do it suddenly, with as little wind-up as you can muster. Once completed, move on with your lesson plan as if nothing has happened. Make no mention of the cartwheel and ignore exhortations for a repeat performance.

2. *Puppet with its strings cut.* When describing the importance of having a well-articulated research question, I like to illustrate the point with the analogy of a puppet without any strings. While miming how I imagine a puppet moves, I explain that a research question gives purpose and guidance to research. The question gives you the answer of where to look next, and tells you when you've found what you need. But without the research question, you are like a puppet without any strings: paralyzed. Then I mime holding scissors and pretend to snip a string above my head. At the moment of snip I let my entire body go limp and I collapse into a boneless heap, hard, onto the floor. I remain in that position just long enough to make my point, maybe two or three seconds, before picking myself up with exaggerated dignity. As with the cartwheel, make no production out of this and move on immediately.

3. *Trip and fall.* This one is useful to shake the class up and get them paying attention to you. I don't love how it is disingenuous (it is a faked accident, after all), but when you are facing a distracted class, what counts is refocusing their attention on you and, by extension, the instruction they are about to receive. This technique is one that should be saved for special occasions when students really needs to get their collective minds pulled out of the clouds. When such a moment occurs, continue with whatever you were saying, but make your way over to an empty area on the floor, preferably in view of the entire class. Find something nearby to trip over, or just tangle your feet together. What matters isn't why you fall, it is how you fall. I like to make my fall into a dive roll for extra effect. I trip, throw my head forward and under my body while tucking to roll, then I extend my body immediately upon exiting the roll, slamming my entire side and one arm against the ground to arrest my momentum before I let myself go limp. If you've studied judo or aikido, it's a basic dive roll with a side fall and some playacting at either end. The big motion of my fall, followed with the loud slap of my legs and arm against the ground, brings everyone to instant attention. At that point I dust myself off and resume the class.

4. *Dancing.* This technique requires two personal traits: fearlessness and a total inability to dance. This technique is best applied in situations similar to the trip and fall: the class is a little distracted or unfocused, and you want to bring them around. Have some contemporary music queued up on a sound system you can control remotely. Trigger it when you feel attention flagging. Dance enthusiastically and entirely without shame. Do it badly. If you can, bust out the Sprinkler or the Shopping Cart, or any other dance moves that are awkward and campy. This is key: the juxtaposition of contemporary pop music that the students are sure to recognize with awkward dance moves executed with fearless joy. If you like, choose a student or professor and dance at him or her. Say nothing, just dance. Persist in your dancing for the duration of the song, about three minutes. The audience

will become uncomfortable after about 20 or 30 seconds, which is to be expected and desired. Your commitment to the behavior and lack of shame generate the humor.

5. *Looking startled.* When teaching one-shot instruction sessions, usually I prefer to introduce myself. It gives me more latitude to express myself than an introduction from a professor and is usually more accurate. When I cannot introduce myself, I like to have fun I with my response to being introduced. When the introduction starts, or just before, take a relaxed pose and pretend to look at something interesting on the ceiling or a computer screen or the floor. I like to mime watching a fly buzz around the ceiling. The moment you hear your name called, jerk to sudden attention, as if waking suddenly from a daydream. Your body goes suddenly tense, and your eyes and head need to dart in two or three directions as if fearing attack. This goes on for maybe three seconds. At the end of that time, adopt a big, false smile and wave to the class.

6. *Just keep moving.* This last one is less about generating humor on its own and more about laying the foundation for your other techniques to work. The concept is simple: stay in motion throughout the class. Professional comedians do this to lend a feeling of energy to the atmosphere, and it has the same effect in the college classroom. By moving around the classroom, you force students to track you, which keeps them alert. Your shifting position gives you different perspectives on the class, making it harder for students to conceal a mobile communications device. Standing and moving around raises your heart rate, which fills your presentation with more energy and makes you more compelling to listen to. Taken all together, the effects conspire to improve how you teach the class and how your students experience the class.

For the first three techniques, athleticism is a prerequisite. They are dangerous and must only be executed by those with sufficient conditioning and training. There must also be an environment with lots of space. You should never risk coming into physical contact with a student. There should be enough distance between you and them that a complete failure on your part will only result in consequences to yourself. More importantly, practice these well enough that you have a zero percent failure rate. Before I ever attempted any of the first three techniques listed here in the classroom, I performed tens of thousands of cartwheels, dive rolls, and falls under supervised conditions. For the last three techniques, all you need is a total lack of shame and a willingness to play using motion. A good pair of shoes, however, never hurts.

The purpose is to startle the class, and by so doing focus their attention onto you. There are many ways to startle an audience, but these physical performances are powerful because they are so utterly out of place. Students are not accustomed to seeing teachers perform athletic feats under any circumstances, and certainly not in the classroom. Having established that something out of the ordinary can happen in your classroom, students will be on the lookout for further displays for the remainder of the class. Whether or not you give them any further physical performances, they will tend to maintain their attention on you and pay attention to whatever you decide to talk about for the rest of the session. It should also be noted that these techniques are all most suited for lecture-style classes in which student attention can wander. For active learning environments where the emphasis is less on the teacher and more on an activity, such extreme attention-getters might not be worth the effort.

For the first three techniques, students react with surprise and excitement. The cartwheel and the puppet with its strings cut are especially effective crowd-pleasers. Whichever of the three is used, the effect tends to be the same: initial surprise followed by an increase in focus on you. Technique four, dancing, inspires some looks of abject horror but also enthusiasm. Students eventually buy into the activity and cheer you on or laugh. Any tension in the room dissipates, leaving a relaxed environment in which students seem to have an easier time interacting with you and each other.

NOTES

1. Hartlaub, P. (2009, July 26). A stand-up lesson from Apatow. *San Francisco Chronicle (CA)* Advance 4 ed., Q12. Retrieved November 21, 2009, from NewsBank online database (America's Newspapers).

2. Available at your local old west saloon-inspired chain restaurant/bar.

7

Evaluating Sources

INTRODUCTION

The techniques in this chapter are characterized by their use of humor to introduce or kick-start a discussion or activity involving critical thinking. Much of what we do in library instruction involves training, as opposed to teaching. We demonstrate specific, repeatable behaviors: click here for this, click there for that. In training, strictly lower-level cognitive skills are brought to bear. Students are learning how to manipulate specific tools. These techniques, however, seek to teach, to get students using critical thinking skills to solve problems or to evaluate situations. Students are learning why they would want to manipulate those tools. This approach asks a lot of students and can be intellectually demanding on the instructor. "Crazy Cat Librarian Lady" is an especially excellent contribution, as is "An Absurd Story."

PURPOSE

These techniques use extreme or absurd examples to generate discussion on an information literacy–related issue. Their humor derives from the extremity or absurdity of the example and is usually focused at the beginning of the technique, where it functions as an introduction and attention-getter. By using such examples, underlying issues are made more readily apparent and easier to engage with. The "crazy cat librarian lady" is both more memorable and more easily discussed than a reasonable, educated, and sane pet owner, even if the two people actually suffer from the same misinformation. By engaging students in critical thinking exercises or discussions, they have little choice but to actively think about the material. Distractions are minimized and participation increases.

ADVANTAGES

Students have to use higher-level cognitive skills. They have to think about the subject matter in the session. Going through the motions, mechanically recording where to click for what, ceases to be an option. Teaching, as opposed to training, requires more mental effort on behalf of the instructor but results in less tedium as well. It is more stimulating to both the teacher and student. When students are engaged in discussions or exercises, their attention is less likely to wander, so they have a better chance of benefiting from the session. The skills they learn in such sessions are also broadly applicable, so they are ultimately more useful. Understanding how to search a particular database is a fine thing, but getting an understanding of what they should be searching for and why it is valuable is far more useful in the long term. Database interfaces are forever changing, but the intellectual underpinnings of information literacy are stable, so our time is more wisely invested when teaching in this way.

DRAWBACKS

As valuable as teaching is, training is more obviously useful, especially to a faculty member who wants students to stop using free online search engines or who has an assignment constructed around a specific database. Depending on your student body, higher-level subject matter might not reach all of your students, especially if some of them are not intellectually prepared to absorb it. There is also a developmental aspect: upper-level students will be more receptive to, and benefit more from, this kind of approach. First-year students are more likely to lack both the experience and cognitive development to fully appreciate higher-level instruction. From that perspective, it can be better to train everyone than to teach only some. These techniques require a lot of preparation and are usually associated with a specific class or subject, so it only makes sense to develop such a technique for a class in high demand. It also means that adapting a lesson plan to include one at the last minute would be problematic at best. Teaching higher-order thinking requires higher-order thinking, which can be exhausting for the instructor if the class must be repeated more than once or twice in a single day.

Crazy Cat Librarian Lady

Beth Lander, associate professor and director of library services,
Basileiad Library, Manor College

I was invited by the education coordinator of our Veterinary Technology program to come into her Small Animal Clinical and Emergency Procedures class to discuss how to locate and evaluate information specific to the vaccination of small animals. The Vet Tech program is a two-year program, and this class is a 200 level class. Approximately 30 students were in the class. I was given 75 minutes of class time for the presentation.

I am a Crazy Cat Lady (CCL) in real life. Although I grew up with dogs, my family got a cat, Miss Kitty, a gorgeous Siberian tiger, 6 years ago. I accept that my future will hold a double-wide littered with books, yarn, chocolate, empty vodka bottles, and about 17 cats.

I asked the professor, herself a crazy cat lady personally and professionally, if I could come into the class in character, and pretend to be the kind of client that I have the potential to be—one who knows more than the vet, because, as the parent of Miss Kitty, I know my cat better than any idiot vet who does little more than express my cat's anal glands every six months.

I told the professor that my point in doing this was to separate myself as Librarian from the Vet Tech students, all of whom I know very well, and many of whom have seen my general schtick in EN101 courses, or some other class. I didn't want to bore them, because I knew if I did, I would lose them within 8 minutes. And, as far as I'm concerned as a crazy cat lady, I want really, really good Vet Techs who can talk me out of my tree when I show up at the emergency room in a total panic because my cat just spent the last 20 hours puking all over my house.

I burst into the class with a stuffed cat under my arm—the students were disappointed that the real Miss Kitty didn't attend—and I started immediately in character. I spoke in a high pitched voice, ending every statement with the pitch going up, speaking in such a way that it would be difficult to get a word in edgewise, all about how everyone says my cat needs vaccinations, but I know that vaccinations have side effects, don't people get autism? and that I treat myself holistically, and how that would be more healthy for my cat, and how I found this really great website on the Google that told me why vaccinations are bad, and obviously I know what's best for my cat, because, well, because she's my cat.

I was really, really annoying. At first the students had no idea how to respond, but then they started to question my motives, which was great. And I wouldn't budge out of character, which they then took as a challenge. When the students started talking to the CCL about these sources that contradicted her Google site, I asked them how they knew that there sources were better than mine; where did they find them? Why was their author better than the "doctor" who wrote the Google site? Why couldn't holistic treatment of humans be transferred to animals? In my questions, I focused on getting them to think about the evidential value of what they were saying, and how that evidence could be used persuasively against misinformation.

The CCL stayed for about 25 minutes of the class. I broke character by asking this of the class: You will be in practice in less than a year, and you will face a client like this at some time in your professional life. How do you handle this client in such a way that ensures the proper treatment of the animal, and doesn't offend the client to the point that the client takes their business elsewhere?

The remainder of the class was a conversation in response to that question, as well as a discussion prompted by the professor about resources available for peer reviewed material outside of the databases provided by the Library. I ended the class by walking the students through the resources listed in the program LibGuide.

I want to get the students to think for themselves, rather than having me just lecture and do demos. By the time these students are in their second year, they should have a grasp of the resources available to them in the Library as well as through professional organizations and governmental agencies. And while the concept of evidence-based practice is not as large a part of the veterinary program as it is in the dental hygiene program, understanding the importance of grounding an argument in evidence is important. Otherwise, the vet tech in practice is little more than another crazy cat lady.

I also stressed to the students that they needed to start thinking like professionals, and NOT like students, who are looking for a quick fix to some assignment they have to complete. The heart of the technique is to shift to a higher level of critical thinking in the face of practical need ("If I offend this patient, they may leave the practice, and my boss will lose money . . ."),

In the end, I'm trying to teach them to think on their feet like professionals; to understand the resources available to them as students might not be the same resources available to them in practice; to understand that equally valid evidence can be obtained through professional, governmental and other educational institutions; and to understand that they may be the first professional a client sees, and that their client's first impression will set the tone for continued interaction with the practice. I also discovered that humor used with a specific intent, rather than humor used to lighten the mood or regain attention, can be a very powerful tool to motivate responsiveness. Use of humor seemed to free the students from the fear of being wrong in their responses—they seemed much more willing to contribute to the conversation, to criticize me as the CCL and to criticize each other, in constructive ways.

To execute this technique, you will need a stuffed cat, Internet access, an audio/video system, a cooperative faculty member, and a lack of self-consciousness. Expect students to react first with laughter, then some doubt, and finally settle into playing along with the scenario. The class environment should be freeform and energetic, filled with boisterous conversation. The only control should be exerted by the professor to shift the focus among the various forms of professional information that are the subject of the session. While this session is entertaining for the students, one its biggest strengths are that it is fun for the instructor. If the instructor is not completely engaged with the class or the material, the students sense that and become distracted.

Being immersed in a role-playing scenario puts the students off balance, especially when they are forced to engage in discussion about resources apart from the ones provided by the library. Students at this level might be accustomed to using academic databases but have little or no experience evaluating veterinary program websites or websites representing professional organizations. This experience can be uncomfortable, but it creates a forum for students to apply the skills they have learned in the library for evaluating sources to real-world problems. Ideally, it also results in a lot of positive interaction, both between student and instructor and among the students.

A Recipe for Information Literacy

Anne Driscoll, lead reference librarian,
University of Maryland Eastern Shore

When teaching students about how to evaluate websites, we discuss what to look for (i.e., authority, currency, dead links, etc). I use my cooking skills as an example of something you might find on the Internet that was not what it seemed. It goes something like this: Most people have the ability to create a Web page via their Internet service providers. Having the ability to put up a web page doesn't mean you are an expert on a subject. For example, my idea of making biscuits is to go to the frozen food section of the Food Lion and getting one of those bags of biscuits. I throw them on a cookie sheet, pop it in the oven, and if I don't forget about them, they are perfect every time. (I mime throwing them on the cookie sheet). Suppose I go home tonight and put up a page titled "The world's best biscuit recipe". You look at it, the ingredients look okay. But what you don't know is that the last time I made biscuits from scratch they came out like little rocks. They were so nasty that my dog wouldn't eat them. (Everyone laughs). Do you REALLY want my biscuit recipe??? Well, maybe if you want to make rocks.

The point is, just because I put it on the Internet, there is no way of knowing that I don't know what I am talking about. But if you go to Rachel Ray's (substitute whatever famous cook) website, you know she is an expert in the field.

This anecdote illustrates the problem of authority on the free web and the dangers of relying on search engine results without critical reflection. Although the experts can also be wrong, it is a lot safer to rely on what they have to say than it is to trust the ideas of someone with indeterminate credentials. This lesson tends to come across as rather preachy, so it is helpful to defuse that impression by using yourself as the target of some gentle mocking.

Wikidom

Kate Rubick, reference and instruction librarian,
Lewis & Clark College, Portland, Oregon

I showed the Stephen Colbert clip on Wikiality (http://www.colbertnation.com/the-colbert -report-videos/72347/july-31-2006/the-word—wikiality) to a class of Sociology/Anthropology qualitative methods students who were learning about analyzing Web sites as a cultural object. I used the video clip to jump-start a discussion on how to look critically at Wikipedia articles to recognize bias. And I had them do an exercise on Wikipedia where they tried to identify authorship or controversies associated with the page. The lesson in this case was that Wikipedia could be used as an object of cultural analysis—rather than as a place to go for information. And that anthropologists and sociologists will often use the Web in this way.

This was a part of an information literacy collaborative project funded by the library. The professor has proposed a project to team up with a librarian and build information literacy into the curriculum of the course. The professor was paid a stipend for this work and was required to assess the program. The assessment was done at the end of the semester in the form of a survey. Unfortunately, the students felt that the assignment relating to looking web sites as objects of cultural analysis was tangential to the rest of the course, so that assignment was not repeated. The use of humorous video was not really assessed on its own. But I have not had another opportunity to reintroduce this fabulous video. More's the pity.

This video is useful for any session in which Wikipedia will be under discussion. It should be noted that while the video does call Wikipedia's approach to truth by consensus into question, the examples used actually demonstrate how Wikipedia manages to correct for deliberate misinformation. As a tool for livening up a session, this video is effective. Stephen Colbert is popular among undergraduates, and the humor in the video can bring a lot of laughter into the class. It can also be effective for students to see a celebrity bringing up points instead of a librarian. As Jonathan Swift demonstrated in "A Modest Proposal," it is better for unpalatable arguments to be attributed to an absent third party. If anyone wants to attack the source of the argument, they cannot, while you are free to suggest responses the absent third party might make to your audience's objections. The video also gives students a break from listening to yet another instructor, which tends to be rather welcome.

An Absurd Story

Kathleen Irvine, Subject Librarian,
Highland Health Sciences Library

I use absurd examples—locating weird research papers ("how many people have been killed by soda pop machines?"), for example. Teaching critical appraisal, to inform the class about research design, I suggest I am about to conduct a study of the efficacy of the homeopathic therapy for piles[1] (a conker[2] in one's pocket—strange but true) and then suggest absurd flawed study designs that the class criticise, so eliciting information on randomisation, sampling, etc. I suggest that my dodgy paper was published very easily as the results were so surprising, and that a much larger, better designed study that refuted my findings was rejected as "stating the bleeding obvious", to illustrate the problem of publication bias. I also use storytelling—with and without explicit humour in various contexts, e.g., telling the story of the back-to-sleep campaign and why it was ever necessary (a cautionary tale about favouring expert opinion over evidence).

For this technique to work best, you will want to have solid public speaking skills and enough force of personality to overcome the oddness of talking about hemorrhoids in front of strangers. Having a few horse chestnuts on hand to give out as prizes makes for an entertaining conclusion to the session. This technique covers skills for searching databases as well as critical evaluation of resources. Students enjoy the unusual references and focus better on class materials.

Celebrity Gossip and Peer Review

John Watts, outreach and reference librarian, Coastal Carolina University

---

This is an interactive module that requires six to eight minutes or longer, and illustrates the differences between scholarly and popular sources. I use pop culture references to give students a familiar foundation from which to discuss scholarly and popular sources. This module consists of three parts: Solicitation, explanation, and evaluation. The humorous elements occur at the beginning and end of the module.

1. *Solicitation.* Introduce the activity and ask students to volunteer names of information sources. "Hello everyone. You are here because you have questions. Huge questions. Questions like: Why is [insert inexplicably popular, untalented celebrity here] famous? I have a question for you, and I want you to just yell out answers as they occur to you. The question is this: Where do you get your information?" Write the results on the board. Students inevitably list popular magazines and websites. Continue until you have enough to work with, more than three, but hopefully closer to ten. If the class is reticent, give them hypothetical scenarios: "At the hair salon, you read what? At the doctor's office? What about on the Internet? In the morning, what websites do you visit? What about in the evening?" Some of the more goody-goody types will actually name academic databases. Praise them.

2. *Explanation.* Address each item on the board, explaining what each source is known for. The idea is to make sure that everyone in the class understands each source. For example, not many students read *The Atlantic*, but the occasional smarty-pants student will bring it up. There are usually opportunities to ad-lib during this part.

3. *Evaluation.* This last part consists of a mini-lecture on peer review and the differences between scholarly and popular sources. List observable traits of scholarly and popular sources. After the lecture, point to each source and ask the class to evaluate which ones are suitable for academic research (The faculty I teach for require peer-reviewed sources for their students' essays). Cross out the ones they reject, and reinforce their evaluations with some color commentary. For example, when rejecting a magazine that features celebrity gossip (always a popular choice), I like to say "Sure, this magazine is great for finding out what [insert drug-abusing celebrity here] is putting up [his/her] nose these days, it is less useful for determining the physiological and psychological effects of continuous cocaine use on rats."

An interest in popular culture and a commitment to staying current are fundamental for getting effective use of pop culture references in instruction. Pop culture has a memory of about three weeks at the outside. Sure, there are exceptions when a piece of gossip is deeply embedded in the cultural awareness, but in general you need to come up with new references at least that often. Ideally, use the most current gossip for the best effect. This means a lot of "research" must be conducted on a daily, or at least weekly, basis. If you try referencing old news, this technique can backfire, confirming you as an out-of-touch old fogey. Part of what gives this technique power is that students do not expect a librarian (or probably any professorial type) to be current with popular culture.

The purpose is to introduce students to the differences between scholarly and popular sources and involve them in evaluating which sources are best for scholarly inquiry. Ideally, it also prevents students from becoming defensive and shutting down in the face of what they can perceive as condescension from the instruction librarian. If I come across as sharing at least a few of their values, maybe they will be more inclined to listen to what I have to say.

If you drop a good joke about a celebrity, especially one that is at all racy, count on a big laugh and, at least for the first time you do it, surprise. The younger the batch of students the better this approach seems to work. By demonstrating that you are current with information that students find relevant (as depressing as that might be from an educational perspective), you align yourself with their values and appear more trustworthy. Humor bookends this lesson and pops up occasionally throughout it, making an otherwise tedious topic more lighthearted and easier to swallow. Any discussion of scholarly versus popular sources seems to inevitably paint popular sources in a negative light, which creates a problem. Students tend to rely on and enjoy popular sources. In our students' eyes, we appear to be attacking those sources. This perceived attack can make some students feel defensive, and that shuts down the learning environment. By proving that you read and enjoy those popular sources, you seem less like a pedantic fuddy-duddy talking down to them. After all, we are not trying to get them to reject popular sources, just not to rely on them for serious scholarly inquiry more suited to scholarly books and articles.

Good versus Bad, Quality versus Quantity, Etc.

Scott Sheidlower, assistant professor and head of information literacy,
York College of the City University of New York

Whenever I teach, I know that I must prove to my students that the library has something special to offer them. It cannot be just plain old information. Information, to my students, is what you find on the Internet. Just type your topic into a search engine and voilà: you have all the information you need. Since I am trying to teach them to critically evaluate sources (ACRL's standard three), I feel that I must get them to think about information differently. I also want to capture their attention. To do this I ask them to define "good' information. Usually they cannot do it. I then say I'm going to give them an example of "good" information. I hop on one foot and rub my tummy. I say that I am now curing the common cold.

The only real requirement for this technique is the physical coordination to hop up and down while rubbing your tummy and a willingness to do so in public. The purpose is to get the students to pay attention and to provide an entertaining context for introducing ACRL's third standard. Most importantly, students laugh. They pay attention, and they get that there is such a thing as "bad" information. It is then much easier to glide right into teaching them about "good" information. The technique seems to work well with the students, but it can sometimes result in colleagues teasing you.

NOTES

1. Hemorrhoids.
2. Horse chestnuts.

8

Searching with Humor

INTRODUCTION

Demonstrating database features and proper search strategy are among the things we do the most and that students appear to enjoy the least. It is boring to do and boring to watch, and it is during this portion of our classes that we observe our students starting to die inside. It is not surprising, then, that we received the greatest number of contributions for this book on the subject of teaching students how and where to search for quality information. Despite the large number of techniques, they tend to use one of two approaches: humorous examples or humorous analogies. Humorous examples simply take the place of mundane examples. Instead of demonstrating a search for health care reform, you substitute a more entertaining topic that yields useful results. Humorous analogies take the place of explanations, connecting an unfamiliar concept with one that is familiar but absurd or surprising. David Ettinger, for example, compares the LC classification system and how it groups related items together to the likelihood of a pretty girl having an even prettier roommate.

PURPOSE

Although they do both share the purpose of making a dull subject more appealing, humorous analogies and humorous examples serve different purposes. Humorous examples are used for the same purpose as mundane examples: they give you a subject to demonstrate searches with without having to drag one out of what might be a totally unprepared class. A canned subject also gives you control over the demonstration, since you know ahead of time what results will come up. The purpose behind using a specifically humorous example is to maintain student attention and suggest that the instructor is not a complete fuddy-duddy. There are only so many times you can demonstrate how to search for articles on abortion before going stark raving mad. If you have to use a canned example, the thinking goes, you might as well use an entertaining canned example. Humorous analogies are meant to promote student comprehension by connecting an unfamiliar concept to one that is familiar and often absurd. The more absurd the analogy, the more memorable the lesson.

ADVANTAGES

Humorous examples, like mundane examples, give you a predictable subject for demonstrating effective search strategies but also lend a bit of levity to a dull topic with no added cost in time, either during the session or during your preparations. A humorous example takes the same amount of time to trot out as a mundane example, and if you are going to use canned examples, you need to come up with them in advance whether they are mundane or humorous. Humorous analogies are a lot more fun to relate, and fun to listen to, than some long-winded, literal explanation. They are also more likely to be remembered long after the session has ended.

DRAWBACKS

For humorous examples, there are significant dangers. In some cases, students will not have encountered such documents as peer-reviewed articles before and might be skeptical of the value of academic databases. Humorous examples often lead to silly or silly-seeming search results, which can reinforce a skeptical student's already negative attitude toward the very resources you are trying to promote. To a serious-minded faculty member, a humorous example could make you seem to be making light of resources that cost the university large amounts of money. It is also tempting to use examples that appeal more to your own sensibilities and less to those of your students. Humorous analogies are a safer approach but are still not without drawbacks. If the analogy used is not apt, it can create confusion instead of resolving it. Unless you are lucky enough to have entertaining and apt analogies come to you in the moment, inventing them on demand involves a lot of work. As a teaching tool, analogies are fairly inflexible. Each analogy is only apt, and therefore useful, for a single concept. For an instructor who teaches a variety of classes, implementing humorous analogies can mean a lot of memorization. Finally, if the needs of your class change at the last minute, you will have a difficult time adapting the analogy to a concept that is even slightly different.

Bookstore vs. Library

David Ettinger, Ph.D., international affairs and political science librarian, Gelman Library, George Washington University

I ask students about how books are arranged in a bookstore and a library. I then ask which arrangement is most advantageous to the researcher. After establishing that the subject arrangement is preferable, we talk about how, because of this arrangement, it is easy to find related books on one's subject, since they are in the same area. Indeed, sometimes one goes up to the stacks in search of a particular book and finds the one sitting right next to it is even better, sort of like going to your girlfriend's place to pick her up and discovering that her roommate appeals to you more than she does.

This technique covers both the basics of LC classification and the advantages of browsing the immediate area around a useful book. The hope here is that by using a familiar and slightly off-color analogy the lesson will be more memorable and lighten the mood in the classroom.

Blind Date

David Ettinger, Ph.D., international affairs and political science librarian, Gelman Library, George Washington University

---

Seeing students almost spontaneously eliminate from consideration the results of database searches based on the most superficial examination of a particular record, I tell them their actions remind me of what happens to me when I go to a bar. I approach a woman and she immediately tells me, "Sorry, I'm not interested." Isn't this a rush to judgment, I ask. Shouldn't she at least take a few minutes to get to know me before she rejects me?

This analogy uses self-deprecating humor, making it illustrative and entertaining at the same time. The purpose is to convince students to more carefully evaluate sources before dismissing them, such as considering the abstract or introductory paragraph. It is more efficient to make use of the sources immediately available than to be expend time and energy looking elsewhere. The efficacy of this technique, at least in the short term, is easily tested by observing students in class as they search. If they linger on sources long enough to read the abstract, you are successful.

An English Lesson Gone to Pot

Billie E. Walker, reference librarian, Penn State University, Berks Campus

---

I hear often that some library instructors are bored with the topic of marijuana in their instruction. However, I have found every time I employ it for teaching keywords I get laughs. In introductory level English classes, when teaching keywords, I tell the class I know they already know how to search, but my role is to help them become better searchers. I then ask them, when they're searching for information on a topic do they sometimes get back information that does not seem to be relevant? You might get a few nods of agreement if you're lucky. I then proceed to say imagine searching the topic "marijuana" and for some strange reason your search came up empty, what are other words you could use to describe the same search? This is where the fun begins. If the students are quiet I say I am not the PoPo (slang name for police) so you can feel free to speak. All students might not participate, however there are usually one or two showoffs that help provide the humor. Many times students say "weed" or "pot" as synonyms of "marijuana". If so, I say "Yes, they are synonyms of marijuana but if you type in only those words you aren't guaranteed to get what you are looking for". I then point to the grass and weeds outside and say "There are weeds and grass right there, do you want to smoke that?" They laugh. I then say "if you want to use words like weeds and grass then you need to be more specific by adding keywords such as "illegal drugs." Students also often mention "pot" as another keyword for marijuana. I then say "if you simply type the word pot, the search may also bring up information on 'pots used for cooking' and that is not what you're looking for so you need to add another keyword to make your search more specific." Of course students also shout some of the new slang names for marijuana. They shout out such names as "sticky icky", "devil's lettuce", "giggle bush", and many more. I usually laugh at these terms, and say "times have surely changed." Sometimes a student will suggest "cannabis" as a term and if not I do it myself. I say to the students "Cannabis is a really good word to use for college level research and in particular in database searching because it is the scientific name for marijuana." I then proceed to show students using the ProQuest database, what happens when you type the terms "marijuana", "weed", "weed and illegal drugs", "cannabis" and "sticky icky". For example, in the ProQuest database there are a couple of articles on "sticky icky" as a drug, as well as an article titled, "Yikes! A Smart Girl's Guide to Surviving Tricky, Sticky, Icky, Situations." This is another teachable moment.

For this technique to be possible, you will need an audio/visual projection system and an Internet connection for demonstrating relevant databases. For this technique to succeed, you will need to project a relaxed and playful demeanor so that students will feel comfortable interacting with you on the subject of marijuana. The goal is to introduce students to keyword searching in academic databases and underscore the importance of using controlled vocabulary (even if it is never referred to by that name) to return relevant results. By deliberately using ill-chosen search terms as well as suitable ones, students are able to immediately see the differences between effective and ineffective keyword searching.

This technique is probably best reserved for instructors who are experienced at creating relaxed classroom environments and are able to come across as the students' ally or confederate. The class must feel comfortable in order to participate in a constructive manner for this lesson. One caveat: some students can get a bit riled up by this technique, and it is best to identify students who are likely to derail the lesson and interact with them directly to keep their contributions on topic.

After the lesson, if there is time remaining, give students time to work on their own research problems. Take time to talk with each student briefly about his or her topic, suggesting helpful keywords or soliciting them from the class. Try to make the search process at least somewhat social, emphasizing the value of collaboration to come up with effective keywords.

Searching for the Dog

Corrine Syster, reference and instruction librarian,
Harrisburg Area Community College

When I teach students about using databases, I always tell them that computers are not smart, and need specific direction. In thinking of a way to explain to students the concepts behind database searching (Boolean logic, giving a computer context, giving specific commands) I realized that a perfect comparison was my 3-1/2-year-old chocolate Labrador Retriever, Angus. Angus employs Boolean logic when thinking about what to eat (Beggin' Strips OR Frosty Paws OR (Kong Bone AND Kong Treat) NOT Dirty Socks), when trying to figure out what we're saying (When we begin a word with "W" he fills in W*alk* so W*) and even when I'm asking if he wants to do something with me. The actual activity is a wildcard, because he doesn't care what it is as long as it start with the invitation ("Angus, do you want to . . .") and ends with (". . . with mommy?"). He won't come if it's ". . . with Daddy?" As a result, I prepared a Power-Point presentation starring my best friend in the whole wide world that teaches these principles and shows how they are applied.

Here are the things needed to do this technique:

- One totally awesome dog
- Digital camera
- PowerPoint
- Aviary.com, Gimp, or other image editing program

I took pictures of the dog's stuff (toys, treats, etc.) on a white background and edited them at Aviary.com to remove the background, which makes the image look cleaner. I then used good old fashioned PowerPoint to create an interactive presentation that does certain things with certain clicks. I did this with the Custom Animations features built into PowerPoint using entrances, exits, and triggers. The triggers tell the animation to happen when you click on something specific.

Often you end up having many things going on at the same time, so it's important to think about what all needs to happen. For example, in a slide about his food, all of the things he would eat are pictured outside a box. Inside of the box are three reasons he might get food. When you click on "Dinner", the other two reasons disappear, while the word "Dinner" moves to the top of the box, the dinner items (bowl, food cup, gravy) move into the box and a plus sign appears between them. When I click "Dinner" again, everything resets. I also took videos of the dog performing tricks and embedded them into the slides, and the videos play when the corresponding command is clicked. This was actually the easiest to set up, since the videos can be set to hide when not being played (so there's no need for exit and entrance animations).

I tell students that Angus is a retriever, and even though he is pure-breed and his father was a master hunter, Angus isn't very good at retrieving. However, he does have the skills to become great. That seems to set them at ease and make them more comfortable with the idea of putting the skills to use. Additionally, when they're having trouble I can say "Remember Angus? If you say 'walk' he wants to go for a walk—but if you say 'W' he'll be content with either a walk or going to visit his friend Willie." What was really nice was that I didn't actually demonstrate the database. I gave them the theory, told them how it related in a few screenshots and then gave them a worksheet to fill out using the database that we worked on as a class.

I used this method of teaching with our Human Development students, who are students who have tested below the college level in at least two entrance exams. Many of these students feel uncomfortable using computers in a more advanced fashion. While I had to explain that the asterisk was the star above the 8 and that you had to press "Shift" and the button to the left of "Enter" to get the quotation marks (as opposed to pressing that button twice), the students were using these techniques and understanding how and why they worked. Because I gave them the worksheet, they were getting hands-on practice using the database and all students were able to find the information for the worksheet.

To implement this technique, you will need to be familiar with PowerPoint or other presentation software. Although it can be tempting to add effects for their own sake, please keep in mind that bells and whistles often only detract from your message and should only be used when they directly contribute to making a specific point. This technique should be followed up with hands-on searching so students can immediately practice the concepts covered by the lesson.

So "Das" How You Search It!

Stephanie Rosenblatt, education librarian, Pollak Library,
California State University, Fullerton

I use a soda analogy to describe that different sets of information are described in different databases. So, when introducing Academic Search Premier, I describe it as the "suicide" of databases. In case you don't remember, a suicide is when you go up to the soda fountain at 7-11 and drop a little bit of every kind of soda into your cup: some Hawaiian Punch, a little Coke, some Sprite, Dr Pepper, etc. Academic Search Premier (or Wilson Omnifile) is like that: a little bit of every discipline, or a suicide. However, if you love Dr Pepper, or need more information on adolescents and depression, Academic Search Premier isn't going to make you happy, you're going to have to go to PsycINFO, the Dr Pepper of databases, or the database you'll want to consult if you need more information on a topic in psychology.

This analogy is meant to illustrate how databases, unlike publically available search engines, are designed to provide access to what are often very specific subjects. While not hilarious *per se*, the idea is to transmit the concept of subject-specific databases by drawing from students' preexisting knowledge. To be most effective, it is best to demonstrate one or more subject-specific databases to drive the point home.

On the "Joisey" Shore

Amy Springer, government and business information librarian,
College of St. Benedict/St. John's University

I went for humor and shock value that their librarian was actually familiar with *Jersey Shore*. I was trying to break the typical librarian stereotypes (boring, old fashioned). I blogged about it here: http://ch-ch-chchanginglibrarian.blogspot.com/.

In my first attempt to integrate *Jersey Shore* into the instruction, I put the letters "GTL" on the screen and asked them what that meant. The class was called Work and Values in a Diverse Society. The students were thrown off and confused about why I'd be referencing their favorite show on MTV. There were several chuckles and nervous whispers of "Gym, Tanning, Laundry?" I then told them that today's library instruction was going to be *Jersey Shore* themed, but we'd need to change it to "Gym, Tanning, Library." Then, I used various scenarios from the show to prompt our search strings.

I presented the class with an image of Pauly D, an aspiring DJ. We were going to do some research on his behalf. We used these keywords: "music industry" and "gender discrimination."

In the second session of this class, I used a different scenario, and it was more successful. We searched on behalf of J-WOWW and Snooki. They are well known for their unusual choices of apparel. I showed an image of them, and we discussed which keywords to use. We tried the keywords: "dress code" and "gender management."

Passing familiarity with *Jersey Shore* is a minimum prerequisite for this technique. You will also require images of the characters and presentation software. Because of the questionable reputation of *Jersey Shore*, you should consult with faculty beforehand to make sure the subject matter is acceptable. Furthermore, this theme should only be used for classes with compatible research interests, such as gender or social conventions. Provided the theme is suitable for a class, this technique can be effective initially as an icebreaker but later for building rapport. Students consider *Jersey Shore* to be an artifact of their generation and are typically surprised that someone in a position of authority would possess a working knowledge of it, and even more surprised if you demonstrate any degree of fondness for it. By showing that you share at least one of their interests, you make yourself more approachable and trustworthy.

A Communication from Gilligan's Island

Kate Rubick, Reference and Instruction Librarian,
Lewis & Clark College, Portland OR

I used the Wikipedia article on *Gilligan's Island* to show Communication 100 level students how to use Wikipedia appropriately in academic work. In the interest of full disclosure, this technique only worked because the assignment was for students to research prominent American speeches and the example I used was Newton Minow (while Minow was the head of the FCC, he gave a speech known as the American Wasteland speech, which was very critical of television. In response to the speech the television program *Gilligan's Island* decided to name the ship that got wrecked in the show the S.S. *Minnow*). It just so happens that the Wikipedia article on Minow at that time pointed out the connection between him and the show.

I clicked on the link to the article on *Gilligan's Island* in Wikipedia in order to show how much fun research can be—but also to show how easy it is to get distracted when using hyperlinks. I also used the Wikipedia *Gilligan's Island* article to show how, using the discussion pages and the references, it was possible to discover to citation-worthy academic sources relevant to the Minow topic.

Well, the joke was kind of on me (and the professor) because we had both thought it would be a fun and funny technique. And it was—except for the fact that the students were too young to know what *Gilligan's Island* was! So it was definitely one of those "I feel old" moments. I think the class was still animated and fun, and the students liked the Wikipedia example, but the humor was not so relevant to their experience. Context is everything when it comes to humor. But I could see how, using a more contemporary example, this could have been really great.

Basically, just reading the room gave us all the information we needed about whether it was as effective as we thought it would be. I think, though, that once I realized that the students were not getting my out-of-date pop culture reference, I was able to admit to them that

I had underestimated our age difference. I told them that since I still shop at Forever 21, I fool myself into thinking that I still am 21. I think that my self-deprecation was well received and made the student laugh (even if the *Gilligan's Island* example did not). In the end, I would say that this class worked as I wanted it to.

As it turns out, it is crucial to use cultural references familiar to the target audience. However, a failed attempt, provided it is executed with enough good nature or warm self-deprecation, can still achieve the purpose of building rapport with a class and making the librarian appear approachable and possibly even fun. While the specific theme of this technique might not be directly applicable to typical undergraduate-level instruction sessions, the underlying idea of using a reference from popular culture to connect course material with students is sound and is worth pursuing whenever possible. This kind of subject-integrated humor is an efficient use of classroom time and has the added benefit of giving students a pleasant instructional experience in place of the dull and tedious droning they might expect upon entering a library instruction classroom.

Our Hero?: Mark McGuire

John E. Adkins, director of the Schoenbaum Library, University of Charleston

When explaining basic Boolean logic I have a running Mark McGuire joke. When I discuss the effect of the operator "OR" I use "steroids" and "Mark McGuire" as my A and B examples. When I move to my "AND" example I ask what they would expect to find, explaining that the funny answer is the same set as before. Then we do "Not" where I explain that the funny answer is a null set.

The purpose for this technique is to use a cultural reference as a connection between students and the otherwise abstruse course material. Boolean logic is rarely an exciting topic and can be confusing to students, many of whom attend library instruction without the expectation of being introduced to new logical constructs. The drawback is that the reference is beginning to recede into the past; not all students are familiar with Mark McGuire, and that drawback increases each semester. However, the structure of this technique can be readily adapted to other cultural references. One need only choose a celebrity whose problems with chemical dependency are current and well documented.

Progress, Not Perfection

David Ettinger, Ph.D., international affairs and political science librarian, Gelman Library, George Washington University

Addressing student frustration about failing to find items that contain all their search terms, I admonish them about seeking perfection. Targeting the women and analogizing to myself, I say: "Suppose you are looking for the perfect boyfriend. He's 5'8", balding, and wears glasses.

Must he really be all of these things for him to be acceptable to you? Maybe someone who is just balding and wears glasses would do just fine."

The use of self-deprecating humor helps the instructor direct students to more effective search strategies without coming across as condescending. It also provides a forum for giving advice about using Boolean operators without actually mentioning them by name, which really never does seem to go over well. The analogy is apt, given the typical undergraduate fixation on dating, and is pretty much timeless. Even if audiences are older, they are still likely to understand and appreciate the humor.

Volunteers, Step to the Front!

Sarah Blakeslee, interim university librarian, Meriam Library,
California State University, California

The most success I had with humor when I did teach was when I directed students to search for particular things (a scholarly journal article on the mating habits of Capybara for instance) in groups and then had one student come up to demo the search they did and what they found. Typically the student who volunteered to come up was more gregarious than the others and they often were very funny. Even if the student wasn't particularly funny, having them do the demo provided more opportunities for me to interject ad lib humor so that every time it was something new and never canned.

Comfort with ad-libbing is instrumental for the success of this technique. Student presenters are likely to take the discussion in surprising directions, sometimes in directions you would rather they avoided. Especially in these instances, it is best to always say "yes," to accept the direction the students have chosen and support their efforts. Do not let them feel as if they are being railroaded. They will resent the effort, and the atmosphere of the class will suffer. This technique takes much of the focus off of the instructor and gives students meaningful activities to work on during class. Even more importantly, it generates a dialog between you and the class: you get to observe how each group of students approaches their research problems, and that knowledge can help direct your instructional efforts with more precision. Unlike the "sage on the stage" model, this method promotes learning by both the students and the instructor.

In the Neighborhood

Norman Boyd, assistant librarian, Anglia Ruskin University
(incidents below were at Barking College)

I have often used informal "connections" to encourage listening. To demonstrate to students that evaluating skills are things they know intuitively already, I might say "My wife insists I buy a mobile phone as I'm late on my journey home quite often. You guys know about them, tell me where and how to buy . . ." They will offer many answers all of which are fielded in a humorous light-hearted way. For example:

Me: Thanks for your answer. So I have to go to the shops? I walk into [insert bakers or something silly]?

Them: No, you go to Vodafone.

Me: Ah, so I go to Vodafone and ask for a phone and that's it? That was simple! [and so forth].

This technique is not unlike the Socratic Method. By asking carefully designed questions and feigning ignorance when advantageous, students can be nudged into discovering truth for themselves instead of having it forced upon them. The underlying idea here is that the students already possess and implement the fundamental skills needed for effective research, but they do not realize it. The challenge exists not so much in teaching new skills as it does in revealing to students how the skills they already possess can be applied to new problems. By taking on the persona of someone slightly out of touch and ignorant of things which the students are highly conversant with, the instructor avoids creating an antagonistic environment. Students are made to feel confident as they expound on a familiar subject, and that confidence bleeds over to the other facets of the class.

A Pregnant Pause

Els Mertens, librarian, Katholieke Hogeschool Kempen,
Centrale Mediatheek

When explaining how to define search terms, I always tell them that when you search on "pregnancy", you don't need to add "women" to your search terms. At least not for the time being.

This technique emphasizes the importance of avoiding redundancy in keyword searches. The unusual image of a pregnant man suggested by this technique illustrates the concept while lightening the mood in the classroom at the same time. Odd and memorable examples such as this are advantageous as they require the same time commitment as mundane examples but are more fun and more memorable.

Pirates and Ninjas and Zombies, Oh My!

Margaret G. Grotti, assistant librarian and coordinator of library instruction,
University of Delaware

I find that an easy way to bring humor into the classroom is to use examples that make use of pop culture phenomena such as pirates, ninjas, zombies, vampires, and so on. I particularly like to use these concepts in first-year classes when I illustrate the importance of developing keywords from a single concept (rather than just typing the first thing that you think of into a search box and hoping for the best). Students don't realize what incredible vocabularies they have when it comes to concepts that are familiar to them (especially if they are fun or funny). For example, I often show the most comically terrible rendering of a stick-figure pirate that I can find and place that drawing up on a power point. I ask for synonyms, related terms, and alternate forms of the word for pirate. Students usually get right into this, citing anything from "Jack Sparrow" to "privateer" as synonyms, and "treasure", "ships", and "booty" (an apparent favorite) as related terms. If the class is slow to warm up to this exercise, I typically pause to tell stories of the zany things that other classes have done when they get a little too enthusiastic about the game. For example, I've had students stand up and put their leg on a chair to pose as "The Captain", brandish an imaginary sword, and shout out "gentleman of fortune". This kind of funny portrait often breaks the ice for more reticent groups.

I use this technique to illustrate the importance of developing keywords from a single concept (rather than just typing the first thing that you think of into a search box and hoping for the best). I have often been asked by colleagues why I do not use a research topic to illustrate the usefulness of synonyms, related terms, and alternate forms of words. There are two reasons for this. First, because I think that it is sometimes important to divorce the concept from the subject matter of a search when teaching. This funny exercise typically forces students to think about applying the technique to *anything*, rather than just searching within library resources. It is my hope that this underscores that the information literacy skills learned in my class are applicable in libraries and in life in general. Second, I feel that using humor and a subject matter that is deeply ingrained in the popular culture backgrounds of almost all of the students is a better way to stimulate engagement and keep students focused.

Before implementing this humorous approach, I typically used a research topic to break things down, lecture-style. I had two constant problems with this approach: First, the students clearly tuned out after I'd been speaking too long on a fairly simple subject, and second, when I introduced a follow-up activity in which students had to apply these concepts, I often got questions such as "what do you mean by related term" after I'd just lectured on it. Clearly this approach was not working for the students, or for me. Using humor and even encouraging disruption to the flow of the lesson has solved both of these problems and led to a much smoother, student-centered lesson.

I have not formally assessed this activity, however, I have paid close attention to the products that students have generated as a result of the follow-up exercise, both before I implemented this approach, and after. Immediately after this conceptual, whole-class activity, I break the class into groups and have them work together to generate keywords for their own research topics by using synonyms, related terms, and alternate forms of each of their core concepts. Since implementing the "pirate" approach, I have been amazed at the improvements that students have shown in this follow-up classroom activity. Students are able to identify synonyms, related terms, and alternate forms of words for each of their core search terms to a much greater and more focused extent. They correctly differentiate between synonyms and related terms, for example, and generate many more examples of viable keywords for their research needs. Prior to this exercise, student work showed clear confusion, a lack of creativity (e.g., only a small number of potential search terms were generated and these were incredibly general in nature and did not, in my mind, represent full learning of this concept).

To implement this technique, you will require an image of whatever pop culture meme you wish to introduce. Images can be hand-drawn, projected, or even mimed, if you are up for a challenge. Flickr contains numerous images under Creative Commons license if you want fast and easy access to an existing image. As students can become unruly as a side effect of this technique, it is helpful for the instructor to be both comfortable with a little bit of chaos and possess effective classroom management skills to settle the class down when it is time to work. As an exercise in relaxation and creativity this technique can be effective, but it is necessary to always encourage student contributions, whether or not they are all on task. Any hint of judgment on your part will stifle creativity and inclination to participate on theirs. Always say yes, and find a way to integrate every contribution into the session, no matter the content.

Sweet Searching

Janet Morton, faculty team librarian,
University of Leeds, United Kingdom

I demonstrate a keyword search. Before typing in the chosen keyword I preface it by saying that it is my favourite topic. I then type the word "chocolate". That is when they usually laugh, as it must touch a sweet spot! It then leads on to Boolean searching, truncation, subject searching, modifying and limiting to searching in different formats, and different locations as we have four libraries which are open to all our students. Of course I can then demonstrate how to place reservations for popular books which are out on loan, and then that enables me to mention recalls and the system of fines if e-mails are ignored.

This technique is primarily used with nontraditional students, with whom it is popular, but it might not be stimulating enough for traditional undergraduates. Combining this technique with complimentary chocolates for the class would be likely appreciated and could help to improve its reception. The promise of a treat can do wonders for focusing the attention.

Searching Is for the Birds!

Ian McCracken, learning resource center manager,
Govan High School, Glasgow, United Kingdom

When I am preparing to teach information literacy, I look for what I call "good bad examples". These are enquiries that show the dangers of searching without proper techniques by getting students or staff to laugh at the silly examples that appear. For example:

1. I ask people what the top answer is in Google (UK version) for the search "Canaries", and tell them that it's neither the islands nor the birds—there are always a number of funny guesses (which is very effective for encouraging the participants to enter into the fun of it). And the answer—It's Norwich City Football Club, who are nicknamed "the canaries".

This is great for introducing the fact that search engines like Google do not speak English and are not intelligent. This leads onto me asking people to suggest ways of finding information about the Canary Islands or canary birds. By being engaged in the process of sharing ideas and having gained confidence from the "fun" part, pupils are now much more keen to suggest how to do this—we then go on to whatever actual topic they have been given and do the same with it—thus having gained the skill of using two or more keywords without even realizing it.

2. To get participants thinking about the ways in which information may not be all it seems to be, I use the site http://www.cityofglasgow.org/recycling.htm (last accessed April 8, 2010).

It usually takes a number of wrong but amusing guesses before it's realised that the "Glasgow" in question is Glasgow in Kentucky and not Glasgow in Scotland. Because of the enjoyment generated in this fun "spot the error" exercise, participants are now much keener to look at other sites more thoroughly to see what mistakes they can spot—my way of trying to eliminate assumptions in the selection of information.

These examples are only samples—it is a good idea to collect as many examples as you can find to illustrate the points above. The skills would include lateral thinking, perseverance, information literacy skills, a sense of humour, presentational skills and the ability to see connections. As well as computers for participants to work on, it is necessary to have the examples in a large format, such as PowerPoint. A flipchart for writing down participants' suggestions is also useful.

I tried for years using various techniques without success, but noted along the way that students' attention also perked up if I made reference in passing to some silly example I had found. I therefore revised my entire approach to focus on the fun element (as shown in the examples above). This has changed the nature and scope of my work considerably: Very favourable reaction from students and teachers has been constant since the change of technique. Colleagues in other establishments, with whom I have shared the ideas, have also been very enthusiastic, and have recommended my work to others, resulting in a presentation to a large conference from Education, Health and other sectors.

The purpose of this technique is to engage students more actively in the research process. The ubiquity of information and the ease of typing a bunch of keywords into a search engine have yielded a generation of unengaged, relatively passive researchers. By exposing them to problems that illustrate the complexity of the situation and making the experience enjoyable, students become more inclined to take research seriously, even if only for a few minutes during the session.

For the best results, choose examples that fit with the overall theme for the lesson at hand. The better adapted this technique is to your lesson plan and persona, the more success you will have. Try to avoid letting the class focus too heavily on the fun aspects of this technique and get out of control. The emphasis should remain on using effective search strategies. The specific examples listed in the technique are only a sample of what is possible. Using those as a model, try to collect your own examples. While any example will do, provided it requires the use of critical thinking to interpret, students respond best to ones that are entertaining or humorous. Once you have the examples in hand, you only require a sense of humor, a classroom containing computers, a board, and something to display the examples on so the entire class can see.

Wikipedia, Searching, and My Mother's Gin-Soaked Breath

Anonymous

In almost any discussion of where they find information, students bring up Wikipedia (that is, unless their professors have broken their little spirits already). While Wikipedia's reliability as a source actually seems to be pretty good, in general, professors look down upon it and request that I address it during library instruction. The real reason Wikipedia ought not to be used in college level work is that it is a general encyclopedia, and therefore is just as inappropriate as using a Britannica article. However, that reason never resonates with students, so I try a different, more memorable tactic. I invoke my mother.

I use this as a cautionary tale: "Occasionally my mother will over-imbibe and make a beeline to the computer to edit her favorite article on Wikipedia: The entry for Mother Theresa. While the faceless experts of Wikipedia might seem trustworthy in theory, if you use Wikipedia for your research, you might end up drawing from, or worse, plagiarizing something my mother wrote after Easter dinner while nursing a vodka stinger. Is that really a risk you are willing to take? Do you want to gamble your grade in a college class on my mother's gin-soaked analysis of Mother Theresa's life story? Can you live with that?" Being intimately familiar with the effects alcohol can have on the human brain, students appear to take this tale to heart.

My mother is also helpful when discussing effective search strategies in academic databases. Occasionally, when I'm home for a visit, my mother will request that I refill her wine glass when she finds herself not up to the challenge. Inevitably I will have to report that the box of wine she has been engaged with since noon is finally empty. Hollering from living room where she is watching Fox News, my mother will share some nuggets of wisdom she has acquired from her longstanding relationship with boxed alcohol. "Tip it,"[1] she'll scream, "and if that doesn't work, take out the bag and squeeze it." I will often relate this story to illustrate the need to not stop before you have truly exhausted all of the possibilities of any given search. Too often students look at the first page of results and declare victory. Or defeat. Much like it is with a box of wine, a little extra effort can yield valuable results.

This technique only requires a willingness to relate fairly personal anecdotes in front of complete strangers, but delivery is also pretty important. It works in three ways: One, it teaches through storytelling, which is often more palatable than traditional lecture. Two, it is personal. Self-disclosure can help build rapport with students. Three, it paints a humorous picture. Funny anecdotes tend to be more memorable and promote attention. Responses from students are fairly typical: the majority laugh, a few express moderate horror, and some do not get it. Generally, the anecdote about Wikipedia mostly engages the young men in the classroom. It also lightens the mood in the room. By using real-life examples and apt analogies, these anecdotes are better able to communicate topics that would otherwise be uninteresting. Students appear exhausted with being talked down to about Wikipedia and really do not want to hear about the importance of thorough searching, so an approach like this one makes the subject matter tolerable and might even help create a lasting impression.

On the Use of Humorous Props and Examples; Also, Something about Cats and Beards

Joshua Vossler, information literacy and reference librarian,
Kimbel Library, Coastal Carolina University

In relation to using humor in the classroom, props fall into two categories: Humorous examples and humorous objects. Humorous examples are funny versions of the things that you were already planning to play show-and-tell with. Books and articles with funny or odd titles are the classic examples. Humorous objects are things that have nothing explicitly to do with the subject matter at hand but are meant to be an amusing addition to class—a rubber chicken, for example, or costumes. At this point, I must confess that I have an unhealthy fascination with props. I have been known to teach classes while pretending to ride a 6-foot stuffed catfish, wearing samurai armor, and dressed as the eponymous character from the film *Beetlejuice*. On separate occasions, naturally. I have also used every weird or funny example I could find or invent. I share this unfortunate fact about myself to establish that I quite like using props, although in the next two paragraphs I will discuss the problems they present in the classroom. If you are in a hurry to see my actual technique, skip the next paragraph.

What I have learned from using props is this: Humorous objects usually aren't. In my experience, they operate as a distraction. Once the initial shock value has dissipated, you find yourself trying to do your job whilst caked in oily makeup, wearing an itchy wig, and wishing you had a respectable reason for being dressed like a weirdo, like a lost bet or witness protection. Props of this kind always seem brilliant when you first come up with them. But, like every apartment dweller who ever impulsively acquired a pet raccoon, you discover the reality of a situation can diverge from your imagination. At best, humorous objects solicit a chuckle, but that chuckle comes at a steep price: loss of audience attention. Instead of watching you, they are now watching the object. Unlike you, the object will grow quickly boring, leading to wandering attention. Sure, you can recapture it, but usually not before losing a few of the more flighty audience members. Humorous examples are better, but still present challenges. The temptation is to use them in place of regular, boring examples of the kinds of documents your students are going to be searching for. Although this is fun for you, it can present problems for your students. A student who has never seen an academic journal article and is skeptical of their value for research is not going to be helped by seeing silly books and articles. In that situation, the humor undermines your purpose in providing examples instead of supporting it. You can be funny, but the materials and services you are discussing should not be. It is already an enough of an uphill battle convincing students to use professional-level research resources instead of free search engines without making those resources appear ridiculous.

The trick to getting props to work in the classroom is having a well-defined purpose. Think of an infomercial. Humorous examples are used, but only in relation to their competitors' products, never their own. The product being sold is always shown to work elegantly. In the classroom, I like to do this with free search engines versus academic databases. I ask the class to choose between two descriptions of the Internet (neither being perfect, but if you had to choose . . .).

1. The Internet is an orderly, carefully administered repository of reliable, vetted information produced by experts.

2. The Internet is a howling repository of urban myths, goat tranquilizers disguised as herbal impotence cures, and the baseless opinions of people who live in their parents' basements.

Students always choose option two, with the occasional wag claiming number one is the better option. To illustrate my point, I have students call up the search engine of their choice and search for the phrase "cats and beards" and click on the first link that comes up. That link leads to a web page entitled "Feline Reactions to Bearded Men."[2] It is a false document made to resemble an academic journal article written about an experiment examining the reactions of a test group of cats to photographs of men with old-timey beards. It has all of the paraphernalia of a legitimate article but is clearly ridiculous. My reason for pointing out this article, which I explain to the students as well, is not to warn students that there are weird documents on the Internet. They already know this. I want to illustrate how free search engines waste their time by including weird documents among with legitimate ones without any accountability. Academic databases, on the other hand, include a much smaller proportion of useless articles, so all of a student's time is spent examining and evaluating legitimate sources of information, not sifting crazy from sane. As a side note, I make a point of not coming across as anti–search engine, as I suspect that would damage my credibility. I stress that search engines are fine things for day-to-day use, but that for specialized projects like academic research, you want to use a specialized tool, like academic databases. Search engines are good, but academic databases are better for the task at hand and certainly a lot faster.

Apart from the prop, all you need for this technique is a clear understanding of your purpose. Without a specific purpose in mind, the prop is just a toy and should probably be left at home. For the article on cats and beards, you need classroom presentation equipment or at least student computers with an Internet connection. The purpose of using the article is to illustrate how evaluating and dismissing irrelevant documents found using a free search engine wastes time that could be saved by using academic databases. Some students laugh, some smile, and a fair amount express mild outrage at the oddness of such an article's existence. Every now and again a single student will find the article deeply amusing and will laugh uncontrollably for 10 or 15 seconds. I also think that the article drives home my point about wasted time, judging from student reactions to the instruction that follows.

When the prop is well chosen and really fits the subject matter under discussion, it makes a memorable point without you having to say a darn thing. The prop prompts students to come to the appropriate conclusion on their own or at least serves to create a memorable image. Either way, it requires fewer words and effort from the instructor and more attention and thought from the students. However, this technique seems to work best when it is a one-and-done: subsequent props do not work as well, at least in my experience. Excessive prop use also draws too much attention away from the instructor. Props should be used as a tool in support of the instructor's message, never in substitution of the message itself or as objects to hide behind. "Feline Reactions to Bearded Men" functions as a *reductio ad absurdum* in this context. Almost everyone has had the experience of finding weird documents on the Internet, so the use of a document whose humor derives from weirdness is suitable for the point I am trying to make. Also, like an infomercial, the product I am trying to steer my audience away from is made to appear unreliable, while the product I am championing works like a charm. So long as I don't belabor that situation and instead allow students to draw their own conclusions, the humorous example also ends up helping steer students toward using academic databases.

The URL for "Feline Reactions to Bearded Men" is http://www.sree.net/stories/feline.html.

Searches with Benefits

John Watts, reference librarian, Kimbel Library, Coastal Carolina University

---

College students think about the opposite sex a lot, and they always seem to get a kick out of references to dating during library instruction. Here are two (hopefully) funny dating references I use when teaching students how to search academic databases.

1. When I cover the use of quotes in databases, I use this gimmick. When you enter a phrase of two or more words into a database search box, for example, puppet cancer, the database will look for results that contain the word puppet, the word cancer, or both words together. As you can imagine, this can lead to weird or useless searches. If you want to make sure every result you get back actually contains the phrase puppet cancer, you enclose the words in quotes. This ties the words together, making them into a couple. An item. Or maybe they're just talking. Whatever they want to call it. (The idea here is to anthropomorphize the search terms and talk about them as if they are young couple walking in the mall.)

2. I often see students using search terms like "benefits" along with their topics. Soft search terms like that need to be eradicated, so I use a funny explanation to help it stick. Think about the word benefits. What else can it mean? You are thinking about the word as referring to beneficial aspects of something, like marijuana use or exercise. But what about health benefits from having a job? Or friends with benefits? Sure, I think we all would like to have both of those last two things, but using that word in our searches usually just muddies up the waters.

All you need for these techniques is a willingness to make jokes that reference sex. Although they are slightly racy, these jokes lighten up the mood and add some energy to an explanation of best searching practices, which can be frightfully dull. Students respond best to example 1, which riffs off of the adolescent confusion over what to label burgeoning romantic relationships. Reactions include laughter and smiles. Example 2 generates laughs as well, but usually more in the form of snickering. There are also surprised looks, likely in response to a librarian talking about sex.

Bouillon Logic

Kwasi Sarkodie-Mensah, Ph.D., manager of instructional services,
Boston College Libraries

My use of humor always seem to come spontaneously in class, but there is one story that freshmen in all my First-Year Writing Seminar sessions (Boston College's English 101/Introduction to Writing) have reacted to very well. As a result of the experience that gave rise to this story, I have come to believe that any type of contribution in class is acceptable and should be lauded.

Several semesters ago I got excited because one of the freshmen for the very first time in about 15 years knew what Boolean was. After about 15 seconds of silence after my question "Does anyone know what Boolean is?" she very confidently replied: "Oh Boolean!!! I use it every single weekend when I cook. When I drop it in my soup or sauce, it changes the taste completely. Everything tastes better".

The students usually will stare at me for another 10 seconds after I tell my Boolean story, and then they all begin to burst out laughing, either agreeing with the explanation, or blatantly concurring how stupid the answer was. The yellow bouillon cube can really have an impact on one's cooking in spite of the ridiculousness of the comparison. When I give them my own reaction to the story about how correct the student answering the Boolean question is, they all seem to agree that making use of Boolean in searches can truly make search results palatable, manageable and when necessary comprehensive.

With web 2.0 we may be moving away from Boolean concepts, but we need to engage students in our instructional sessions. The purpose of my story is to be sure that students are with me. To get them engaged and to walk with me. If we have to go through Quest, which is Boston College's library catalog, and we go from 200 hits for a general and broad term to another applying Boolean concepts and getting 6 hits, in our Catholic tradition, I can ask: So do you guys now have faith in Boolean? Along with the giggles will come statements like "Now we are cooking" or "I will never forget about the yellow cubes."

This technique has two distinct applications. For the first application, it can be used as described but will likely be less powerful when told secondhand. Furthermore, teaching Boolean logic during instruction sessions seems to be increasingly falling out of favor, so this anecdote might not be relevant for many instruction programs. For the second application, it can interpreted as a new imperative for library instruction: welcome and integrate any and all student comments, no matter how strange or off topic they might initially appear to be. By being open to anything students wish to add, you will have more success encouraging students to speak up. Often, only a handful of naturally gregarious students will contribute to a session. The more reticent ones remain silent, and their concerns are never addressed.

NOTES

1. This is also the title of a book by Maggie Griffin, Kathy Griffin's mother. It just so happens that Kathy and I have mothers who share similar interests. My mother was hollering "Tip it!" at me all the way back in the 1990s.

2. I cannot recall where I heard first about this article, but I am certain I am not the first librarian to use it in class. My thanks go to that anonymous individual who first revealed "Feline Reactions to Bearded Men" to the library community.

9

Using Jokes

INTRODUCTION

This chapter is for devoted to jokes. These are one-liners, short anecdotes, and humorous analogies. Some of them relate to information literacy, some to the life of a librarian, and some are better off not described. The techniques in this chapter seek to earn laughs and will sometimes go to great lengths and walk some fine lines in pursuit of that goal. As you read through this chapter, please keep in mind that what you are reading are really only the desiccated corpses of jokes that once were. To be living and breathing, these jokes need to be delivered by a human voice, told within the context of a specific persona, and in front of an appropriate audience. Language that might appear odd or harsh in text can come across very differently when voiced by a practiced comic. There is also the issue of taste, which warrants a disclaimer here. We do not guarantee that these jokes are suitable for your audiences. Only you know your audiences, and you have to make your own determinations. We also do not guarantee that just anyone will be able to make these jokes funny. It can take hard work and planning to make a joke funny, and some jokes will never work for some people. Finally, taste is of sufficient concern that I will even invoke the Bard: "A jest's prosperity lies in the ear of him that hears it, never in the tongue of him that makes it."[1] There is a joke in this chapter about being too poor to eat anything but cat meat. It might seem monstrous to some but wildly funny to others. Use your best judgment before trying anything you find here in front of a live audience.

PURPOSE

Laughter is a means for maintaining attention and building rapport. Telling jokes in class produces laughter (ideally), which students enjoy. Once a teacher has demonstrated that funny or entertaining moments can occur in class, students start to watch for out them. They pay attention to the boring material in the hope that you will tell another joke. This approach is essentially a ruse: the medicine goes down easier if it is encased in something delicious. The jokes convince the students to pay attention. In the spaces between jokes, you try to teach them something. The secondary purpose, building rapport, is less complicated. It is as simple as this: people who tell funny jokes are easy to like. In the case of humorous analogies, the purpose is to entertain and promote understanding and retention of what is often an alien or difficult concept.

Because jokes are often brief, they can be used as a canary in a coal mine. Especially when they are used in the opening moments of a class, jokes are a fast and low-risk way to test your audience's reaction to your comedic material. If they are receptive to your first few jokes, they will likely be receptive to further attempts at humor. If they respond well to a joke about your appearance but not to one about your emotional problems, you can use that knowledge and adjust your material accordingly. Gleaning this kind of information about your audience can prevent you from trotting out material that will not work. Finally, those first quick jokes can reveal who your allies and enemies are. If you can identify one or two people in the audience who are especially appreciative of your humor, you can take advantage of their enthusiasm later in the performance. Conversely, if you can identify the grouches, you will be better able to deal with them.

ADVANTAGES

In exchange for what amounts to only a few minutes or less of class time, it is possible to increase student attention as well as your own charisma using a single, repeatable technique. One-liners and short anecdotes take seconds to tell, and once you've memorized and practiced them well enough they require no preparation. Maintenance, while necessary, only needs to be done periodically, usually only in response to a change in how your audience responds to any given joke. As far as devices for improving student attention, this one is quite effective. It uses intermittent positive reinforcement, which is the most effective kind of reward system for motivating behaviors. It is the same system that casinos rely on and that makes fishing so compelling. For the human brain, connecting a specific action with a specific reward is advantageous but boring. However, if an action produces a reward randomly, the human response is to obsessively repeat the action. In this case, the action is paying attention, and the jokes are the reward. By delivering them intermittently, you reinforce student attention far better than if you told a joke every 10 minutes exactly. You do not even need all that many of them to produce this effect. Three or so good jokes are all it takes.

DRAWBACKS

There is no such thing as a free lunch. Using jokes in class can be extremely effective, but this approach comes with challenges and drawbacks aplenty. Making an audience laugh requires more than the right combination of words. Delivery is crucial, and comic timing can make or break a performance. Practice is also an impediment. It is only through repetition that you learn to deliver and time your jokes properly, and that repetition has to occur in front of a live audience. You learn on the job, and the learning process is often painful and fraught with failure. Jokes will fall flat and audiences will turn on you. If you are using someone else's material, like the jokes included in this chapter, you have to make sure that they are compatible with your stage persona, the version of yourself that the audience sees. If you are thin, making jokes about feeling fat will be a hard sell. The same goes if you wear a wedding ring and make jokes about being lonely. If you write your own material, you are in for some very hard work. Really good jokes are rare, and it might take you more than a year of work to come up with even a handful of excellent jokes. Even if you have your jokes and know how to deliver them well, if your audience changes, you might be in real trouble. Jokes that work well for first-year college students might very well flop in front of an audience of juniors, or worse, a roomful of deans. As luck would have it, a failed joke is quite a bit worse than no joke at all. Joking is a high-risk endeavor. You either win big or lose big, and there is not usually much middle ground. Jokes also retain the audience-and-performer relationship and do not especially promote much besides attention and reaction from students. Not a lot of interaction results from this technique.

The Rule of Pants and Amusing Comments Regarding Citation

Joshua Vossler, information literacy and reference librarian,
Coastal Carolina University

The Rule of Pants is an analogy I came up with back in graduate school while I was working as graduate assistant teacher. Faced with a classroom of English composition students who didn't understand why formatting and citation were important, I flailed about for a way to explain it to them that connected to their way of looking at the world. After becoming a librarian, I adapted it to introduce the importance of citation before APA and MLA workshops for first-year students. The Rule of Pants is an analogy, and it goes like this.

"I have a question for the class, and it is important that you answer it honestly. Do you believe I am an articulate, reasonably intelligent person who possesses knowledge and skills that would be beneficial for you all to learn?"[2] Wait for the class to agree. "Okay, now for another question. Are my intellectual abilities influenced by what I'm wearing, or are they an intrinsic part of me?" Wait for the class to say that those abilities are intrinsic. "Excellent. Just one more question. What if I took my pants off right now, and finished today's class only wearing a shirt?" Let this question sink in for a moment. Encourage replies, and respond to anything worthwhile. "Okay, clearly my pants are an important part of me, even though they don't actually alter my intellectual abilities. My pants indicate that I am part of a society that operates according to rules that govern conduct. Just like speaking English and not biting people I disagree with, wearing pants is a signal that I respect the rules of the society I am a part of, and by extension, all of the other people in that society. Here's where I get to my point. The university is its own society, and it has special rules. Citation styles are part of those rules. People who take the effort to cite correctly are wearing pants, and people who do not are pantsless weirdos. Your teachers will judge you based on your adherence to these rules. Like citation, wearing pants can be uncomfortable and awkward, but it is something you do out of respect for others and out of a desire to earn their respect in turn."

Citation, perhaps because it really is so deadly dull, seems to be fertile ground for generating humor. That's fortunate, since something is necessary to break up the tedium of talking about citation. Here are a few amusing comments I use when discussing citation, especially citations that are generated by websites or databases.

1. When introducing the idea that many library databases contain readymade citations, I ask: "I'm going to show you something that lazy people love. Who here is lazy? Raise your hands. Okay, those of you who didn't raise your hands, close your eyes. You can keep doing things the long way." If the whole class raises their hands, I observe that truly lazy people wouldn't raise their hands at all, and suggest that we skip this next part.

2. After demonstrating where to find readymade citations in a database, I say this: "I'd like to share something about myself. I like to keep all of the people around me on a constant emotional rollercoaster. It keeps me from getting bored. Now that I've made you happy, I have to crush your spirits. Citations that you don't make yourself are almost never entirely correct."

3. I use this analogy to emphasize the importance of not blindly copying database citations: "Is anyone here familiar with either *The Matrix* or the *Terminator* films? There's an important lesson to be gleaned from science fiction films that pertains directly to database citations. I'm absolutely serious here. This is the lesson: Do not trust the machine. It will let you down." At the end of the class I ask them to repeat what they have learned about trusting the machine.

4. While going over database citations for errors, if I encounter a name in all capital letters, I ask: "Look here. See this name? Is this person's name JOHN SMITH (I yell this name rather loudly), or is it John Smith (I say this name at a normal volume)?" I am playing off of the Internet convention that all capital letters represent yelling, usually to great effect.

The only skill needed for using any of these techniques is comic timing, although a projector and computers with Internet access are helpful for the comments dealing with citation. For the Rule of Pants, the purpose is to communicate the importance of citation in terms the students understand and can respect. It is also an opportunity to establish a playful persona and a warm, friendly learning environment at the beginning of class. For the amusing comments, the purpose is to punctuate the dry material with humor so that students will continue paying attention. The comedic elements are also present to make the session more entertaining for the instructor.

For the Rule of Pants, students smile and a few chuckle to themselves. There also a few stares of mute horror. However, when the actual citation portion of the workshop gets underway, classes exposed to the Rule of Pants take the activities more seriously. The four amusing comments are where the laughs come from. Numbers 1 through 3 earn chuckles and small laughs, while number 4 is the big crowd pleaser. This one always results in a solid round of laughter. College students just seem to deeply enjoy yelling.

Grounding a subject as abstruse and broadly disliked as citation in terms that resonate with first-year students seems to overcome the initial resistance they have to citation in general and citation workshops in particular. Citation ceases to be like eating your vegetables when you are 9, and becomes more like eating your vegetables when you are 40. They are able to not only grasp but also appreciate its importance. Regardless, the humorous elements help warm the class up for what is at its heart a dry, tedious activity that will never compare to boxes of puppies or ice cream.

The Librarian Will Get You If You Don't Watch Out!

David Ettinger, Ph.D., international affairs and political science librarian, Gelman Library, George Washington University

---

I ask how many students have worked with a librarian or sought a librarian's assistance. Typically, only a few hands, if any, go up. What about the rest of you, I ask. What is holding you back? What have we ever done to you? Why are so afraid of us? When is the last time you walked down the street and someone yelled out "Watch out, a librarian's coming!" It never happens.

The purpose of this technique is to emphasize how librarians are friendly and helpful by juxtaposing the mental picture of a librarian inspiring terror. This somewhat jarring image is also humorous on its own merits and can result in laughs or chuckles. Students are also likely to be surprised by hearing this come from a librarian, which can be helpful for increasing student attention.

Rated PG

David Ettinger, Ph.D., international affairs and political science librarian, Gelman Library, George Washington University

---

Invoking a sexual analogy, I tell students that selecting an interesting and viable topic, what I refer to as the "intellectual foreplay" of doing research, is, arguably, the most important part of the research process, more critical than the execution itself. I also warn students not to yield to the frequent tendency to abandon a topic too soon if it seems difficult to research, "premature evacuation."

The purpose of this technique is to emphasize the value of taking time and care to select a research topic and to remain committed to the topic in the face of difficulty. Students enjoy the risqué elements, and that enjoyment can contribute to building rapport with the instructor.

A Professional Class

Tracey Simon, director, Floral Park Public Library

The mission: To provide a basic overview of reference services to library assistants/technicians and potential librarians in a professional development course. Since my program was on a Saturday morning, I was more inclined to use a bit of humor. Note: Most of the class was made up of native-born English-speakers. Much of the humor probably would not have gone over as well if the class had a different construct. Humor is very subjective.

The highlights are as follows:

First off, I wore a t-shirt with the words "Frequently Asked Questions" on it, courtesy of the Unshelved folk. I also wrote on the blackboard: "How many reference librarians does it take to change a light bulb?" I used this riddle to start a discussion on the nature of reference work. Answer: I don't know, but I can look it up for you.

On becoming a librarian: When I told my parents I wanted to be a librarian, they were not thrilled with my career choice. "Oh, honey," they said, "You'll never get married. You'll never make money. You'll have . . . cats!!!" They were only partly right. I did get married. I never did make a lot of money. And yes, I have cats . . . (Pause) . . . on my salary, I can't afford real meat!

This was followed by a discussion of the some of the realities of being a librarian. I read aloud a few entries from *Reference Librarianship: Notes from the Trenches* by Charles R. Anderson. I also included fractured titles that people have asked for (I try to collect them from various sources), including "The Autobiography of Malcolm the Tenth," "Tequila Mockingbird," and the more subtle "Sex in the City." When someone asked me if I could help them find "Sex in the City," my first inclination was to say "No, but I can help you find a good time on Long Island." Instead I just corrected the title: "I think you want 'Sex AND the City' by Candace Bushnell."

The reference interview: I told them some true stories about the questions people ask, including this one that happened to me:

Patron: Do you have *Consumer Reports?*

Me: Yes, we do. Is there a particular issue or item you'd like information on?

Patron: I'm interested in purchasing a "soov."

Me: A "soov"?

Patron: (getting a little testy) Yes, a "soov." I'm looking to buy a used "soov." A Chrysler "soov."

Me: (enlightened) Oh! You mean an SUV!

Patron: I know how to spell it, dammit. Now get me the darn magazine!

Practice with delivery and comic timing are the most important skills for implementing the anecdotes in this technique. Internet access and presentation hardware is also helpful. If you would like to acquire an on-topic novelty t-shirt to complete the image of the comic librarian, consult unshelved.com. Students enjoy the anecdotes and usually laugh, though it is important to gauge your audience. International students, for example, might have difficulty understanding and appreciating some or all of the humor. However, when delivered to an appropriate audience, these anecdotes help to liven up what is otherwise a rather dull subject.

Fangs for the Memories

Michelle Blackman, Instruction Librarian, Grossmont College

After I welcome students to the library instruction lab, I introduce myself and tell them I've worked here 15 years, and in that entire time, we've never had to call security and tell them that a librarian bit a student.

This technique can be especially effective if delivered in a deadpan tone of voice and can be a cute way to remind students that librarians do not bite. This technique is most effective if you refer back to it once or twice throughout the session and ask students to say aloud what they learned about librarians today. Repetition, repetition.

Striking a Blow for Information Literacy

Bonnie Petry, reference librarian, College of Natural Sciences, John M. Pfau Library, California State University, San Bernardino, California

---

I once took a college class from a professor who would always put a relevant cartoon or two on the overhead projector before she began lecturing. While my fellow students and I appreciated the cartoons, which were well-chosen and always funny, the professor never smiled or laughed and didn't even make any noise as she placed the transparencies on the projector, waited long enough for everyone to see them, and then took them off. Furthermore, she never referred to the cartoons at all during her lectures. Her unsmiling, plodding delivery of the lectures never wavered one iota. I was mystified. Why would this woman spend so much time and effort to obtain high-quality, interesting cartoons for her class and then give the remainder of the class time all the charm and interest of walking around in wet shoes and socks?

I advocate Integrated Wit. If you are able to blend the informative content of your class with a good measure of humor that arises naturally from that content, you will have a winning recipe you can dish up again and again. And even though you may develop a standard stock of humorous remarks (as I have over the years) it will seem spontaneous to your student audience. Here is a small selection of well-worn examples to illustrate my meaning:

- When trying to convey to a class that the reference desk is THE place to go for assistance, I'll reveal the "secret" that professors also consult reference librarians and then I'll say, "And if they are our good friends like professor X here (professor who brought the class in), we give them correct answers!"
- When computers, databases, networks, etc., go awry during a class, I'll comment, "They always act up when company comes over!"
- When explaining the difference between quantitative and qualitative research, I'll say, "Scientists are not that interested in the people who think they saw bigfoot—they want to CATCH a bigfoot so they can weigh and measure him and put a radio collar on him."
- When explaining the proper construction of a keyword search, I'll tell students, "While databases contain excellent information, they are not SMART so you must explain what you want very carefully and in a way that they can understand."

To use Integrated Wit in class, being able to see the absurd in things is a big plus. Is ERIC the name of the guy who makes this database? Is the OxResearch database all about cattle? Cultivate a warped perspective and share it. For example, if your library subscribes to EBSCOhost, does that make you an EBSCOparasite? Colorful metaphors and similes can liven things up too: "Doing all your research on the Internet is like buying all your groceries from only one aisle in the grocery store." A sense of appropriate delivery and timing are important.

The purpose behind Integrated Wit is to make a persuasive argument that librarians and information literacy are not completely dull and tedious. Students walk into library instruction expecting to be bored out of their minds, and anything that flies contrary to those expectations helps the cause. Students react in different ways. Some engage with you and the material with enthusiasm; others will do so, but with reluctance. Others will never engage. Humor is helpful but not a panacea. However, the serious students will respond quite well and appreciate your efforts to make the class pleasant. Regardless of how well students visibly respond to your humor, you are still making forward progress by revealing yourself to be a pleasant, light-hearted individual, and people like that are easier to approach than people who appear gruff and hostile, as a general rule.

Using "Higher Humor"

Antony Brewerton, head of academic services, the Library, University of Warwick, Coventry, United Kingdom

---

Although I have used costumes at Freshers' Fair events as a way of marketing the library (http://www.sconul.ac.uk/publications/newsletter/31/3.pdf) I tend to find these a bit overbearing and this approach (personally) feels forced to me (the Patch Adams approach leaves me cold) and not appropriate for teaching information literacy. Instead I use a few well placed jokes, plays on words, absurd humour. For example:

1. In an induction I tell students that if other students are annoying them because they are talking to let a librarian know and then we can "ssshhhhhh" them—"we are taught how to do this properly at library school".
2. When I have taught nursing students I explained that with the thesaurus facility you can "explode" the term . . . and then said "let's look at exploding 'leg ulcers' " (nurses are very responsive to gallows humour!).
3. With history students I show them the dangers of "popularist" Web sites—one example starts looking like a history of Florence Nightingale but ends with a link to "see my nurse doll collection".
4. Again with historians I have used the cartoon mentioned on p. 20 of my article as a way of introducing best practice with their thesis.

The purpose of these techniques is to create a sense of camaraderie by laughing together as a group. All of the humor is directed either at the instructor or at a humorous idea, so students will not feel put off or left out. This form of humor is both relaxing and amusing for most students and helps create a constructive educational climate.

Note: The mention herein of "my article" refers to Brewerton (2002).

What Did He Just Say?

Joshua Vossler, information literacy and reference librarian,
Coastal Carolina University

Constructive hostility is the use of seemingly unfriendly statements in such a way that they have an inclusive, friendly effect. This technique should not be confused with sarcasm, which is a friendly statement delivered in a hostile manner and usually alienates your audience.

Constructive hostility is the inverse: hostile statements delivered in a friendly manner, which do not usually alienate anyone. These techniques are helpful for adding variety to your presentation. The hostility also adds an edge to your delivery that helps you come across as more genuine. Real people are not entirely positive all of the time, but paid shills are. A few touches of negativity help dispel the notion that you are just another salesman trying to sell something that nobody actually needs.

Here are a few examples of constructive negativity. Please remember that all of these statements must be delivered with warmth and enthusiasm in order to accomplish their mission. If your soul is filled with hostility that cannot be suppressed, please do not attempt.

1. *After the class has arrived and you are ready to begin the session.* "Are all of the important people here?" Be sure to address the class with this question, not the instructor. The idea is to let the students answer this question for themselves. If someone shows up late, you can accuse the class of being liars, too.
2. *Welcoming the class.* "Hello everyone, welcome to the library. I'm really excited you are here today, because we have some fantastic things for you to learn about. Of course, I'm also really excited about what I have for lunch today, so don't let it go to your heads."
3. *Establishing your classroom as an environment safe for interaction.* Explain that in your classroom, everyone is safe. "As college students, you are supposed to be ignorant, and that's a wonderful thing. It's the only time in your life when nobody can give you crap over not understanding something. That's an amazing advantage, when you think about it. Your instructors are here to help you. If you don't understand something, it is our job to explain it to you. If you ask a question in my class (Choose a student and address him or her directly), here's what I won't do: I won't say 'You! Why would you ask that? What's wrong with you?' (For best effect, raise your voice. I like to pitch my voice up to a shrill screech for added effect, then immediately return my voice to normal for the next statement). I'm not going to do that. Not only is that an ineffective way to help you learn, but I don't want her to squirt pepper spray in my face. It hurt enough when my mom did it that I don't want to repeat the experience."

These techniques all rely on the ability to modulate your voice for theatrical effect. For best results, you need your voice to communicate warmth and friendliness on demand. For technique 3, you need to amplify your volume and alter your voice to achieve the proper effect. Done correctly, these techniques help you come across as more approachable and genuine. Students are accustomed to people trying to sell them things, and they recognize salespeople by their unflinchingly positive attitudes. It is easy for instruction librarians who are enthusiastic about their subject matter to come across as salespeople. To a degree, we are indeed trying to sell our students on the use of academic research materials. By sprinkling in some negativity we can work to dispel the notion that we are just trying to sell them a bill of goods.

For techniques 1 and 2, students usually smile, and a few chuckle. Technique 3 usually earns some outright laughs, especially the final joke about being pepper-sprayed by my mother. The student being addressed will usually shrink back from the volume, but smile or laugh afterward. The class tends to relax a bit after this one, and there are usually more questions and student interaction, both with the instructor and with each other.

Stalking Information Literacy

Joshua Vossler, information literacy and reference librarian,
Coastal Carolina University

In our library instruction sessions, librarians spend a lot of time exhorting students to use library databases for their research, as well as explaining how to locate and retrieve physical books. In both cases, it is hard not to come across as condescending and pedantic. One day, I found that I just couldn't deliver the same serious explanation again, so I tried using an analogy comparing these tasks to stalking, and found the analogy both apt and entertaining for the students. In the classroom, I normally portray myself as an extremely odd individual, so this analogy did not appear out of place.

Finding a book in the library is a lot like stalking someone you want to get to know. Sure, it's nice to know names and phone numbers, but really, you want to know where they live. Books, just like people, have addresses that tell you where they sleep at night. We call those addresses call numbers, and they work just like street addresses.

If you've ever tried to stalk someone, you know that you can learn some useful things from searching in publicly available online search engines. The really juicy personal information, however, is only found in IRS and DMV databases, which are locked away from the general public. Unless you're sneaky. It's the same way when you are researching a college-level essay. Sure, you can flail around in publicly available online search engines and find a little good stuff here and there, but library databases are like the IRS and the DMV: they are where the best information is found.

While not absolutely necessary, an overhead projector aids delivery. Stand directly in the light, so that the projection plays across your face while you relate these analogies in a calm, matter-of-fact tone. The light adds a nice, creepy vibe to the delivery, magnifying the humor. The purpose of using analogies like this one is to catch and maintain student attention but also hopefully to create a memorable image that can promote long-term retention of the material. From the instructor's perspective, it also makes a dull topic more entertaining to teach. This technique usually produces laughter and chuckles. If delivered early in the class, this can work as an icebreaker as well. It dispels tension and opens students up to the possibility that they might enjoy themselves. It also gets them to pay close attention to you, either out of interest in what you might say next or possibly out of mild concern for what you might say next. Either way, they have mostly withdrawn attention from their favorite social networking sites.

Because the analogy takes the same amount of class time to deliver as a literal explanation of how call numbers work, using it costs little or no extra time in an instruction session. The relatively edgy subject matter surprises students somewhat, and you can capitalize on that surprise. Having demonstrated that you are capable of making funny and unexpected comments, students will be more inclined to pay attention to the rest of your presentation. This approach is not unlike intermittent positive reinforcement, which is the most compelling form of reinforcement. Students get something they enjoy, a humorous remark, and have to continue paying attention if they are to get a repeat performance, which may or may not actually take place. Just like feeding quarters into a slot machine and only occasionally winning, the intermittent reward makes the activity associated with it all the more compelling.

"Twelve Steps" to Using Humor!

Heather Nicholson, MLIS candidate and library intern
at the University of Lethbridge Library

I usually start my library instructions with a confession (done in that stereotypical Alcoholics Anonymous tone): "My name is Heather and I completed two undergraduate degrees without ever talking to a librarian." PAUSE. "I realize now that it was a terrible mistake."

I tell them that they might be shocked to discover that librarians aren't born librarians: We have to learn all of the great stuff we know.

I then launch into a description of some of my ill-informed library strategies from my undergraduate days (like aimlessly wandering the stacks hoping to stumble upon a good resource or scouring an entire book on Buddhism for a basic description of the religion rather than using a reference source) and how a librarian could have saved me time. I tell them my mission is to help them avoid making the same mistakes I did. I stress that the ONE thing I want them to learn from my presentation is that they should ask a librarian for help. Throughout my presentation I like to stop just often enough to be slightly annoying and remind them that they really should consult a librarian if they have a question. Did I mention that a librarian could help them with this? If you need any refreshers on this information, you could, ask a librarian? Did you know that librarians staff the reference desk and they LOVE answering questions? etc.

The purpose of this technique is to humorously reveal past errors made by the instructor in the hope of making students more comfortable with admitting ignorance and seeking assistance. While it requires more class time than a simple suggestion to seek help from librarians, it is probably a lot more likely to be successful. As such, it is best used in instruction programs that prioritize individual student appointments.

Lonely and Information Literate

Joshua Vossler, information literacy and reference librarian,
Coastal Carolina University

Self-effacing humor has enormous power to generate goodwill in an audience. This technique is especially useful for instruction librarians because of the condescending position we so often find ourselves in. Standing up in front of a group of strangers and telling them the methods they use to search for information are flawed is not the best way to build rapport. Even if we use clever rhetorical strategies to soften that message, we are still stuck in an oppositional relationship. Revealing yourself as possessing skills and knowledge superior to that of the class might be necessary to establish yourself as a valuable source of information, but doing so usually comes at the cost of likeability. It creates a gap. However, by undermining yourself as a person but not as a professional, you can establish professional competence and build rapport at the same time. To wit, a teacher who knows better than you and is also a confident, happy person can be insufferable. A teacher who knows better than you but is miserable and filled with self-loathing can be charming, provided the references to misery are delivered in a cheerful, upbeat tone.

For the purposes of explanation, I put references to being desperately lonely into two categories, A and B. Category A is for setting the mood at the beginning of class. You use the comments in this category to establish your persona and introduce the idea that you are emotionally compromised. Category B is for recovering from mistakes or unfortunate events while building goodwill and entertaining the class. Please note: you do not actually need to hate your life or be desperately lonely to implement these ideas. But it helps.

Category A: Establishing the Pain You Live In Every Day to Earn Goodwill

1. In the beginning of class, I like to perform a brief self-introduction. My goal is to convince the class that I am competent and worth listening to. I also want to be likeable, though, so I make sure to balance good things I say about myself with at least a few negative things. For example, after relating something positive about my abilities as a researcher, I say: "Of course, these skills that make me a good librarian also ensure that I will die alone and be eaten by cats. Which is weird because I don't have any cats."

2. Expressing joy at being present for each instruction session is a fine thing, but it can ring a little hollow to anyone who does not find library instruction stimulating. Since that includes almost everyone not planning to attend library school, qualifying your excitement is a good idea. This can be done by explaining your excitement: "I'm excited to be here because this is the most social interaction I'll have all day. Well, that is except for when I go to the supermarket just to be around people, even though I don't actually need any groceries." (Pause here, and sigh deeply before moving on.)

3. Much of the subject matter in library instruction is boring to a normal person. I like to acknowledge when something is boring in the hope of earning some goodwill from my students: "I know you might think this is boring, but for me, this is a hot Saturday night. Heck, this is about as much fun as I ever experience in life. (Brief pause, staring out into space, then a break into a big smile.) I hate my life."

Category B: Preemptively Attacking Yourself to Diffuse Audience Criticism

1. In response to a failed search, or anything that required any kind of setup: "All that effort and no payoff. Just like my last date."

2. In response to a long wait for a web page to load, or anything involving an unexpected or inconvenient delay: "Oh, the suspense is killing me. This is more exciting than anything in my personal life, which pretty much just involves waking up alone and going to bed alone. At least here there's uncertainty."

3. In response to failed humor, a missed reference, or anything else unfortunate: "Oh, I'm so alone."

A willingness to mock yourself in front of strangers is absolutely necessary for both categories of this technique. Delivery is crucial as well. Negative self-talk must be delivered in an upbeat, cheerful tone, ideally with a smile on your face. If your attitude is happy but the statements you make are depressing, the discordance between the two signals to the students that it is okay to laugh. This discordance must be maintained to avoid making the audience feel uncomfortable; it communicates that despite your misfortune you are doing just fine. You will know if you are succeeding with this technique if students are laughing or making eye contact with you and smiling. If they look away or become quiet, you have failed.

The comments that make up this technique have no direct educational value. They are used instead to manipulate the social environment of the classroom. Used properly, these comments can get laughs, help you build rapport with students, and recover from failed humor and other classroom setbacks. The comments in category A help make you appear more human and fallible and consequently more likeable. When used in conjunction with a self-introduction that establishes your professional competence, the comments in category A bridge any emotional gaps created by your assertions or demonstrations of ability. This can make it possible to build yourself up as a professionally competent resource without coming across as a self-important jerk. Students will be more inclined to take you seriously as a presenter but will also see you as an approachable human being.

Instead of trying to minimize or ignore setbacks or failures in class, which students always seem to notice anyway, the comments in category B allow you to address those problems and move on quickly. By preemptively attacking yourself, you diffuse any criticism that might arise, especially as a result of efforts to gloss over or ignore those problems. Additionally, the severity of the attack you leverage against yourself can actually garner sympathy from your students. When a confident or pretentious person makes a mistake, the temptation is to use the opportunity to take him or her down a notch or at least to snigger. On the other hand, when a person who is emotionally compromised makes a mistake there is no such temptation. If anything, the students become more inclined to nurture, to reassure the presenter that nothing terrible has occurred. By being self-critical in this way, you can bend the audience's natural human kindness to your advantage.

Students respond with laughter and sometimes even offer emotional support. In response to the comments in category A, students laugh or smile and continue to pay attention. In response to the comments in category B, students laugh. Instead of focusing on your failure, students forgive you and might even speak up to in your defense. Undergraduates appear to quite enjoy hearing their instructor talk about being desperately lonely. It is difficult to overstate how effective this technique can be at getting laughs and building rapport. At this time in their lives, many of our students are intensely involved in their social lives and would be hard-pressed to imagine a fate worse than staying home on a Friday night—or any night of the week, for that matter. I suspect that is why references to isolation and loneliness resonate so powerfully with them. These comments also play on the stereotype of the librarian as a spinster or emasculated, romantically undesirable male. The surprise generated by making playing into the stereotype might also be responsible for our students' strong responses.

This technique is meant to improve how students perceive us and minimize the effects of instruction-related errors or technological failures. It requires little or no additional time commitment; all of the comments are brief. The comments in category A help create a constructive learning environment, and the laughs they can produce in the opening minutes of class suggest the likelihood of more entertaining moments later in the session. That suggestion helps maintain student attention for the entire class. The comments in category B are useful in that they can be applied to almost any classroom mishap or any situation that might be seen as making the instructor look too successful or pretentious. They are arguably most effective when delivered in response to situations that do not warrant such a harsh self-evaluation. The less fitting the comment is to the crime, the funnier students find it. Comment 3 deserves special attention. Instead of needing to prepare and memorize a dozen or more context-specific responses (what to say when the Internet goes down, what to say when your search returns zero results, what to say when a particular joke bombs), this comment acts as a one-size-fits-all response. It should not, however, be overused (for the comments in category B, typically three or four instances are appropriate).

Gimme, Gimme, Gimme, Gimme What I Cry For!

Jenna Ryan, assistant librarian—reference and instruction, Louisiana State University

---

I like to sprinkle in humorous "gimme" questions into my multiple-choice quizzes—it gives the students a few extra easy points, and usually makes them sit up and pay attention. For example, one of my questions reads:
   Which of the following is *not* a good way to contact a librarian for help:

   a. by phone
   b. in person
   c. using smoke signals
   d. by instant message

The obvious (and amusing) answer to that question usually gets the student a few free points and some chuckles, which wakes them up in the morning (I give my quizzes first thing in a 9am class). In addition, the surprise of a silly answer makes them pay more attention to the rest of the question, namely that in person, phone and instant messaging are good ways to contact a librarian. I do the same thing with other questions—asking what floor a particular resource is on and including floors we don't have, like an 8th floor or a mezzanine, among the options. While obviously most questions must be serious in order for the quizzes to have any value, I've found that a few silly questions here or there makes the student pay more attention and builds classroom rapport—if the teacher has a sense of humor, she can't be all bad, right?

   This technique helps to create a more relaxed classroom atmosphere, to surprise students into paying closer attention to the quizzes, and to establish the instructor as having a sense of humor. When adding humorous elements to tests or quizzes, it is vital that those elements be unquestionably funny or silly. If they do not stand out, even to the most obtuse reader, you run the risk of alienating students. When a student misses a joke you tell in class it is mildly lamentable but no great tragedy. If a student misses a joke on a test, and a classmate notices and mocks him or her, that student is forced to endure embarrassment as a result of your instruction session. That should never be allowed to happen. However, when the questions are well chosen, this technique provides an opportunity to introduce levity into a dull situation with no loss of class time whatsoever.

NOTES

1. William Shakespeare, *Love's Labor's Lost*, Act IV, Sc. 2.

2. This question makes some teachers nervous. The fear, as I understand it, is that the class might respond by saying that you are not articulate, intelligent, or possessed of valuable knowledge or skills. I have two responses to this fear. One: I have asked this question in front of more than a thousand students, and never have I gotten a negative answer. Our students tend to think well of us, at least in terms of intellectual ability. I would be terrified to ask my students if they think I'm cool, however. Two: If you really think your students think that poorly of you, then you should probably do something about how you present yourself to them.

10

Webliography

Since video can be an effective educational tool both inside and outside of the class-room, we have included an annotated webliography of YouTube videos. Most of the videos here contain library-specific information; for example, "Librarians to the rescue, part 1" lists all the University of Florida at Gainesville libraries. Citations are modeled after the method presented by the library at the University of Illinois at Urbana-Champaign (Ream-Sotomayor, 2010). The same model was used to cite Vimeo videos and clips from commercial websites such as Comedy Central and MSNBC. These citations are not duplicated in the bibliography.

Most of the clips found here were found by the authors themselves, but some were taken from the blog of Professor Robert Schroeder, reference librarian and coordinator of information literacy at Portland State University in Portland, Oregon, which is entitled *cinfolit: cinema + information literacy* (http://cinfolit.blogspot.com/). We thank him for his kindness in allowing us to use his list of sites. It should be noted also that UCLA also has a great many YouTube clips on information literacy and library use. They are searchable under the name *LITEBite*, with LITE standing for Library Instruction To Everyone. One sample LITEBite is "LITEBite #7: Dude, Where's My Book?" Its URL is http://www.youtube.com/watch?v=ScydzFB3c14&feature=related.

Bennett, D. (Creator). UFlibraries (Poster) (2008, February 15). Librarians to the rescue, part 1 [Video]. Retrieved from http://www.youtube.com/watch?v=CwANhl6QSk8&feature= channel.
    Running time: 9 minutes, 24 seconds.

Bennett, D. (Creator). UFlibraries (Poster) (2008, February 15). Librarians to the rescue, part 2 [Video]. Retrieved from http://www.youtube.com/watch?v=AXUZAzHAAgY&feature= related.
    Running time: 9 minutes, 51 seconds.

Bennett, D. (Creator). UFlibraries (Poster) (2008, February 15). Librarians to the rescue, part 3 [Video]. Retrieved from http://www.youtube.com/watch?v=0nJhKTUFbaM&feature= channel.

Running time: 3 minutes, 47 seconds.

Total running time for these three videos: 23 minutes, 3 seconds.

The previous three videos, all created by Dwight Barnett for the University of Florida at Gainesville's libraries, deal with a team of four students. These students are Barbara (Barbie), the pretty but dimwitted blond; Jimmy, the frat boy athlete; Bobby, the geek or nerd; and Kathy, the smart girl. These four are in a class with Dr. Stern, a no-nonsense faculty member. Four weeks prior to the videos Dr. Stern assigned the class a 3,000-word paper that is due the following week. In order to make the work easier for the students to do, they have been broken up into groups. This group of four students has not yet started the paper, and all four are anxious about doing it. Dr. Stern had told the class not to use either Yahoo! or Google but instead to use the library. At the end of the first video the students are in the campus' Marston Science Library and are asking the librarian for help. In part 2 they learn to use the library, and in part 3 they see the results of their hard work. They get a 92 on their final project.

A portion of each video is University of Florida–specific, such as what the home page looks like, but parts deal with general library services such as the fact that the library has classes that teach students to use databases as well as the serendipity that can occur when one physically looks for books on shelves. Much of the humor is concentrated in part 1.

Comedy Central (Producer). (2005, October 17). The Word---Truthiness [Video file]. In *The Colbert Report*. Retrieved from http://www.colbertnation.com/the-colbert-report-videos/ 24039/october-17-2005/the-word---truthiness.

Running time: 2 minutes, 40 seconds.

In this clip Stephen Colbert introduces the concept of truthiness. Truthiness is the idea that whatever feels correct is correct and is to be preferred over anything that is found in reference books or other research sources. Obviously this could lead to a discussion about using solid, trustworthy sources. It should be noted that the clip discusses the nomination of Harriet Miers for Supreme Court justice by President George W. Bush, and your students may not remember this happening.

Comedy Central (Producer). (2006, July 31). The Word---Wikiality [Video file]. In *The Colbert Report*. Retrieved from http://www.colbertnation.com/the-colbert-report-videos/72347/ july-31-2006/the-word---wikiality.

Running time: 3 minutes, 10 seconds.

In his continuous spoofing of Wikipedia (see also *wikilobbying* in the next entry), comedian Stephen Colbert has defined and coined the word *wikiality*. The word means truth, facts, and reality, whether real or not, which are both controlled by and voted upon by a majority. If the majority votes in favor of the fact it passes from fiction or speculation to reality. This clip, like his other two clips, can be used to speak about two things: firstly, Wikipedia as a reliable or an unreliable source, and secondly, the need for high-quality information.

Comedy Central (Producer). (2007, January 29). The Word---Wikilobbying [Video file]. In *The Colbert Report*. Retrieved from http://www.colbertnation.com/the-colbert-report-videos/ 81454/january-29-2007/the-word---wikilobbying.

Running time: 3 minutes, 18 seconds.

Wikilobbying is based upon the fact that Microsoft was caught paying "an Australian computer expert" to do the work to modify Wikipedia entries to reflect favorably on Microsoft.

Therefore, according to Stephen Colbert, wikilobbying is the use of money to purchase a Wikipedia-based "reality" about companies. There are no current political events mentioned in this entry except for Microsoft being caught changing Wikipedia entries.

DeJesus, O., Ring, J., McBride, J., Vinolo, J., Sadlo, M., & Quintero, E. (Creators). Raromono-media (Poster) (2010, February 3). Steps to becoming a critical thinker [Video]. Retrieved from http://www.youtube.com/watch?v=U3hr-QbmquQ.
Running time: 2 minutes, 10 seconds.
DeJesus and colleagues have written and put together a short, quick song that presents the steps students should use to think critically. While the pictures that match the images are funny, the steps are quite serious. The six steps in the song are:

1. Admit that there are things you do not know.
2. Define terms.
3. Be willing to learn, or as the video says, be open-minded.
4. Produce ideas. This seems to be the point at which one is researching because folded into this is the idea that one should "consider the source" and that one should put something down on paper.
5. Accept the fact that your perspective might change.
6. Finally, "come up with your own conclusion."

While it is true that the tune is simple and the words are basic this clip could certainly be used on an early Monday morning to generate a class discussion.

Elkins, J., Neuhaus, C., Chen, S. H., & Chen, E. (Creators). echen888 (Poster) (2008, December 9). Library and the Internet [Video]. Retrieved from http://www.youtube.com/watch?v=Rk7bV40RyBM&feature=related.
Running time: 2 minutes, 6 seconds.
Here the "hip" Internet tells the "uncool" library what he can do. The library responds he can do the all of the same things except Facebook. The video then changes into a short discussion about using or not using Wikipedia. The video does a good job of explaining some of Wikipedia's drawbacks. The clip has the feel, in our opinion, of the Windows versus Mac commercials, except here the old-school library is the winner.

Hafstad, S., & Aksnes, J. H. (Creators). UniBergen (Poster) (2010, May 27). Et Plagieringseven-tyr [Video]. Retrieved from http://www.youtube.com/watch?v=Mwbw9KF-ACY.
Running time: 5 minutes, 13 seconds.
The title translates as "A Plagiarism Carol," and the video is based upon Charles Dickens' *A Christmas Carol*. This video is the story of James, a college student at the University of Bergen in Norway, who has a paper due at the end of the winter holidays. Although he promises his teacher that he will do it, instead he parties and has sex, thereby putting it off until the day before it is due. As he searches his topic, the "Ghost of Plagiarism" pays him a visit to show him what could happen if he plagiarizes and what could happen if he doesn't. If he plagiarizes he could get caught by the school's "turnitin" program and he could be summarily dismissed and disgraced. If he does his own work he could save the world and be congratulated by the President of the United States and become an international hero. James is impressed but says he can't do it because he doesn't know how. In a big, fun musical number the ghost tells him about a wonderful place where he can get help---the library. The video is in Norwegian, but if you click the closed caption (cc) button on the bottom of the clip, it has English subtitles. The

video is a great deal of fun and addresses plagiarism in a lighthearted way, but the reader should be warned that on the video, at about 23 seconds, right after James has had sex, he is talking to his female sex partner about his need to research and do his paper. Right there (23 second) is a shot of her breasts, from James's point of view, covered by a bra and hence not too revealing. However, it could make some faculty member or some students uncomfortable. Otherwise this is an excellent video to use to discuss plagiarism. To find this video on YouTube, if typing "Et Plagieringseventyr" is too difficult (because you are a non-Norwegian speaker), one can type "plagiarism ghost" and locate the video.

Hammer, C., & Thorne, M. (Creators). YorkTelevision (Poster) (2009, August 24). Draft my paper (HD) [Video]. Retrieved from http://www.youtube.com/watch?v=KGJL8uv_11A. Running time: 11 minutes, 11 seconds.

This video was created at York College of the City University of New York (Full disclosure: Professor Sheidlower was one of the technical advisors). The City University of New York is, by definition, located within an urban setting, and York College is located in a neighborhood in one of the outer boroughs, Jamaica, Queens, and has a strong multicultural street flavor to its environment. This urban street flavor comes though in this video from the students' clothes to their gestures to the rhythm of their speech. The video was created by the York WAC (Writing across the Curriculum) program. It deals with the trails and travails of a student, Marcus, who is taking History 101 and has an assignment to create an annotated bibliography for the class. Marcus starts his research at home, Googling and using Wikipedia. He then takes what he finds to the professor. The professor tells Marcus that the material he has found is not acceptable because the sources are suspect. As Marcus walks the halls of York, he meets Xzibition, the host of *Draft My Paper* (the title of a television show that is loosely based upon *Pimp My Ride*). Xzibition says he can help Marcus, but Marcus will need to go to the library. Xzibition then gathers his crew: C. E, a reference librarian; Shelves, a librarian in circulation; Data, the electronic resources librarian; and Big Margins, a writing stylist. The librarians are all played by York students, and therefore the students viewing the video will feel more connected to them. C. E. then teaches Marcus how to use the OPAC to locate books on his topic. Shelves follows, giving Marcus a crash course in finding books in the stacks. This is followed by Data teaching Marcus the use of an electronic database. Finally Big Margins helps Marcus create the bibliography in the proper style. The Professor is now happy and so is Marcus. Even in 11 minutes with the events in this video being very hurried, the video would be useful to show to a bunch of "gangstas" or "gangsta wanna-bes." Of all of the videos in this list it is the only one which aims at this group of students.

Idiots of Ants (Creators). Idiotsofants (Poster) (2009, February 26). How the Internet really works [Video]. Retrieved from http://www.youtube.com/watch?v=1DW7Rt2xsVg&feature=related. Running time: 2 minutes, 17 seconds.

This short comedy clip from the British comedy group Idiots of Ants concerns a library worker who asks a patron to give up his computer because he has been on it too long, since 1991. The patron is the Internet, and once he stops typing on the computer, the 'Net goes down. The Internet then shows the library worker some of the many things he would have been doing had he not been asked to stop. An example of this is a mailbag full of email. This video clip probably will not teach a digital native anything about the Internet per se, but the librarian could use it to start a discussion as to what the 'Net does. The librarian could also use it to teach people who are computerphobic since the clip personalizes the Internet. It could also make a good icebreaker.

iotaman5 (Poster). (2009, June 7). That Mitchell and Webb Look---Send us your reckons [Video].
Retrieved from http://www.youtube.com/watch?v=OQnd5ilKx2Y.
Running time: 1 minute; 31 seconds.
David Mitchell and Robert Webb are two British comedians who have a comedy sketch show,
That Mitchell and Webb Look on the BBC. In this skit Mitchell and Webb are newscasters
at a news desk who have been denied a quote from a British minister about a major catastrophe. The minister refuses to comment, in fact "she just yawns," and so Mitchell and
Webb invite the viewers to send in their "reckons" about the catastrophe. They do not particularly care about the accuracy of the quote as long as they have something to air. It is
similar to Stephen Colbert's wikiality, that is, truth is meaningless as long as the masses
believe it and vote on it. However, it goes even further in showing how wikiality would
work in the real world. This clip could be used to discuss, among other things, information quality or truthfulness and whether it is important.

MSNBC.com (Producer). (2010, June 28). BP press release theater. [Video file]. In *The Rachel
Maddow Show*. Retrieved from http://www.msnbc.msn.com/id/26315908/#37988491.
Running time: 3 minutes, 40 seconds.
This clip was shown on the Rachel Maddow Show. In it Rachel Maddow satirically shows
some video press releases that include both images and words that were created by the
oil company BP. These clips were press releases made to help buffer the company's image
after the oil spill in the Gulf of Mexico. Maddow has added music to the press releases,
thereby lampooning them. If the reader wishes to see BP's own unedited responses to this
disaster they can go to http://www.aolnews.com/2010/06/24/bp-blog-finds-upbeat-side
-of-oil-spill/. This clip and BP's original information could lead to an interesting discussion of both point of view and source. Be forewarned, prior to running Maddow's clip
an approximately 15- or 20-second commercial will play.

Porterken (Poster) (2008, November 8). A brief history of the Internet (Lotus) [Video]. Retrieved
from http://www.youtube.com/watch?v=FbMHY8I_kQ8&feature=related.
Running time: 1 minute, 51 seconds.
This short video clip, which is an advertisement from the software firm Lotus, was animated
as if it had been produced by the Monty Python comedy troop. It not only gives the story
of the Internet but also the history of the World Wide Web. The clip puts both of these
technological inventions in a sociological and historical framework. For example, it mentions the United States Department of Defense's role in the creation of the Internet.

Rhett & Link (Creators). RhettandLink (Posters) (2010, August 2). Squirrel rights song [Video].
Retrieved from http://www.youtube.com/watch?v=n2vVtSBOos.
Running time: 4 minutes, 14 seconds.
This song, sung by Rhett and Link in a country style while wearing squirrel masks, concerns
the fact that people find squirrels to be cute and often videotape them without their permission. Speaking as the squirrels, Rhett and Link go over some of the reasons people
don't like their images used without their permission and some of the consequences for
doing this. It could lead to a discussion of privacy rights or copyright.

Smith, J. (Creator). Juliansmith87 (Poster) (2010, August 29). What happened to Chris [Video].
Retrieved from http://www.youtube.com/user/juliansmith87#p/u/12/wkkPc2pw2R4.
Running time: 1 minute, 44 seconds.
In this short clip Josh walks in on his friend Julian, who is watching television on the couch,
and asks him what's wrong with their mutual friend Chris, who is slumped over in a chair

next to the couch. Julian informs him that Chris is dead. Josh wants to call the police but for unexplained reasons Julian says not to. They dump Chris's body in the lake and only then does Josh ask Julian how he knew Chris was dead. This is never answered. One could use this video to discuss the process of critical thinking. Josh had a few times at which he could have analyzed Julian's thinking more strictly. We never do find out if Chris is actually dead.

stkatesrefdesk (Poster). (2008, June 22). Evaluating web sources with the library fairy [Video]. Retrieved from http://www.youtube.com/watch?v=GRIW1EhUDSk&NR=1.
Running time: 1 minute, 55 seconds.
In this YouTube clip, two students at St. Catherine University in Saint Paul, Minnesota, have sat down to discuss information which they have found on the Internet. As soon as they start discussing it, the library fairy appears (an obese, bald man in a tutu with a wand) to go over what they've found. He also describes the markers of good web information, such as currency, bias, and so forth.

uinfosydney (Poster). (2008, May 28). Search smarter, search faster [Video]. Retrieved from http://www.youtube.com/watch?v=Oa66AxTbjxA&feature=related.
Running Time: 6 minutes, 54 seconds.
During the end of term a student in a dorm room at college is working on a paper with the topic "What led to the extinction of prehistoric animals in the Australasia region?" He is not enthused by the topic and cannot find any articles in the school's databases to help him write the paper. Supplying their voices, he uses a model Tyrannosaurus Rex and a model Woolly Mammoth on his desk as foils to help him learn how to identify keywords (here called key concepts), use two of the Boolean operators, AND and OR, and finally use synonyms in order to find articles and create a structured search. While not wildly humorous, it is very entertaining.

Vossler, J., Watts, J., & Hodge, T. (Creators). Kimbel Library (Poster) (2010, August 2). The information cycle [Video]. Retrieved from http://vimeo.com/13830031.
Running time: 2 minutes, 35 seconds.
This video was created under a Creative Commons license. It describes the information cycle and various forms of output at each stage of the cycle. It emphasizes that information can be found in various formats, either paper or electronic, and that the format is less important than the information itself. It keeps the technology simple, using only a whiteboard and marker and a sock puppet in addition to newspapers, magazines, books, and iPads as examples of the output of the information cycle.

Vossler, J., Watts, J., & Hodge, T. (Creators). Kimbel Library (Poster) (2010, July 22). Why citation is important [Video]. Retrieved from http://vimeo.com/13547869.
Running time: 2 minutes, 2 seconds.
This video was created under a Creative Commons license. It tells the story of Jim, a smart student who hates wearing pants. One day he stopped wearing them and noticed no one listened to him. They more interested in where his pants were. The creators make the analogy that citing correctly might be a pain (like wearing pants) but helps make your professors listen to you. This video uses paper dolls along with a whiteboard and markers.

Vossler, J., Watts, J., & Hodge, T. (Creators). Kimbel Library (Poster) (2010, July 8). Scholarly sources vs. popular sources [Video]. Retrieved from http://vimeo.com/13186317.
Running time: 3 minutes, 11 seconds.

This video was created under a Creative Commons license. It uses a whiteboard and a sock puppet to make its point---the difference between scholarly and popular sources. It makes the analogy that popular sources are like starlets while scholarly articles are like serious actors. The video then analyzes exactly what makes a source scholarly; for example, scholarly sources have plenty of references, they are lengthy, and so forth. This is followed by a parallel analysis of popular sources; for example, they lack references, they are short, and so on.

Vossler, J., Watts, J., Hodge, T. B., & Schacher, C. (Creators). Kimbel Library (Poster) (2010, July 25). Selecting the right number of keywords [Video]. Retrieved from http://vimeo .com/12861706.
Running time: 2 minutes, 43 seconds.

This video was created under a Creative Commons license. It asks three questions, two of them silly and one real. These questions are: What do chickens and breakfast cereal have in common? What is the meaning of life? How many keywords should you use when searching library databases? This sounds just plain silly, but the last question is real, and when it is answered the creators explain it in relation to a search in Google. They also discuss how to analyze the keywords in order to choose which to use.

References

Ajaye, F. (2002). *Comic insights: The art of stand-up comedy.* Los Angeles, CA: Silman James Press.

Allen, S. (1987). *How to be funny: Discovering the comic you.* New York, NY: McGraw-Hill.

Allen, S. (1998). *How to be funny: Discovering the comic you.* Amherst, NY: Prometheus Books.

American Library Association, Association of College and Research Libraries, Presidential Committee on Information Literacy. (1989). *Final Report.* Retrieved from http://www.ala.org/ala/mgrps/divs/acrl/publications/whitepapers/presidential.cfm#opp.

American Library Association, Association of College and Research Libraries. (2000). *Information literacy competency standards for higher education.* Retrieved from http://www.ala.org/ala/mgrps/divs/acrl/standards/informationliteracycompetency.cfm

American Library Association, Association of College and Research Libraries. (2003). *Characteristics of programs of information literacy that illustrate best practices: A guideline.* Retrieved from http://www.ala.org/ala/mgrps/divs/acrl/standards/characteristics.cfm

Archibeque, O. (1987). Laughter in the library: The use of humor in bibliographic instruction. *Colorado Libraries, 15* (December), 26–28.

Arnsan, D. (2000). Libraries, laughter and learning: The rubber chicken school of bibliographic instruction. *Community & Junior College Libraries, 9*(4), 53–58. doi: 10.1300/J107v09n04_07

Baker, C. (2010). The impact of instructor immediacy and presence for online student affective learning, cognition, and motivation. *The Journal of Educators Online, 7*(1), 1–15. Retrieved from http://www.thejeo.com

Beja, M. (2009, August 24). How students, professors, and colleges are, and should be, using social media [The wired campus]. *The Chronicle of Higher Education.* Retrieved from http://chronicle.com/blogPost/How-Students-Professors-and/7787/?sid=at&utm_medium=en

Berk, R. A. (2002). *Humor as an instructional defibrillator: Evidence-based techniques in teaching and assessment.* Sterling, VA: Stylus.

Berk, R. A. (2003). *Professors are from Mars, students are from Snickers: How to write and deliver humor in the classroom and in professional presentations.* Sterling, VA: Stylus.

Berk, R. A. (2008, April). Humor and the net generation. *Higher Education Advocate*. Retrieved from http://www.nea.org/he

Berk, R. A., & Nanda, J. P. (1998). Effects of jocular instructional methods on attitudes, anxiety, and achievement in statistics courses. *Humor: International Journal of Humor Research, 11*(4), 388–409. doi: 10.1515/humr.1998.11.4.383

Berwald, J.-P. (1992, December). Teaching French language and culture by means of humor. *The French Review, 66*(2), 189–200. Retrieved from http://www.wwu.edu/depts/mcl/french/FR/.

Booth-Butterfield, S., and Booth-Butterfield, M. (1991). Individual differences in the communication of humorous messages. *The Southern Journal of Communication, 56*(3), 205–218. Retrieved from http://www.tandf.co.uk/journals/journal.asp?issn=1041-794X &linktype=44.

Brewerton, A. (2002, Summer/Autumn). 'Laugh? I nearly learnt how to use a database!': a serious article on the use of humour in teaching information skills. *SCONUL Newsletter.* Retrieved from http://www.sconul.ac.uk/publications/newsletter/26/CH7.pdf

Brophy, J. E. (1979). Teacher behavior and its effects. *Journal of Educational Psychology, 71*, 733–750. doi: 10.1037/0022-0663.71.6.733

Bryant, J., Brown, D., Silberberg, A., & Elliot, S. (1980). *Humorous illustrations in textbooks: Effects on information acquisition, appeal, persuasibility and motivation.* Retrieved from ERIC database. (ED196071)

Bryant, J., Comisky, P., & Zillman, D. (1979). Teachers' humor in the college classroom. *Communication Education, 28*, 110–118. doi: 10.1080/03634527909378339

Bryson, L. (2008). Humor deficit: A librarian's guide to being funny and competent. *Science & Technology Libraries, 28*(1&2), 87–99. doi: 10.1080/01942620802096978

Buxman, K. (2000). Humor in critical care: No joke. *AACN Clinical Issues: Advanced Practice in Acute & Critical Care, 11*(1), 120–127. doi: 10.1097/00044067-200002000-00013

Carter, J. (1989). *Stand-up comedy: The book.* New York, NY: Dell.

Carter, J. (2001). *The comedy bible: From stand-up to sitcom: The comedy writer's ultimate how-to guide.* New York, NY: Fireside.

Chapman, A. J., & Crompton, P. (1988). Humorous presentations of material and presentations of humorous material: A review of the humour and memory literature and two experimental studies. In M. M. Gruneberg, P. E. Morris, & R. N. Sykes (Eds.), *Practical aspects of memory* (pp. 84–92). London, United Kingdom: Academic Press.

Chapman, A. J., & Foot, H. C. (Eds.). (1977). *It's a funny thing, humour.* Oxford, United Kingdom: Pergamon Press.

Check, J. (1997). Humor in education. *Physical Educator, 54*(3), 165–167. Retrieved from http://www.phiepsilonkappa.org/public.html

Check, J. F. (1986). Positive traits of the effective teacher—Negative traits of the ineffective one. *Education, 106*(3), 326–334. Retrieved from http://www.projectinnovation.biz/education_2006.html

Conkell, C. S., Imwold, C., & Ratliffe, T. (1999). The effects of humor on communicating fitness concepts to high school students. *Physical Educator, 56*(1), 8–18. Retrieved from http://www.phiepsilonkappa.org/public.html

Cousins, N. (1979). *Anatomy of an illness as perceived by the patient: Reflections on healing and regeneration.* New York, NY: W.W. Norton.

Crump, C. A. (1996). *Teacher immediacy: What students consider to be effective teacher behavior.* Retrieved from ERIC database. (ED390099)

Dickmeyer, S. G. (1993). *Humor as an instructional practice: A longitudinal content analysis of humor in the classroom.* Retrieved from ERIC database. (ED359587)

Downs, V. C., Javidi, M. M., & Nussbaum, J. F. (1988). An analysis of teachers' verbal communication within the college classroom: Use of humor, self-disclosure, and narratives. *Communication Education, 37*(2), 127–141. doi: 10.1080/03634528809378710

Eastman, M. (1972). *The sense of humor.* New York, NY: Octagon Books. (Original work published in 1921)

Elkan, D. (2010, January 30). Locating the brain's comedy circuit: Why do some jokes have us rolling around on the floor, while others leave us simply rolling our eyes? Neuroscientists think they've found the answer. *New Scientist, 205*(2745). Retrieved from http://www.newscientist.com

Fenton, N. (1943). Lillien Jane Martin, 1851–1943. *Psychological Review, 50*(4), 440–442. doi: 10.1037/h0063137

Friedman, H. H., Halpern, N., & Salb, D. (1999). Teaching statistics using humorous anecdotes. *Mathematics Teacher, 92*, 305–308. Retrieved from http://www.nctm.org/publications/mt.aspx

Frymier, A. B., & Weser, B. (2001). The role of student dispositions on student expectations for instructor communication behavior. *Communication Education, 50*(4), 314–326. doi: 10.1080/03634520109379258

Fulton, T. L. (1985). *Plain (well, not just plain) fun: The potential for humor in the academic library "one-shot lecture."* Retrieved from ERIC database. (ED274353)

Garner, R. (2006). Humor in pedagogy: How ha-ha can lead to aha!. *College Teaching, 54*, 177–180. doi: 10.3200/CTCH.54.1.177-180

Glenn, D. (2009, December 15). Matching teaching styles to learning style may not help students. *The Chronicle of Higher Education.* Retrieved from http://chronicle.com/article/Matching-Teaching-Style-to/49497/?sid=at&utm_medium=en

Goebel, B. A. (2009). Comic relief: Engaging students through humor writing. *English Journal, 98*(6), 38–43. Retrieved from http://www.ncte.org/journals/ej

Goldstein, J. H., McGhee, P. E., Smith, J. R., Chapman, A. J., & Foot, H. C. (1977). Humour, laughter and comedy: A bibliography of empirical and onempirical analyses in the English language. In Chapman, A. J., & Foot, H. C. (Eds.), *It's a funny thing, humour.* (pp. 469–504). Oxford, United Kingdom: Pergamon Press.

Gordon, J. (1992, June). Humor in legal education and scholarship. *Brigham Young University Law Review, 1992*(2). Retrieved from http://lawreview.byu.edu/index.htm

Gorham, J., & Christophel, D. M. (1990). The relationship of teachers' use of humor in the classroom to immediacy and student learning. *Communication Education, 39*, 46–62. doi: 10.1080/03634529009378786

Grassian, E. S., & Kaplowitz, J. R. (2009). *Information literacy instruction: Theory and practice.* 2nd ed. New York, NY: Neal-Schuman.

Greig, J. Y. T. (1969). *The psychology of laughter and comedy.* New York, NY: Cooper Square.

Gruner, C. R. (1978). *Understanding laughter: The workings of wit and humor.* Chicago, IL: Nelson-Hall.

Gute, D., & Gute, G. (2008). Flow writing in the liberal arts core and across the disciplines: A vehicle for confronting and transforming academic disengagement. *JGE: The Journal of General Education, 57*, 191–222. doi: 10.1353/jge.0.0026

Haig, R. A. (1988). *The anatomy of humor: Biopsychosocial and therapeutic perspectives.* Springfield, IL: Charles C. Thomas.

Haigh, G. (1999, January 8). Do smile: But don't make too many jokes. *The Times Educational Supplement Magazine.* Retrieved from http://www.tes.co.uk/Home.aspx?navcode=486

Hashem, M. E. (1994). *Play and humor in the college classroom: Using play as a teaching technique in interpersonal communication classes.* Retrieved from ERIC database. (ED372442)

Hauck, W. E., & Thomas, J. W., (1972). The relationship of humor to intelligence, creativity, and intentional and incidental learning. *The Journal of Experimental Education, 40*(4), 52–55. Retrieved from http://www.tandf.co.uk/journals/titles/00220973.asp

Hill, D. (1988). *Humor in the classroom: A handbook for teachers (and other entertainers).* Springfield, IL: C. C. Thomas.

Hoare, J. (2004). The best medicine. *Nursing Standard (Royal College of Nursing (Great Britain), 19*(14–16), 18–19. Retrieved from http://nursingstandard.rcnpublishing.co.uk/

Hobbes, T. (1651). *Leviathan: Or the matter, forme, & power of a common-wealth, ecclesiatical and civill.* [Project Gutenberg version] London: Crooke. Retrieved from http://www.gutenberg.org/dirs/3/2/0/3207/3207-h/3207-h.htm#2HCH0006

Holland, N. N. (1982). *Laughing: A psychology of humor.* Ithaca, NY: Cornell University Press.

Holy Name University. (n.d.). *International Society for Humor Studies.* Retrieved January 24, 2010, from http://www.hnu.edu/ishs/index.htm?

James, D. (2004). A need for humor in online courses. *College Teaching, 52,* 93–94. doi: 10.3200/CTCH.52.3.93-120

Kaplan, R. M., & Pascoe, G. C. (1977). Humorous lectures and humorous examples: Some effects upon comprehension and retention. *Journal of Educational Psychology, 69,* 61–65. doi: 10.1037/0022-0663.69.1.61

Kher, N., Molstad, S., & Donahue, R. (1999). Using humor in the college classroom to enhance teaching effectiveness in 'dread courses.' *College Student Journal, 33*(3), 400–407. Retrieved from http://findarticles.com/p/articles/mi_m0FCR/

Korobkin, D. (1998). Humor in the classroom: Considerations and strategies. *Classroom Teaching, 36*(1), 154–158. Retrieved from http://heldref.metapress.com/app/home/journal.asp?referrer=parent&backto=subject,4,13

Kuhrik, M., Kuhrik, N., & Berry, P. A. (1997). Facilitating learning with humor. *Journal of Nursing Education, 36*(7), 332–334. Retrieved from http://www.journalofnursingeducation.com/

Layng, A. (1991). Sexism and classroom humor. *College Teaching, 39*(2), 43. Retrieved from http://www.tandf.co.uk/journals/titles/87567555.asp

Lefcourt, H. M. & Martin, R. A. (1986). *Humor and life stress: Antidote to adversity.* New York, NY: Springer-Verlag.

LoSchiavo, F. M., & Shatz, M. A. (2005). Enhancing online instruction with humor. *Teaching of Psychology, 32,* 246–248. doi: 10.1207/s15328023top3204_8

MacAdam, B. (1985). Humor in the classroom: Implications for the bibliographic instruction librarian. *College & Research Libraries, 46,* 327–333. Retrieved from http://crl.acrl.org/

Malvasi, M., Rudowsky, C., & Valencia, J. M. (2009). *Library Rx: Measuring and treating library anxiety, a research study.* Chicago, IL: Association of College and Research Libraries.

Mandler, G. (2007). *A history of modern experimental psychology: From James and Wundt to cognitive science.* Cambridge, MA: MIT Press. Available from http://site.ebrary.com/lib/librarytitles/Doc?id=10185591

Markiewicz, D. (1974). Effects of humor on persuasion. *Sociometry, 37,* 407–422. doi: 10.2307/2786391

Marshall, J. (2002). *What would Buffy do? The use of popular culture examples in undergraduate library instruction.* Retrieved from ERIC database. (ED468217)

Martin, L. J. (1905). Psychology of aesthetics I: Experimental prospecting in the field of the comic. *The American Journal of Psychology, 16,* 35–118. doi: 10.2307/1412228

Martin, R. A. (2000). Humor and laughter. In A. E. Kadzin (Ed.), *Encyclopedia of Psychology.* Oxford, UK: Oxford University Press.

McDowell, E. E., & Yotsuyanagi, N. (1995). *An exploratory study of communication apprehension, willingness to communicate, and sense of humor between college students in the United States and Japan.* Retrieved from ERIC database. (ED396349)

McMorris, R. F., Boothroyd, R. A., & Pietrangelo, D. J. (1997). Humor in educational testing: A review and discussion. *Applied Measurement in Education, 10*, 269–297. doi: 10.1207/s15324818ame1003_5

McMorris, R. F., & Kim, Y. (2003). Humor for international students and their classmates: An empirical study and guidelines. *Journal on Excellence in College Teaching, 14*(1), 129–149. Retrieved from http://celt.muohio.edu/ject/index.php

Millard, E. N. (1999). Humor can be serious strategy. *The Delta Kappa Gamma Bulletin, 65*(3). Retrieved from http://www.dkg.org/site/c.meJMIOOwErH/b.5841719/

Newton, G. R., & Dowd, T. E. (1990). Effect of client sense of humor and paradoxical interventions on test anxiety. *Journal of Counseling and Development, 65*(6), 668–672. Retrieved from http://www.counseling.org/Publications/Journals.aspx

Oring, E. (1984). *The jokes of Sigmund Freud: A study in humor and Jewish identity.* Philadelphia, PA: University of Pennsylvania Press.

Osborne, N. S. (1992). *Librarian humor in classroom and reference.* Retrieved from ERIC Database. (ED349018)

Peresie, M., & Alexander, L. B. (2005). Librarian stereotypes in young adult literature. *Young Adult Library Services, 4*(1), 21–28. Retrieved from http://www.ala.org/ala/mgrps/divs/yalsa/yalsapubs/yals/currentpastissues.cfm

Petry, B. L. (1998). Adding zest to OPAC instruction: Humor and the unexpected. *College & Research Libraries, 5*(2), 75–85. doi: 10.1300/J106v05n02_11

Powell, J. P., & Andresen, L. W. (1985). Humor and teaching in higher education. *Studies in Higher Education, 10*(1), 79–90. doi: 10.1080/03075078512331378726

Radford, G. P., & Radford, M. L. (2001, July). Libraries, librarians, and the discourse of fear. *The Library Quarterly, 71*, 299–329.

Radford, M. L., & Radford, G. P. (1999, June/July). *Media images of librarians in modern popular culture.* Paper presented at the annual conference of the American Library Association, New Orleans, LA.

Radford, M. L., & Radford, G. P. (2003). Librarians and party girls: Cultural studies and the meaning of the librarian. *The Library Quarterly, 73*(1), 54–69. doi: 10.1086/603375

Rareshide, S. W. (1993). *Implications for teachers' use of humor in the classroom.* Retrieved from ERIC database. (ED359165)

Ream-Sotomayor, N. (2010). YouTube video. In *APA citation style: Publication manual of the American psychological association, 6th edition, for education, psychology, and other social sciences.* Retrieved from http://www.library.illinois.edu/learn/tutorials/apa.html

Romal, J. B. (2008). Use of humor as a pedagogical tool for accounting education. *Academy of Educational Leadership Journal, 12*(1), 83–106. Retrieved from http://www.alliedacademies.org/Public/AffiliateAcademies/ael.aspx

Russo, M. C. (1992). Recovering from bibliographic instruction blahs. *RQ, 32*(2), 178–183.

Sarkodie-Mensah, K. (1998). Using humor for effective library instruction sessions. *Catholic Library World, 68*(4), 25–29. Retrieved from http://cathla.org/catholic-library-world-clw

Saunders, L. (2002). Teaching the library: Best practices. *Library Philosophy and Practice, 4*(2), 1–8. Retrieved from http://www.webpages.uidaho.edu/~mbolin/saunders.html

Shatz, M. A., & Coil, S. R. (2008). Regional campus teaching ain't a joke but humor can make it more effective. *AURCO Journal, 14*, 105–117. Retrieved from http://aurco.org/journal

Silver, B. & Hansard, P. (2004). *What Bird Did That? A Driver's Guide to Some Common Birds of North America.* Berkeley, CA:.Ten Speed Press.

Strean, W. (2009). Laughter prescription. *Canadian Family Physician, 55*(10), 965–967. Retrieved from http://www.cfp.ca

Sultanoff, S. M. (1993). Taking humor seriously in the workplace. Retrieved from www.humor matters.com/articles/workplace.htm

Sutherland, N. R., & Winters, C. M. (2001). The A, B, Z's of bibliographic instruction: Using real-life analogies to foster understanding. *The Reference Librarian, 35*(73), 293–308. doi: 10.1300/J120v35n73_06

Swidler, D. (2010, December 14). First make them laugh [Letter to the editor]. *The New York Times,* p. D4.

Tierney, J. (2010, November 15). When the mind wanders, happiness also strays. *The New York Times.* Retrieved from http://www.nytimes.com

Torok, S. E., McMorris, R. F., & Lin, W. (2004). Is humor an appreciated teaching tool?: Perceptions of professors' teaching styles and use of humor. *College Teaching, 52*(1), 14–20. Retrieved from http://www.tandf.co.uk/journals/titles/87567555.asp

Trefts, K., & Blakeslee, S. (2000). Did you hear the one about the Boolean operators? Incorporating comedy into library instruction. *Reference Services Review, 28*(4), 369–377. doi: 10.1108/00907320010359731

Vereen, L. G., Butler, S. K., Williams, F. C. Dang, J. A., & Downing, T. K. E. (2006). The use of humor when counseling African American college students. *Journal of Counseling & Development, 84,* 10–15. Retrieved from http://www.counseling.org/Publications/Journals.aspx

Walker, B. E. (2005). Using humor in library instruction. *Reference Services Review, 34,* 117–128. doi: 10.1108/00907320610648806

Wandersee, J. H. (1982). Humor as a teaching strategy. *The American Biology Teacher, 44,* 212–218. Retrieved from http://www.ucpressjournals.com/journalBuy.asp?j=abt

Wanzer, M. B., Frymier, A. B., Wojtaszczyk, A. M. & Smith, T. (2006). Appropriate and inappropriate uses of humor by teachers. *Communication Education, 55,* 178–196. doi: 10.1080/03634520600566132

Warnken, P. N., & Young, V. L. (1991). Application of training principles and techniques for successful library instruction. *Reference Services Review, 19*(4), 91–96. doi: 10.1108/eb049142

White, G. W. (2001). Teachers report of how they used humor with students perceived use of such humor. *Education, 122*(2), 337–347. Retrieved from http://www.projectinnovation.biz/education_2006.html

Wilder, S. (1996, April). The age demographics of academic librarians. *ARL: A Bimonthly Newsletter of Research Library Issues and Actions,* 185. Retrieved from http://www.arl.org/bm~doc/agedemo.pdf

Ziv, A. (1976). Facilitating effects of humor on creativity. *Journal of Educational Psychology, 68*(3), 318–322. Retrieved from http://www.apa.org/pubs/journals/edu/index.aspx

Ziv, A. (1979). *L'humour en education: Approche psychologique.* Collection Science de l'éducation. Paris, FR: Editions Sociales Francaises.

Ziv, A. (1981). רומוהה לש היגלוכיספ [The psychology of humor]. Tel Aviv, Israel: ידחי.

Ziv, A. (1984). *Personality and sense of humor.* New York, NY: Springer.

Ziv, A. (1988). Teaching and learning with humor: Experiment and replication. *The Journal of Experimental Education, 57*(1), 5–15. Retrieved from http://www.tandf.co.uk/journals/titles/00220973.asp

Index

About the Authors

JOSHUA VOSSLER is an information literacy/reference librarian at Coastal Carolina University.

SCOTT SHEIDLOWER is an assistant professor in the library at York College/CUNY. He is the head of information literacy at York College as well.